Decoding History

Also by W. J. R. Gardner

ANTI-SUBMARINE WARFARE

Decoding History

The Battle of the Atlantic and Ultra

W. J. R. Gardner
Historian
Naval Historical Branch
Ministry of Defence

Foreword by

Geoffrey Till
Dean of Academic Studies
Joint Services Command and Staff College
Bracknell

NAVAL INSTITUTE PRESS
Annapolis, Maryland

First published in Great Britain in 1999 by
MACMILLAN PRESS LTD
Houndmills, Basingstoke, Hampshire RG21 6XS
and London

Published and distributed in the United States of America and Canada by
the NAVAL INSTITUTE PRESS
291 Wood Road, Annapolis, Maryland 21402–5034

Library of Congress Catalog Card Number 99–74458

ISBN 1–55750–158–0

Contents

List of Tables

List of Figures

Foreword

The Battle of the Atlantic was the great maritime encounter of the Second World War in Europe. In this campaign, or battle, as it is usually if confusingly known, a continental power sought to exploit the vulnerabilities of the maritime coalition that threatened it by attacking its weakest link, namely the shipping that crossed and recrossed the broad Atlantic, carrying military equipment and personnel and all the requirements of the British war economy. It was one of the few battles that regularly kept Churchill awake at night, for he knew how crucial its outcome was for Britain's capacity to survive, let alone prosecute an offensive war.

It was a huge affair, involving hundreds of U-boats, thousands of ships, aircraft and people and it lasted for the better part of six years. Naval personnel on both sides, the merchant sailors of many different countries, airmen, scientists, code-breakers, logisticians, dockers and factory-workers all had their crucial roles to play – and suffered accordingly. To use Jock Gardner's own analogy, it was the great maritime drama of the war and it ran and ran.

Not surprisingly therefore, when confronted with such a huge and complicated matter, most people seek, and often need, a guide to what really mattered, to what worked, to what made the crucial difference. This applies as much to historians bewildered by the mass of sometimes conflicting but always competing data as it does to participants in the battle who want to understand, or at least to confirm (since they usually exhibit strong experience-based views on this already), how their efforts fitted in to the whole.

Accordingly, books about the Battle of the Atlantic usually refine the complexity and focus on particular aspects of the case. And the explanations came in waves. First was the obvious focus on the dramatic operational and tactical levels of the campaign, sustained by the processing of official Admiralty and German naval records and a flood of gripping personal reminiscence from both sides. At first this was almost exclusively the domain of the professional military on both sides, but soon important contributions to an evolving debate were made by the chief victims of the battle, the merchant sailors who suffered so much in the Allied cause. Very soon books which sought to compare and contrast the role played by the forces of the various nations involved in the campaign began to appear, a field in which Canadian historians were particularly prominent. In this first generation, the points at issue were questions of tactics, of the availability of effective weaponry and the planning of the campaign. Who was right, who wrong. What worked, what didn't. A second wave developed from the first. It went further into ultimate causes. What made the strategy of convoy-and-escort so successful apart from the fighting skill and equipment of the protagonists? When details of the role of, first, operational analysis and then, even more dramatically, operational intelligence in the shape of Ultra appeared, many people concluded that here at last was the essential truth about the Battle of the Atlantic. In some cases, this encouraged works that concentrated on the efficiency of the planning and administrative regimes at the headquarters staffs on both sides. How important was the Operational Intelligence Centre? What contribution did Dönitz's surprisingly amateurish planning approach make to the German defeat?

Another aspect of the second wave involved pushing upwards into the grand military strategic level of war in search of the crucial determinants of victory. If, at the tactical and operational levels of war, the importance of air-power was clear, perhaps this was true at these higher and more rarefied levels, too. Perhaps it was the outcome of the struggle for large aircraft resources between the proponents of maritime air and of a bomber offensive that would include the attack on U-boat bases that was the critical illustration of the Second World War as a grand clash between the elephant [land-power] and the whale [sea-power].

Imperceptibly, such considerations led to a third wave of analysis which is still with us – namely, a focus on the efficiencies and inefficiencies of industrial states at war. These were studies which looked at production schedules of ships, aircraft and submarines, at the effectiveness of transport systems to, at and from the docks, and more broadly yet, at the integration of the requirements and the products of this campaign into the rest of the war economies of Britain and its allies on the one hand and of its continental adversary on the other.

Against this background of the growing extent and complexity of explanation about the Battle of the Atlantic, what contribution does this book make to a debate apparently growing too difficult fully to comprehend? To me, this review of the way in which the Battle of the Atlantic can and should be approached, is valuable, and indeed unique, for two separate but connected reasons. First, it challenges the hidden monocausal assumption. Jock Gardner puts everything

together in a way which makes the unwisdom of focusing on single ✓✓
issues, however important they seem, quite crystal-clear. This argument is particularly strongly made in the sophisticated analysis of the
role of Ultra which follows.

Secondly, the book convincingly demonstrates the dynamism of
history in general and of war in particular. War is a relationship
between two sides who decide actions in response to what they perceive the other side to be doing. Nothing stays the same, therefore. So ✓
what may have been the crucial factor at one stage was no longer so at
another. Moreover, this was a campaign of such breadth that what was
true of one aspect of it in one geographic location was not in another.
The message that comes out here, loud and clear, is that there are no
quick and simple conclusions – and probably no decisive causes either. ✓
To return to Jock Gardner's analogy, in this theatre of explanation we ✓
find a cast without stars; everyone is a supporting actor.

So what we are faced with is a kind of postmodernist 'Well, it
depends...', when confronted with the claims of any explanation
about the outcome of the Battle of the Atlantic. What we need, there- ✓
fore, is some sort of guide to help us through the thicket, to point out
the traps and to identify the issues that real explorers need to be aware
of. *Decoding History* does precisely this and will, I suspect initiate a new,
fourth wave of analysis designed, in the terminology of the 1960s, 'to
get it all together'. The quality of this work, moreover, is an encouraging sign that with this wave, we may at last be approaching a real and
comprehensive understanding of this most important and most
complex campaign of the Second World War.

GEOFFREY TILL
Joint Services Command and Staff College, Bracknell

Acknowledgements

Any book has to start somewhere and although concentrated work on this one did not begin until more recently, its origins lay in being asked by J. D. Brown to give a paper in 1988, posing the question whether resources or intelligence were more responsible for the Allied victory over German submarines in the 1939–45 world war. As an American academic commented some time later, the question was not really answered by my subsequent paper. He was almost certainly right; this book, therefore, explores the topic more thoroughly.

Serious study of the problem demands assimilation of much material and I have been lucky to have had the help of a number of industrious and perspicacious guides. Derek Law not only wrote one of the best bibliographical guides to the Royal Navy in that conflict; he has also kept it up to date and I am grateful for full and free access to his further work. I was very well served by the staff of the Ministry of Defence Library in Whitehall for their assistance in identifying and obtaining some of the rarer books on the subject. Mavis Simpson and Jean Clayton were particularly helpful. Rachel Magowan cooperated with me on an earlier unrealised project, but very few efforts are wasted and the work she did then has provided a valuable insight into German intelligence efforts. Similarly, I have to thank Naomi Waters for introducing me to the work of Kevin Smith.

Assistance with archival material has been very generous. In this country, David Ashby has been most energetic on my behalf and, in the United States, I was generously received by Bernard Cavalcante and Kathleen Lloyd of the Naval Historical Center. At the National Archives and Records Administration at College Park, I was most fortunate to benefit from the guidance of that great expert, John Taylor.

A number of recognised authorities have been very free with their time and experience. In particular, I would mention Jeffrey K. Bray, Michael Gannon, David Lees, Marc Milner, Alfred Price, Jürgen Rohwer and Kathleen Broome Williams. A special mention should be made of D. W. Waters, surely the doyen of Battle of Atlantic analysts and historians, both by his literary longevity and distinction. David Syrett has been a formidable disputant as well as being a source of much of the soundest work on the subject. I am most grateful, too, for an advanced sight of his forthcoming volume on the topic for the Navy Records

Society, for which I must also acknowledge the cooperation of Michael Simpson, the Honorary General Editor of the Society. Before his death, some years ago, Edward Thomas, the author of the naval sections of the British official history of intelligence, was able to clarify some important matters for me. Over the years since 1988, I was able several times to discuss the subject of the current book with Sir Harry Hinsley. We did not always agree on causation and significance but the discussions we had were always enlightening, stimulating and good-natured. I regret that his death in 1998 has deprived me of the opportunity of a culminating discussion on the subject.

As the book was written, I was immensely thankful for the efforts of a number of critics who were able to correct errors of fact, flaws of reasoning and infelicities of expression. As is customary, I still claim the credit for the residual problems, but the efforts of R. M. Coppock, Sebastian Cox, Ralph Erskine, Arnold Hague and Kevin Smith should all be noted. However, the prize for either industry or masochism has to be awarded to Paul Sutcliffe who undertook the arduous task of looking at several chapters. I ~~would like to~~ thank John M. Smith at Macmillan for rigorous but helpful editing skills, an essential complement to the imperfect historian.

Geoffrey Till has not only contributed a distinguished foreword to the book but has been a consistent source of constructive criticism and encouragement over many years. Lastly, I ~~should like to~~ thank Terry Dean and Tim Gardner for allowing another time-absorbing project to be carried out at the same time as I was working on this book.

Glossary

Abwehr	Foreign and counterintelligence department of the high command of the German armed forces
AIO	Action Information Organisation
Alberich	U-boat rubber hull coating
Aphrodite	U-boat radar decoy balloon
ASV	Air-to-Surface Vessel (radar) – despite its name a useful device versus surfaced submarines
ASW	Anti-Submarine warfare
ASWORG	Anti-Submarine Warfare Operations Research Group
BdU	*Befehlshaber der U-Boote* – Commander of U-boats
Bold	Underwater decoy – see also SBT
BP	Bletchley Park
CAOR	Chief Adviser Operational Research
CIC	Combat Information Center – American term for AIO
CinCWA	Commander-in-Chief Western Approaches
COMINCH	Commander-in-Chief (US Fleet)
CTL	Constructive Total Loss
CVE	Escort aircraft-carrier
DE	Destroyer Escort
DNOR	Director of Naval Operations Research
EG	Escort Group
Enigma	German machine cipher
FAT	*Federapparat* – German torpedo carrying out search-pattern
Fido	American anti-submarine homing torpedo
Fliege	German, lit. Fly – radar detector
Frontboote	Operationally ready submarine
GC&CS	Government Code and Cypher School – cover-name for Bletchley Park
glückliche Zeit	Fortunate or happy time – period(s) of greatest submarine success
GNAT	British name for German acoustic torpedo – see also T5
GRT	Gross Register Tons
HF DF	High-Frequency (radio) Direction-Finding

JIC	Joint Intelligence Committee
Knickebein	German radio navigation system
KTB	*Kriegstagebuch* – war diary
Kurier	German radio transmission compression device – see also Squash
Kurzsignalheft	Short signal book
LUT	*Lage unabhängiger Torpedo* (Position independent torpedo) – German torpedo carrying out search-pattern
MAD	Magnetic Anomaly Detector
Metox	German radar detector
MF	Medium Frequency (radio)
Mücke	Mosquito – German radar detector
NID	Naval Intelligence Division – of Admiralty
nm	nautical mile(s)
OEG	Operational Evaluation Group (US)
OIC	Operational Intelligence Centre
OKM	German Naval High Command
OR	Operational (or Operations) Research
ORS	Operational Research Staff (or Section)
Paukenschlag	lit. 'Roll of drums' – operation in 1942 against USA east coast shipping
PC	Patrol Craft
RCN	Royal Canadian Navy
RFP	Radio Finger Printing
RNR	Royal Naval Reserve
RNVR	Royal Naval Volunteer Reserve
Rudeltaktik	Pack tactic – often translated as 'wolfpack'
SBT	Submarine Bubble Target – see also *Bold*
SC	Submarine Chaser
SI	Special Intelligence – i.e. Ultra
Sigint	Signals Intelligence
Sonne	German oceanic navigation system
Squash	British name for *Kurier*
T5	German acoustic homing torpedo – see also GNAT
TA	Traffic Analysis
TBS	Talk between Ships
Thetis	German floating radar decoy
TINA	Method of recognising individual German radio operators – and thus their submarines
Tonnageschlacht	Tonnage warfare

U-Bootwaffe	The submarine arm
Ultra	Decryptions of Enigma coded signals (general usage)
VHF	Very High Frequency (radio)
VLR	Very Long Range (aircraft)
Wanze	Bug – German radar detector
xB-Dienst	German naval equivalent of Bletchley Park
Zaunkönig	Wren – German acoustic homing torpedo – see also GNAT and T5

List of Convoys Mentioned in the Text

GUS   Gibraltar to USA
HG   Gibraltar to UK
HX   Halifax to UK
OG   UK to Gibraltar
ON   UK to North America
ONS   UK to North America – slow
OS   UK to Freetown (West Africa)
SC   Sydney (Canada) to UK
SL   Freetown to UK
TM   Trinidad to Gibraltar
UGS   USA to Gibraltar
WS   'Winston Specials' – special purpose convoys – no single route

1
The World War and the Atlantic Campaign

In order to understand the significance of one aspect of the Battle of the Atlantic properly, it is first necessary comprehend the whole. This is not as obvious as would at first appear, for a number of reasons: the conflict's great scope, reading the strategic role of the Battle correctly and the distortions introduced into understanding wrought by over 50 years of historical literature.

This chapter will attempt that broader comprehension, first considering the nomenclature and nature of the Battle. Next, it will move on to consider its strategic importance from a number of different perspectives: national viewpoints, the link to other operations, especially those on land, and some points connected with doctrine. From there, the difficulties of chronicling and analysing such a large-scale conflict are considered, together with a brief view on how these challenges have been met over the half-century since the events to which they refer. Lastly, a pattern for assessing the overall problem is put forward so that a reasoned re-assessment of the importance of one particular aspect of the multi-faceted struggle can be carried out, that of code-breaking intelligence – generally known as Ultra.

The Battle of the Atlantic – size and significance

The term 'Battle of the Atlantic' can be misleading as a battle is normally perceived on much smaller scales of time and space. Normally, campaigns are seen as comprising several battles together with the manoeuvres which connect them. Here, this is reversed and a number of campaigns – and some other components – comprise the Battle of the Atlantic. Despite this difficulty of definitions and names the term is useful shorthand that describes the most important part of the German anti-shipping strategy: perhaps more significantly 'the Battle of the Atlantic' is now hallowed by long usage.

The conflict spanned the entire war and consumed a great amount of resources on both sides. The Germans built over 1000 submarines, of which some 830 participated in operations at one time or another.[1] Of these 450 were lost to enemy action or accident and a significant number of the 40 000 U-boat men were lost. In return they sank nearly 2800 merchant ships, exceeding 14 million gross tons. This was warfare on a very large scale indeed. The principal cause of shipping loss in the war was the submarine and most were sunk in the North Atlantic. However, although it is worth remembering the submarine's rightly and richly deserved reputation as the merchant-ship-sinker *par excellence*, it was not the only method and the North Atlantic not the only place where such action took place.[2] The other point worth noting is that the effort deployed at any one time in the Battle, although often very large, did not approach the numbers mentioned immediately above. At a peak, about 100 submarines might be deployed, around 800 000 tons of shipping sunk in a month and there might be around a dozen convoys at sea in the main area of interest, the North Atlantic, ultimately each of 60–100 ships protected by perhaps eight escorts and some aircraft. This was hardly insubstantial but in terms of numbers of submariners, they would barely have manned a brigade on land.

This is perhaps a useful point at which to introduce the concept of levels of warfare. Such terms were not in contemporary use and, it might be argued, the peculiar features of the war at sea in general and this struggle in particular ill suit the application of definitions whose origins lie in land warfare.[3] For current purposes, the definitions used are those which appear in *British Maritime Doctrine*.[4] The suggested examples from the Battle of the Atlantic are, however, defined separately.

There are obviously some difficulties with applying the four levels of war both to the five military activities in general and, perhaps, to the Battle of the Atlantic in particular. One obvious example might be when relevant scales of military forces are applied to the level of war. Obviously as the levels ascend, so too does the likely commitment of forces. Thus, for example, the submarines committed to a campaign would involve little more front-line manpower than a brigade on land – which would almost certainly be considered as tactical in the land case.[5] Nevertheless, an understanding of relative levels of war as defined by such a system is an essential tool in understanding both the Battle of the Atlantic as a whole and the applicability and utility of Ultra intelligence to its conduct.

3

Table 1.1 The levels of war

Level	Definition	Military activity	Battle of the Atlantic example activity
Grand strategic	All resources including economic and technical. Government or alliance decisionmaking	War	Shipbuilding, the management of shipping as a resource, allocation of materials and production to ASW
Military strategic[a]	Application of military resources to gain grand strategic objectives	Campaigns[b]	The convoy system, allocation of ships and aircraft to ASW, attacking U-boat building and base facilities
Operational	Planning and conduct of campaigns and major operations	Major operations	Conduct of operations in specific large areas, the general conflict taking in several convoys and submarine groups
Tactical	Direction of military forces to gain operational objectives	Battles, engagements	Individual convoy actions

Notes
[a] Sometimes given in literature as 'strategic'. However, the use of 'military strategic' avoids ambiguity.
[b] There is a tension between the definitions and the layout in Figure 2.1 of *British Maritime Doctrine*, suggesting that campaigns are both the concern of strategic and operational levels. No attempt is made to resolve this here.

High-level perspectives – alliances and nations

In a very important sense, at the level of grand strategic interests the Battle of the Atlantic was not symmetrical to either alliances or to their constituent nations, and unless this is understood then it is difficult to see the series of campaigns in a proper perspective. Looking first at alliances, there are some fundamental structural points to consider. These indicate the diversity nature of such associations.

The German–Italian–Japanese axis was very loose at best, and had little coincidence of interest other than to prevail over their opponents and (individually) dominate the world. Each of these implicit aims was latterly about as realistic as the other. Further, both mutual respect and coordination were lacking in attitudes to each other and strategic target-setting. There were relatively few spheres in which any large-scale cooperation was carried out. Indeed, joint military ventures, such as in Africa and the eastern Mediterranean were characterised more by a sense of one side – the Germans – bailing out another – the Italians – whose strategic ambitions were at odds with their abilities to achieve them. There were some attempts to bring together aspects of submarine warfare against the Grand Alliance. The smaller of these was in the Indian Ocean and Far Eastern areas but these were not wholly effective, not least because Japanese base support of German submarines was inadequate.[6] An apparently more thoroughgoing effort was made in the Atlantic by Italian submarines.[7] However, this suffered from a number of problems, some material, some doctrinal and others probably caused by lower operational effectiveness.[8] Certainly the Italians were poorly regarded by the Germans. As such, they could hardly be said to have aided Axis solidarity. Looking in strategic terms at the Battle of the Atlantic from an Axis perspective, success would not automatically have resulted in the Axis winning the war. It would have been a very important enabling step but would not immediately or certainly given a victory to that side. This is an important aspect of the asymmetry of the Battle.

The strategic situation of the Grand Alliance, whose principal members were Anglo-Saxon and Russian, could hardly have been more different. The means of connection of the strategic and economic might of the USA with the European war was entirely Atlantic-borne. A loss of the ability to use the ocean for such a purpose would have certainly ruled out any useful form of Allied victory, far less the unconditional surrender demanded latterly. For the Axis, the Battle of the Atlantic might represent the last, best chance to delay or prevent the

Allied re-occupation of mainland Europe: for the Alliance the Battle had to be won. But success at any given time was not sufficient: Allied dominance had to continue to ensure that American economic strength and Allied logistic capabilities could both be exploited to the maximum. Further, it was not just in strategic importance or aim that the Alliance differed from the Axis: it was far more of a real combination, with significant depth and breadth, both dimensions lacking from the Axis. It is true that there were many Allied quarrels, with sides often being split along national lines. In particular there were severe differences of opinion on the allocation of resources and strategic plans, as well as lower-level disputes. But the strength of the Alliance lay in its ability to resolve these and to continue to do business and cooperate in a number of different ways. Thus the great amphibious operations from late 1942 onwards never involved less than two nations, as did the European bombing campaigns as well as the Battle of the Atlantic.

It is perhaps worth expanding the Allied perspective in terms of four individual nations: the USSR, Canada, USA and the UK. The first of these is not normally considered a participant in the Battle, as the Russians took no part in the main actions, but it would be wrong to ignore it entirely.[9] The demands of supply to Russia certainly put extra demands on the Battle in two ways. firstly, there was a necessity for a certain amount of material to move across the Atlantic in addition to that heading for the UK. Admittedly some of this was diverted rather than being an extra imposition, but the amount was not insignificant. The second aspect was the diversion of protective assets to cope with a very much wider range of German threats than would be considered normal for the main Atlantic routes during most of the war. Admittedly some of this made demands on ships which had little role to play in the Battle of the Atlantic such as cruisers, but the German northern combination of submarines, surface ships and aircraft also tended to absorb large numbers of destroyers and other escorts when they might have been used on the transatlantic routes. The climactic conditions imposed an extra burden, sometimes themselves creating damage which further delayed the return of these largely British units to Atlantic service.[10] Some might argue that the Arctic convoys are a part of the Battle of the Atlantic, but they are very much a subset of the main experience with significant differences in terms of amounts of cargo delivered, together with their climactic and warfare environments. What was perhaps their most noteworthy feature was the strong political imperative to run these convoys, both to support the

Soviet Union materially and as a significant gesture in the direction of – cynics would say instead of – a second European front.[11]

Canada was another nation which, for different reasons, was unlikely to have her direct national security affected by the Battle of the Atlantic. On the other hand, her geographical placing was of extreme importance for the Battle. After leaving ports in the north-eastern USA, eastbound convoys still had a considerable distance to travel before leaving the north American continental landmass behind.[12] This made air and naval bases on this coast of great importance in being able to support convoys with relative ease, most especially before the entry of the USA into the war. There can be little doubt, too, that the Canadians made a considerable contribution to the fighting of the Battle. However, many of their good intentions in this direction were degraded somewhat. This was largely attributable to the problems of starting from a very small base in a number of ways – force size, technology and competence.[13] Despite these disadvantages, Canada provided escorts for a great number of ocean convoys and a part of the escort force, out of proportion to her naval strength. Relations with her larger collaborators, the Americans and British, were not always harmonious: the former either tended to ignore Canada or else consider it a British possession with no requirement to be treated otherwise, whilst the latter was often highly critical of Canadian tactical performance. It is certainly true that some of the heaviest maulings suffered by convoys were to those under Canadian protection, but it is only fair to point out that the Canadians escorted a higher proportion of the slow convoys which were, by their nature, more vulnerable.

The United States of America was again not directly at risk from German submarine activities. Nevertheless, damage could be wrought on its interests and there was throughout an economic vulnerability. For the first part of the war, up until December 1941, America was little touched by the Battle of the Atlantic as initially deployed submarines lacked the capacity to reach into the western hemisphere. Nor did they, with the targets available to them off Europe need to do so. In the latter part of 1941, the Germans were constrained by their leadership from deliberate attack on American ships. However, a form of going to war by degrees was practised by both the Americans and Germans. The situation changed completely by 1942 with America now fully in the war. The operational-level details are in the next chapter. The importance of this to the Battle of the Atlantic was not perhaps immediately obvious. A significant part was played in convoy escort, in much the same way as the Canadians and British were undertaking such tasks, although full implementation of the convoy system did not occur until after substantial losses had been incurred. What was of much greater significance was the provision of war material. This had already been undertaken, but the spur of full participation in the war turned a relative dribble into a veritable torrent. Technological innovation was a key factor but perhaps the most important matter was the sheer volume of war material which came from the American war production machine. Of these, probably the most notable achievements were long-range aircraft, escort carriers and – surely the most important of all – vast numbers of merchant ships.

The United Kingdom was the only Allied European participant of substance throughout the war. This fact, together with the realisation that economic strangulation if not physical starvation was a possible outcome of the Battle, lent British efforts an urgent motivation that was unusual in its intensity and probably matched by no other nation, except possibly the Germans. Despite Churchillian flirtations with premature dreams of hunting groups; despite considerable other claims on scarce naval and air units, the aim of shipping protection and its principal engine of execution – the convoy system – was maintained throughout the war. Further, the British often took the lead in matters of strategy and tactics and, despite efforts at defence diplomacy on their part, this was sometimes to the annoyance of their American allies and the irritation of the Canadians. Nevertheless, this steadfastness of aim, combined with a sometimes almost terrifying intensity of application, was an important determinant of victory. So too was a comparative receptiveness to new ideas, sometimes emanating from what would have previously been thought of as somewhat strange quarters. Thus, the two fields – unfamiliar at the outset – of codebreaking and operational research gained initially respect and later enthusiastic acceptance.

Returning to the level of Alliance grand strategy, the importance of the Battle of the Atlantic lay in its power as an enabling and empowering mechanism. It was the containment of Dönitz's submarines in 1942, their defeat in 1943 and the continuing efforts that kept them down from then onwards that allowed the massive buildup of men and matériel that culminated in the successful invasion of Europe in 1944 and, ultimately, the winning of the western European war. To emphasise the importance of this continuity, the Battle of the Atlantic had to be won and it had to stay won.

Some further strategic points

A number of other points deserve to be made in an overview of the
Battle of the Atlantic. These concern the non-submarine components
of the threat to shipping, the subject of so-called sea lanes, connections to land warfare and, lastly, a brief mention of the economic
dimension.

There can be little doubt that the principal agent of merchant-ship
destruction in the Battle of the Atlantic was the submarine, as viewed
statistically and from the standpoint of history. But it was by no means
the only problem which faced the Alliance at sea and it is appropriate
to mention the other problems caused by enemy action. One of the
biggest perceived threats both acutely in reality and potentially as a
chronic factor was that of the German heavy surface ships. There were
only a few of these and their number was never added to significantly
as the war progressed.[14] Their sorties were a source of great concern as
much for their disruptive effect as for actual achievements in sinking
ships. They also tended to induce a reaction which would lead to all
possible available battleships, aircraft-carriers and cruisers, as well as
many other units, including aircraft being mobilised in an attempt to
find and destroy them. On occasion, this would even mean the redeployment of ships from other theatres such as the Mediterranean. The
best example of this is almost certainly the *Bismarck* Atlantic sortie in
May 1941 when one German battleship accompanied by a heavy
cruiser absorbed the efforts of eight battleships/battlecruisers, two aircraft-carriers, 14 cruisers and five flag officers at sea.[15] Later in the war,
her surviving sister *Tirpitz* resulted in the commitment of significant
effort without even leaving the protection of the Norwegian coast.

Another threat based on the surface was that of the disguised raider,
effectively cruisers posing as merchant vessels. Clearly, these could
only function effectively in areas where there was a low density of
Allied opposition, as the submarine's ability to disappear immediately
was denied such ships. This meant in practice that their operating areas
were largely those remote from the North Atlantic. As there were also
difficulties in sailing these ships from German ports covertly against a
reasonably effective reconnaissance effort, they tended to be a diminishing asset. This is reflected in the fact that they sank no ships at all
after 1943 and their wartime total globally was only about 830 000
tons as against over 14 million for submarines.[16] For the purposes of
the Battle of the Atlantic, therefore, such activities should be noted but
no further account will be taken of them.

In overall terms, a more potent means of ship-sinking was the mine, which accounted for some 1.4 million tons of shipping. These could be laid by surface minelayer, aircraft or submarine. Although both significant and reasonably economical in German effort, there were drawbacks to such campaigns. Although suited to coastal waters and port entrances, mines could not be used effectively in deeper water, a product of technological limitation and the general property that deeper water is nearly always wider water, thus generating a quite unrealistic demand for mine numbers. There are three basic difficulties to be encountered in planning a minefield off or near an enemy's coast: accurate placement, which is necessary for efficient minefield design; the vulnerability of the minelayer; and the ease with which an enemy can counter a mine offensive. The latter is to some extent determined by the mine technology used. In the early years of the war, the advantage here clearly lay with the Germans, but a marked British effort to find out the nature of the mines used by the Germans and then considerable application in dealing with them meant that the mine's use as an effective weapon peaked in 1940 and declined thereafter.[17] Probably the area most affected was the Thames Estuary (and thus the Port of London) but this was, in any case, to be rendered much less important than in peacetime by its marked vulnerability to air attack. Thus the mine and the countermeasures to it played a significant part in the war, but hardly one that was central to the Battle of the Atlantic.

Aircraft, too, posed a risk to shipping. Their overall global wartime achievement in terms of numbers and tonnages of ships sunk stands second only to submarines – but a long way behind.[18] It is less easy to be very specific and make reasoned comparisons about their achievements in the North Atlantic area.[19] Certainly, they had a marked effect on coastal shipping around the UK coast and in the North Sea and this, together with losses in harbour, resulted in the diversion of the main stream of traffic from southeastern to northwestern ports. In the open ocean it is fairly clear that results were of a relatively low order, and peaked in the latter part of 1940 and the first half of 1941. After that, with the large-scale diversion of aircraft to other places, especially Russia, little was achieved. In any case, it can be argued that the greater danger from aircraft such as the Focke-Wulf 200 came not from its performance as a bomber but from its reconnaissance potential. If this had been properly worked up with Dönitz's submarines, if more generally Luftwaffe-Kriegsmarine cooperation had functioned on a basis of mutual trust rather than antagonism, then not only would the aircraft have been more useful but the submarines, too, would almost certainly have done better. Overall, however, other than for very limited periods of time German aircraft did not play a significant part in the Battle of the Atlantic.

It is now necessary to consider an item of mythology as far as shipping, attack on it and its defence is concerned: the matter of 'sea lanes'. This is a terminology – or at least a meaning – which probably derives from the nature of transport and warfare on land and is rarely, if ever, applicable to matters maritime. There are, of course, a number of places around the world such as various straits where free passage is restricted by either dry land or limited depths of water. But on a planet which is mostly covered by water and whose landmasses are more continental than archipelagic, these are relatively rare. This contrasts sharply with the position on land where, ever since the advent of the modern era, options for mass transport – and thus the passage of armies – are rather more constrained. It is true that there are some areas of the world which have almost maritime characteristics, such as parts of the American Midwest, and in North Africa and the Russian steppe, but these are not perhaps representative of the areas in which most conflicts occur.[20] On land, roads and railways are vitally important in war. It may well be possible, indeed it is normally necessary, for frontline troops and their equipment to move across and fight in untracked territory, but it is vastly more efficient for some, if not all of an army's logistic support to move on clearly defined and thus vulnerable paths. These tended to be defined by both placement and use. Although these lines of communication may be built or upgraded to ease military movement, most of them already exist. The requirements of warfare, especially at high tempos, also suggest reasonably high density of military traffic. It is therefore worth an enemy's while to consider interdicting such a route *as a route* most especially where alternatives are scarce or, better still, non-existent. Such considerations do not apply in oceans. Their sheer scale permits many alternative routings under most circumstances and, in any case, traffic density at any one point in the open ocean at any one time is very slight. For these reasons sea lines certainly do not exist and any practical definition of sea lane would probably have to be so broad as to negate the normal sense of 'lane' as being a narrow passage. One dictionary gives two main meanings, both with the connotation of constriction.[21] The important point to note in oceanic warfare is that neither lanes nor lines can legitimately be attacked: only ships can be targets.

This spatial property of the oceans has another implication, in this case for any nation who wishes to use it. Under most circumstances, it is not possible to control the sea absolutely, everywhere and at all times. This might be possible in certain littoral areas for some of the time, but in the open ocean such a dream of total control would not just be hopelessly uneconomical in resources but practically impossible. Sea control, therefore, by most modern definitions is temporary and partial.[22] For an opponent, countering such control, generally known as sea-denial, is clearly aided by invisible deployment – as was the case for submarines at least in the early part of the war. The ability to exercise any form of sea-control or sea-denial is critically dependent on intelligence and reconnaissance.

A further aspect of the Battle of the Atlantic which should be considered is the interaction of its maritime action with that on land. The dependency of the latter on the former has already been mentioned in this chapter.[23] But there is also a relationship in the other direction too, with land operations having significant impacts on the Battle as well. There are two especially good examples of this, although others may be found. It can be argued with considerable force that the greatest strategic step forward that was made by Dönitz and his U-boats happened not because of any tactical or material advances in submarines, or because of allied deficiencies at sea, but was made rather by German armoured and other land and air forces in the summer of 1940. The remarkably rapid fall of France allowed the setting-up of submarine bases in western France on the Atlantic coast, giving much easier access to the Atlantic than had previously been the case. Similarly, it was the demands of the land campaigns in north Africa and their consequent seaborne logistic support, together with the inadequacy and impracticability of providing German surface naval support, which generated the demand for the transfer of U-boats to the Mediterranean in the latter part of 1941. Historical hindsight and Dönitz's contemporary view both suggest that the Atlantic would have been the better long-term choice for the Germans, but the important point is the linkage with the battles on land, not the correctness or otherwise of the decision. It might be thought logical to extend this process to the air, but this would appear to deny the universal importance of the air to engagements both at sea and on land. Indeed, it might be argued that there is rarely such a thing as a modern campaign that takes place in a single environment. Certainly on going down the levels of warfare, there is a tendency for conflicts to be more heavily weighted to two or even a single environment, although this is not an invariable rule.[24] In the context of the Battle of the

Atlantic, it would be difficult to argue that air warfare was not an important part of the conflict – even if, from the perspective of both sides and especially the Germans – it was never fully integrated.

It is perhaps proper also to introduce the idea at this point that economics is important to an understanding of the Battle: this need not be the daunting prospect that it might appear to some.[25] Not only were both Allied and German aims easily expressible in economic terms – the transfer of a desired amount of a cargo across the Atlantic, and the thwarting of that aim, respectively – but many other aspects of the Battle can be viewed more clearly, even down to the tactical level, in the light of views which draw on both economics and operational research.

One final observation: in the centuries leading up to 1939, very little of maritime warfare occurred very far from land. More advanced naval nations might operate at oceanic ranges from their home ports, but warfare tended to remain robustly coastal. It could be argued that the Battle of the Atlantic was the first instance of true ✔ oceanic warfare.[26]

It can thus be seen that the Battle of the Atlantic did not exist in some form of strategic vacuum but, despite some of the points of difference with other forms of warfare, that it was very much part of the strategic continuum of the Second World War.

The Battle of the Atlantic and its history

For the historian, the Battle of the Atlantic sets a challenge, or rather a series of challenges. The fundamental problems are those of size and complexity. So before ending this chapter by setting out how it is intended to deal with the problem of assessing one particular aspect of it – Ultra codebreaking intelligence – it would be wise to ✔ review the essential nature of the Battle, how the writing of history has approached this phenomenon, and in turn what effect this has had on perceptions of the Battle. If this body of literature is considered to be flawed, then suggestions for corrective action are also needed.

Some allusion to the extent of the Battle of the Atlantic has already been made in this chapter, but it is worth re-emphasising some of these. They can be summarised as:

- the size of the area in which the conflict occurred, only exceeded by the Pacific theatre

- the length of the conflict, which took in the entire span of the European war from 1939 to 1945
- the deployment of considerable amounts of high technology combined with the importance of national economies to the conflict
- the strategic significance of the Battle
- the importance of 'soft' fields of activity such as intelligence, training, organisation and operational research.

All this is suggestive of a maze; not perhaps an ordinary, two-dimensional one, but one which exists in at least three dimensions. This analogy may be a helpful one in seeing what type of problem exists: it does not necessarily, however, provide a guide to navigating through the maze.

There have been several approaches adopted over the decades to the problem.[27] Like the Battle of the Atlantic itself and its archival legacy, the mass of secondary material is large. There is no space here to conduct a full historiographical review of the field, but a few general areas of study can be sketched out.[28] These are the time period, the theme and the general survey and they may exist singly or in some degree of combination.

Time periods rarely take in less than the passage of a single convoy but there have been a number of monographs both in book and article forms dealing with such subjects.[29] It is rare for any of these to deal with convoys which experienced no substantial encounter with the enemy.[30] Other works consider the span of campaigns or parts of them.[31] Another approach is to look at single subjects, such as the activities of a single type of ship involved, equipment or individuals.[32] General surveys ought to begin with the official histories of Roskill and Morison, but there have been more recent instances, too.[33]

Some general comments can be made about the body of literature as a whole. Obviously, and this will become more pronounced as participants disappear from the scene, the historian is limited largely to the available primary material, setting an obvious limit to both scope and depth of research. This has been described as a 'looking under a lamppost' phenomenon.[34] But it might be argued that street-lighting is both absolute and relative. Total darkness (lack of material) precludes further search (study). Low levels of light (comparatively scanty material or difficulty in interpreting what is available) may turn students away from subjects. But this does not mean that the rejected, or less popular subject is either impossible to pursue or – more critically – less important in understanding the general picture. One example of this is high-level shipping policy.[35]

As has been suggested by the preceding argument, there has been a clear bias in the published literature to the benefit of incident instead of routine, of action over non-event, and of front-line happenings in preference to subjects such as administration. This is one form of historiographical distortion. This is so because, in the case of the Battle of the Atlantic, what did not happen is perhaps as important as what did. Marc Milner has noted this in two ways, drawing attention to the avoidance of action as being of significance.[36] To him too belongs the phrase 'Happy is the convoy that has no history'. In fact, despite the assumption that might be drawn that these statements refer to the same thing, two distinct phenomena are being alluded to here. In the first case, it refers to those convoys which the Germans wished to engage, and made efforts to do so, but were not successful for whatever reason.[37] The second refers to convoys which were not even exposed to attempted molestation. Here, the explanation might be simply a lack of German capacity in one of several different ways, or else a perception as occurred at several points in the conflict that for reasons, positive or negative, that their interests lay elsewhere than attacking convoys, either generally or particular ones.

One particular distortion that has been evident almost throughout the historiography of the Battle of the Atlantic has been about Ultra. For some 30 years after the end of the war this was a closed subject, unknown except to those involved in it and a very few others. Those who were aware of it were under considerable constraints both legal and, to the credit of the overwhelming majority, of honour too, not to reveal their knowledge. There were a few instances of pushing such discretion to its limits, Donald McLachlan's 1969 book driving a substantial dog-cart if not a coach and horses through the wall of silence, even if this would appear to have gone largely unrealised at the time, except by those already knowledgeable.[38] A more interesting and elegant hidden indicator was given by no other than the official historian of the maritime war, Stephen Roskill, as early as 1956. He wrote:

> Though it runs ahead of the stage now reached in our story, it is relevant to mention that it was not until May 1943 that the discomfiture of the highly skilled German cypher-breakers was

made complete and final. The reader should not, of course, assume that we British were meanwhile idle in achieving the opposite purpose.[39]

The distortion in these decades running up to 1975 was that historians in general were able to take no overt account of the Ultra factor in their analyses. That year saw the publication of *The Ultra Secret*.[40] For the next decade or so, the distortion flipped in the opposite direction and assumptions of Ultra's potency were made which were not justified and rarely supported by analysis of decent rigour.[41] This is what might be described as the 'Ultra as magic ingredient' phase of historiographical distortion. The proper palliative lay in works such as the British official history, and indeed this disposed of some, if not all, of the more extreme claims for Ultra.[42] Unfortunately, its publication was not completed until 1988 by which time the 'magic ingredient' school had built up considerable impetus resulting in what has been called the Ultra myth.[43] Consequently, it would be premature to claim that all distortions have now been overcome and that a fully balanced view of the significance of Ultra now exists. Nor is it likely to be approached, far less achieved, unless proper regard is paid to three categories of historical question: what, how and why.

It is the contention of this book that the balance of prior literature on the Battle of the Atlantic has been strong (if patchy in coverage) in respect of what; considerably less good on how and unacceptable on why. The purpose of what follows is an attempt to remedy that deficiency as it applies to one subject, albeit an important one.

Navigating through the maze

In attempting to give an indication of the true significance of Ultra to the Battle of the Atlantic, it is necessary to make two preliminary points. The first is that such an analysis, or to be more accurate, series of analyses, can only be carried out because of prior work carried out by a number of others in the field.[44] Second, there will be times in the chapters which follow when points will be repeated. This is necessary because the events and phenomena which are described had overlapping characteristics. Further, the trail of occurrences and thought of the book is complex, and sometimes long and thus some repetition is not only desirable but essential; no apology is offered for doing this.

The method adopted is initially to present the Battle of the Atlantic as a whole together with Ultra in a number of different perspectives or contexts: chronology and time, economics, a German view, convoys, technology and finally signals intelligence. These are then used to inform two case studies, the first on the calendar year 1941 and the second on the period from the summer of 1942 to May 1943. Finally, the findings of all of these are brought together to produce an argued view of the overall significance of Ultra in the Battle of the Atlantic.

2
Chronology, Time and Measurement

It is very difficult to understand specific parts of the Battle of the Atlantic – whether they are defined by period or subject – without having at least a basic knowledge of the whole series of campaigns that form the struggle. This is probably best done by means of chronological presentation and the case studies which are given later in the book should, in particular, be viewed in such a context among others. Although these can be read as monographs, some of their value is lost without an appreciation of the whole of which they form part. The Battle of the Atlantic underwent several changes of scale, nature and intensity and was never lacking in strategic significance. In this work, which is concerned with assessing the overall impact of one specific field, Ultra, on a larger whole, it is nec- ✔ essary to comprehend this whole before turning to looking at the particular. A chronology is probably one of the most practical ways of achieving this purpose.[1] However, the mere chronological presentation of information is sometimes derided in historical writing, but as well as being significant in itself it is an essential foundation for much subsequent analytical work. This latter point is expanded on in two ways in the latter part of this chapter. Firstly, it is suggested that time is woven so deeply into perception of events and their meaning that its proper significance has a tendency to be ignored, or at least underestimated: here it is intended to redress this imbalance. Secondly, this raises the even less regarded area of measurement, despite its undoubted importance. In order to conduct analyses which have any significance, they must be founded on two sound pillars – data and method. The last part of this chapter will concern itself with some characteristics of the problems of measurement of data. Perhaps, this is an appropriate point at which to reassure readers that this examination will be conducted almost entirely in words and without recourse to complex mathematics.

The Battle of the Atlantic – a chronology

There are many different places where a chronology of the Battle of the
Atlantic might be found, including the official histories of Roskill and
Morison.[2] These works cover the whole war at sea from British and
American perspectives respectively. The entire naval conflict is also
described in a more detailed and overtly chronological format in the
book by Rohwer and Hummelchen.[3] There are also a number of works
which adopt a largely chronological approach to the topic. It would,
however, be fairly difficult to take issue with the classification adopted
by two of the leading authorities on the subject, Barley and Waters,
and Jürgen Rohwer.[4] In this classification, eight phases of the Battle of
the Atlantic are identified, and it is intended to describe these briefly,
to provide a time-related frame for the succeeding chapters.

The first starts with the outbreak of the European war in September
1939 and runs up to the overrunning of the Low Countries and France
in June 1940. Its main characteristics are of only a few, predominantly
small submarines deployed relatively close to Germany, being constrained by the limiting strategic geography of Germany's position in
the North Sea. Despite these disadvantages these boats had a significant
impact, averaging some 100 000 tons of shipping sunk per month ✓
during the period. Swings in performance were dictated as much by
the operational tempos of a small force and weather as by anything
their opponents did. The majority of the ships sunk were sailing inde- ✓✓
pendently, indicating that the British (and others) were unable to have
as extensive a convoy system as they wished.[5] At sea, unlike on land,
there was to be no 'phoney war' or *Sitzkrieg*, as the conflict started on
the first day with the sinking of the liner *Athenia*, actually against
German directives. The incompleteness of the convoy system gave the
Germans no incentive to seek the more difficult targets. Nevertheless
they carried out the first trials of the *Rudeltaktik* – what became known
to the Allies as wolfpack tactics. Although efficient and reasonably productive in themselves, submarine operations on such a scale were
unlikely to cause serious strategic or economic damage to Britain. The
46 boats operationally deployed at the outbreak of war were depleted ✓✓
by 17 submarines lost in the Battle of the Atlantic and the Norwegian
campaign.

The second phase, also of about nine months, was from July 1940
until March 1941. The German conquest of France gave the great
advantage of the Biscay bases, allowing the deployment of submarines
into the Atlantic both with shorter passage-times and without many of

the operational difficulties implicit in North German basing. At the same time the British were weakened not only by the demise of their French ally but also by losses of surface ships sustained in the campaigns which had resulted in the German successes. Worse still, the heavy demands of anti-invasion operations meant that even fewer escorts were available to support the convoy system. Some use was made of the *Rudeltaktik*, with results that were encouraging for the Germans. This meant that the Germans were able not only to continue to reap significant dividends from sinking independents but also to see good results from attacking the relatively weakly protected convoys. As a result, the still fairly small number of submarines managed to sink about 250 000 tons monthly, split roughly equally between independents and convoyed shipping.[6] Such results were starting to become the true stuff of tonnage warfare and had such levels of achievement been maintained by the planned expansion of the submarine fleet, then a decisive result could have taken place.[7] It was for these results that the period became known to the Germans as the first of two *glückliche Zeit* or 'Happy Time'.

The characteristics of the period from March to December 1941[8] were quite different, however, from its predecessors. The first point to note is that during 1941 the submarine fleet grew over threefold, from about 80 submarines at the beginning of the year to over 250 by the end of 1941. Secondly, the British – by now alone – were able to increase their activities in the important area west of the United Kingdom and Ireland. As a result of a number of poor submarine operations in this area and British pressure, the Germans decided to move their operations to the west, particularly intending to put themselves out of reach of British air activity. The latter happened, but in solving one problem two others were created. Firstly, effective application of the *Rudeltaktik*, by now the predominant method of attack in open ocean was partially thwarted by the sheer size of the area of operations, and consequently submarine packs had problems in locating convoys. Secondly, the longer passage times from base detracted from submarines' overall productivity – defined as number of tons sunk per submarine at sea for a given time.[9] They were no less deadly once they found a convoy, but this happened less often and it took them longer to reach such areas. At the same time, the British were not only making progress with their material but were also able to use intelligence with increasing effect. In the first third of the period, sinkings averaged about 300 000 tons monthly but fell back latterly to about 120 000 tons. At the strategic level there were substantial diversions of submarines, especially to the Mediterranean. The other important development was the growing involvement of the United States in *de facto* convoy escort effort in the western hemisphere, leading to a German order not to operate against such shipping. In December, Hitler declared war on the USA. The overall summation of the period is one of German initial promise thwarted by different varieties of Allied action.[10]

From January until July 1942, the character of the Battle of the Atlantic changed radically. Some of the longer-range submarines were despatched to the US east coast and there enjoyed a second *glückliche Zeit*. Despite the very long passage there, the results not only returned the U-boat fleet to its previous high levels of productivity, it surpassed most of 1941. This was because there were many targets available on that seaboard; they sailed independently without immediate protection and such action as was taken was largely ineffective.[11] The key to this was the lack of a convoy system, whatever the underlying reasons for such a deficiency. Sinkings averaged about half a million tons monthly in this period. Later, convoy systems were introduced and, as they came into effect, the measure neutralised the initial German effort. However, Admiral Dönitz responded to this by moving his submarines to areas where there was as yet no convoy system. Thus the Germans moved successively into the Gulf of Mexico and the Caribbean. Such deployments were, of course, at ever-greater distances from Europe but they continued to bring rewards in terms of tonnages sunk. However, by the middle of the year, it was becoming clear to the Germans that the attack on the Americas had all but exhausted itself and a new strategy was needed.

This process started by degrees from about July 1942 when oceanic warfare against convoys was resumed, a phase which continued until near the end of May 1943, by which time this was the main activity of Dönitz's submarines.[12] The main characteristics were very large deployments of submarines and hard-fought battles against relatively large numbers of both air and warship escorts. But unlike the convoy battles of 1941, when it seemed that a group of submarines had to do little more than to make initial contact with a convoy before sinking a significant number of ships, resistance was now much stiffer. The main consequence of this was a drop not just in submarine productivity but in their ability to sink ships at all. Nevertheless the scale of commitment meant that Allied losses were significant. In the last half of 1942, they averaged over 500 000 tons monthly; in the succeeding six months, the corresponding figure was under 300 000. From the beginning, too, there were some submarine sinkings to encourage the Allies but these did not reach large figures until right at the end of May 1943, accompanied by a poor return for the large commitment of effort. Dönitz then withdrew from attacking convoys on the main cross-Atlantic routes. This phase could justly be described as the climactic one of the Battle of the Atlantic: before it, U-boats enjoyed their greatest success; afterwards, they scrabbled for fragments.

After this came a short spell of only three months (June–August 1943) in which the Germans made a few abortive efforts against convoys in the central Atlantic. These achieved little and led to the further significant losses of submarines. Some attempt was made to take the U-boat war to more remote areas where the Germans assessed that there was less protection for shipping. However, these efforts were on a small scale compared to those in the previous period and the net result was a fall in tonnage sunk to about 150 000 tons per month. Worse still, the efforts long applied by the British to the submarine transit routes through the Bay of Biscay bore particularly good fruit in this phase and the German decline continued.

The Allies became even more dominant between September 1943 and May 1944. Again losses of merchant ships declined and submarine sinkings stayed high. The Germans had hopes of various technical innovations both in the near- and medium-terms. The former depended on such techniques as a homing torpedo, intended largely as an anti-escort weapon, and measures to counter the great potency of aircraft against submarines. A combination of rapidly applied countermeasures to these innovations, skill and superior force gave the Allies dominance over the German efforts. The net result was a further fall in tonnages sunk to averages of under 100 000 tons monthly. Limited attempts to return to convoy warfare failed. Further ahead, the Germans looked to the potential of advanced technology propulsion to make their submarines, then little more than submersible torpedo boats, into something close to the true submarine. The Allies, aware of such developments and rightly concerned about them, started a series of countermeasures designed to stop or at least greatly slow their operational deployment. Despite considerable efforts, the German decline continued.

The last year of the submarine campaigns and of the war itself saw the continuing theme of German effort being maintained despite a further decrease in achievement. The introduction of the schnorkel did something to improve the survival of submarines, most especially in making them far less vulnerable to both aircraft and radar. It also made feasible the deployment of submarines to inshore waters. However, operating in this fashion allowed no more effectiveness than before and despite the large size of the overall submarine fleet, average monthly sinkings were in the order of 50 000 tons and the number of ships sunk never exceeded 20. Perhaps the last best chance for German submarines to have influenced Allied strategy lay in their potential to disrupt the invasion of France in the summer of 1944. Certainly, it was a possibility that the Allies took extremely seriously. As a result, extraordinary efforts were made to deny the routes from the assembly ports to the beaches – these were entirely successful. More widely, the much-vaunted new technology submarines were now in production, but despite substantial numbers of them undergoing training, no effective operational deployment took place before the German surrender in May 1945.[13]

Thus ended the longest, most destructive submarine assault on shipping that the world had ever seen. It had involved the efforts of about a thousand submarines and some 40 000 men at sea. It is very difficult to produce a useful single series of figures for the Allied effort pitted against it, but it is safe to say that it amounted to many more ships, aircraft and people than were at any one time at sea on the German side. There were also many resources not at sea devoted to both sides of the struggle and it is probably even more difficult to attempt to quantify these resources. However, the accounts given in this section form a necessary backdrop to the more detailed accounts and analyses which follow.

Time – the central dimension *or* three aspects of the fourth dimension

Setting out a chronology makes implicit use of a sequence of events rendered in the order in which they occurred and introduces the subject of time in its own right. Time is very much one of the tools with which a historian has to work but it is a quantity which can be semi-submerged and thus taken too much for granted. A return to a basic understanding of time and its characteristics at all levels and scales can very much aid an understanding of some of the less evident features of the Battle of the Atlantic.

Time, like all features which are intimately woven into the events of the world, together with its history – both narrative and analysis – runs the risk of being so obvious as to be overlooked. It is not the only subject which tends to suffer from this neglect. Weather, very much the concern of the maritime practitioner, tends to receive less consideration from the

Table 2.1 Looking at time

Names	Frames	Windows	Connections
Characteristics	Objective Post-event Sequence Narrative Observed complex events	Subjective Contemporaneous Opportunities Intended events Different criticalities for different participants	Analytical Post-event Correlation Bases to consider complex phenomena
Typical Time currencies used	Hour → hour Date → date	Relative times	Hours–days–months (operational research) Days–months–years (history)
Examples	The Battle of the Atlantic The east coast of America campaign – first half of 1942	The time available to a submarine pack for attacking a convoy while it is in the air-gap How long can an escort group commander afford to detach escorts	Submarine productivity calculations Changes in convoy warfare characteristics

historian. Yet it did have a very marked effect on both the conduct of operations and their outcomes, and unless this is both known about and taken account of, both chronicles and assessments may either make factual errors or else draw false conclusions. It might be argued that it affects both sides equally and, in the general sense that two naval forces in the same general area experience approximately the same weather, this is correct. However, the problems of keeping a convoy of unlike ship-types together in heavy weather are not the same as those experienced by the submarine group attempting to close them or carry out attacks. Another example is that in an era when the eye was the principal tactical sensor, visibility was all-important and poor visibility tended to work to the benefit of the convoy rather than its attacker, although the problems of convoy management might well be exacerbated. In a different way, economic considerations were omnipresent in the Battle of the Atlantic in a number of ways.[14]

It might be useful to consider time in three different ways, which are explored more fully below. In shorthand these could be referred to as Frames, Windows and Connections.

Frames could be described as the normal way in which narrative history has been addressed, looking at all relevant events within a defined period. It is, or should be, objective and is largely concerned with sequence, that is, the order in which events occur. The events are often complex or compound and selection may be exercised in their presentation. The times selected can vary greatly in dimension but it is rare for them not to be defined, explicitly or implicitly.

Looking ahead to *connections*, this too is very much a label for a commonly practised tool of many different sorts of historians, that of analysis. Although some analyses, for example those of political motivation, can be conducted in an apparently time-free context or at least a less time-based manner, many investigations are conducted with time as one of their important bases. This can often be a useful technique for separating, or at least clarifying, the causations of complex phenomena. Although such correlative studies have been described in terms of being a tool for the historian, there has also been another important user of this technique, the operational researcher.[15] This is important for two reasons. Firstly, as indicated in Table 2.1, there is a clear overlap in the likely time-currencies to be used by the two disciplines, suggesting that each may draw on the other. Indeed from this it might be suggested that the operational research community might have a rather more legitimate claim to being the first rough drafters of history than journalists. Secondly, techniques have been drawn from operational research for use in this book and examples will be found in subsequent chapters.

Turning back to *windows*, this term is used here broadly in the sense expressed in the term 'windows of opportunity'. These are generally contemporaneous matters relating to opportunities in which certain desired outcomes may be achieved or specific dangers occur. They are very much related to the perceptions of the participants, thereby allowing the concept that such judgements may either be objectively false, or at least flawed in the light of hindsight. Nevertheless, that renders them no less important at the time. A significant point is that such a method of looking at phenomena tends to be more concerned with relative than absolute time. It should also be appreciated that there are such things as non-perceptual windows, that is, ones which open and close without the comprehension of a participant. As such uncomprehended events can have no effect on contemporary decisions, they are considered no further here.

Having broken down the consideration of time into these three categories, it is now necessary to make the point that little subsequent study is likely to be confined to a single one of these categories. The understanding, however, that these are separate ways of looking at time nevertheless remains a valid and useful tool in attempting to untangle the complexities of the past. One example of this is trying to discover the 'what', 'how' and 'why' of the Battle of the Atlantic in the second quarter of 1941.[16] In discussing the stages of this, all three ways of looking at time are noted alongside the appropriate aspects of the investigation.

In the spring of 1941, German submarines moved their main areas of operation into the mid-Atlantic (frames). As 1941 went on, the realisation dawned on the Germans that the Americans might eventually enter the war on the Allied side. This would make American industrial capacity available for the construction of merchant shipping. Clearly, therefore, the period until this happened represented an opportunity to significantly deplete British-controlled shipping (windows).[17] They suffered a drop in productivity (connections). In examining the reasons for this, a number of possible explanations were examined. These included the availability of Ultra information (frames) and its timeliness (windows and connections). Another factor looked at was the relative efficiency of submarines in sinking ships once convoy contact was made (frames and connections) as well as whether there were any significant differences in German performance before and after the general availability of Ultra (frames and connections). This exposition of analytical method is intended give a greater insight into subsequent examples in later chapters. Despite this threefold split, time remains indivisible; however, it is strongly suggested that it should be looked at it in more than one way. Certainly, if this under-regarded and implicit dimension is not taken proper account of, then it is likely to lead to flawed conclusions at best.

Time and the conduct of the battle

The threefold way of looking at time has already made the point that a significant aspect of time was not just its value as an analytical tool to operational researcher or historian but that it also played an important part in the conduct of the battle as it happened. This point can stand some further expansion. In particular, there are two areas where it can be suggested that time aids comprehension of the whole series of campaigns: levels of war, and in the treatment of problems.

The levels of war have been described in the previous chapter, which also gave some allusions of scale in the sense of geography and commitment of force. Here it is suggested that there is also likely to be a temporal dimension to such a classification. It is not sound to be too rigid about this connection but, starting from the self-evident reductionist point that grand strategy is as unlikely to be concerned with minutes and seconds as tactics is with years, the following might be suggested. The posing and solution of problems was very much the concern of those who directed activities at the various levels of war and some examples of these help to understand the points already made.

At the levels of grand and military strategy the connected problems of the sinking-rate of merchant ships was closely tied to that of the rate at which they were built.[18] This might be thought to be a simple comparison of two statistics against time and this can stand as an example

Table 2.2   War and time

War level	Probable timescales of interest					
Grand strategic	Years	Months	(Weeks)			
Military strategic	(Years)	Months	Weeks	(Days)		
Operational			Weeks	Days	(Hours)	
Tactical				(Days)	Hours	Minutes

Note   Brackets indicate possible rather than likely timescales of interest.

of how decisions might be more difficult for the policymaker than the historian. An Allied policymaker would probably be able to estimate the building-rate quite well but would have to make either highly speculative guesses or else take large policy gambles on the sinking-rate. ✓ One starting-point to such a problem would be the intended scale of operations over a given future period, a range of German performance and the known industrial capacity of the Allies. Time was clearly of great significance too. If a certain shipping stock was required, say, for a /were the buildup to the Normandy landings, then it would be needed by a certain time and required for a certain further period. If sufficient shipping was only available at some later date, other factors might entail the postponement of the operation, not necessarily just for the same period as the original delay, possibly into the following year. The terms 'time management' and 'time lines' as used in modern business might not have been in common currency then, but many of the concepts were.

At the tactical end of the spectrum stood the problem facing an escort force commander whose force had gained submarine contact. It was fairly self-evident that he should do something about it, but what? A fairly normal reaction was the detachment of one or more other units of the escort to assist the unit in contact. A further action was likely to be the turning-away of a convoy, so that it would take the submarine (and, it was hoped, its fellow pack-members) longer to close the convoy. Returning to the submarine contact, if a reasonably sure submarine-sinking occurred in fairly short order then these ships could quickly rejoin the convoy. But what if this speedy and happy outcome did not ensue? To what extent should the prosecution continue? Another question is that of the acceptable standard of proof of destruction of the submarine. This is often presented in the literature as a resource problem but it is also a time problem and the two aspects are closely related. One of the advantages of the greater numbers of available escorts as the war progressed was that it became more feasible to tolerate longer detachments and thus more prolonged attacks on submarines. This was one function of time playing a part in tactical decisions. But, in order to achieve the escort group commander's short-term requirements it might not be necessary to approach, far less ensure, the submarine's destruction. Depending on the geometry of the submarine's position to the convoy and their relative speeds, all that might be necessary to ensure the convoy's security would be to stop the submarine closing the convoy further for a certain period of time; this was likely to be much less than that needed for sinking the submarine with certainty. Thus can be seen the confluence of time, tactics, geometry and dynamics. The factor common to all these was time. This means that virtually all tactical problems generate time-requirements, just as factors favouring the escort made time, then those working for the enemy took it away. This was one of the reasons why the long-range aircraft was so valuable to convoy protection. In these circumstances, it allowed very quick conversion of almost any detection by a convoy unit into an attack, a circumstance hitherto somewhat rare.[19]

Another example at the operational-tactical level was the operation of submarine groups in the mid-Atlantic in the latter days of such operations in the spring of 1943. It has been an historiographical commonplace to illustrate the 'air gap' in mid-Atlantic as being the dead area between the circles of coverage of various Atlantic air-bases. But this spatial representation should also be seen in temporal terms as well. The distance which a convoy would realistically take at convoy speed in passing through the gap would convert into a period of time. This, in German perception and tactical reality, was the basic time a pack had in which to locate the convoy, close it and carry out attacks before withdrawing to safety, the whole process unhindered by air surveillance and attack. This sounds fairly simple but there were complications. It was obviously more prudent to carry out the most dangerous part of the process, torpedo-attacks themselves, by night, so careful synchronisation was needed. Obviously, the Allies would try as hard as possible to minimise the danger. All of these complex factors were calculable and expressible in either absolute or relative time. The feasibility or otherwise of operations to both sides depended critically on both the absolute existence of such opportunities and the vulnerability of sub-phases in the process to delay.

The last example deals with intelligence in general and especially Ultra. The ideal form of Ultra for anti-submarine operations would consist of information of the correct quality – dealing with current and near-future submarine operations – which was also available in a timely fashion. Equipped with this it might be possible to divert a convoy such that no submarine of the opposing group ever sighted it, far less directed its group to an attacking position. Obviously such a situation was the ideal, and this did not always work in practice. At the outset, one rough approximation by a practitioner suggests that Ultra would have to be decrypted within 48 hours of transmission to be tactically useful: this would seem realistic. But there are many complicating factors: the geometry of convoy and submarine group at the outset,

29

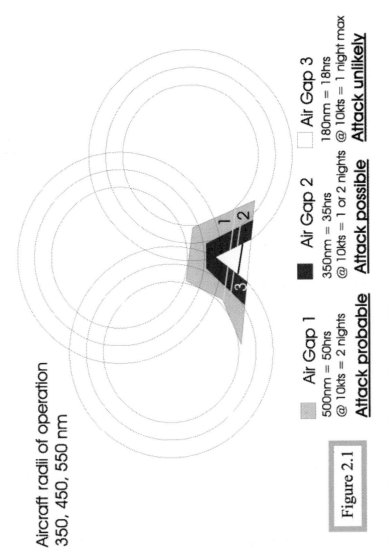

Figure 2.1 Closing the air gaps – distance and time

speeds of both groups, night and day, weather and visibility are just some considerations. To these should be added some complicating factors such as the relative skills of those directing the two formations from shore, navigational (in)accuracy and a degree of luck – such as happened on at least one occasion when a convoy was sighted by a submarine not of the attacking group. Most of these factors could be dealt with – if only in post analysis – by expressing them in terms of time.

Two final observations can be made. Doctrine has long held that the object of convoy is the safe and timely arrival of the ships protected. It should be fairly obvious that these are not complementary but rather competing objectives and that most practical problem-solving involved a degree of compromise of one or both of these requirements. The other point is that with the exception of such processes as the delivery of weapons and astro-navigation, knowledge of very precise times was unnecessary to the conduct of the battle. Indeed with weapons delivery, it was only relative time that was likely to be of importance. In other words, for most purposes, the contemporaneous measurement of time was adequate.

The significance of measurement

It is hoped that it has now been demonstrated that an understanding of the dimension of time is useful to the investigations that follow. But time is only one of several dimensions which have to be considered and such quantities themselves are only the measurable subset of the entire range of facts that have to be taken into account. On this, there is a useful threefold division, often made by practitioners of intelligence when dealing with information and, it is suggested, historians ignore such a discipline at their peril: fact, deduction from that fact and speculation.[20] To use such a system does not mean that everything written for publication should be arranged in three parallel columns or some such style but it should certainly be made reasonably clear in the final exposition which is which. Perhaps more importantly it should be used more rigorously in the analytical work which precedes writing. Measurement applies to a special class of facts: those that are susceptible to quantitative representation; and to a fast glance, that would appear to be that. But unfortunately truth, as has been observed, can lack both purity and simplicity and this can even apply to measurements. All 'facts' should therefore be approached with such an underlying health warning in mind – *caveat emptor*.

A naval historical work which has deservedly received more attention than many in the last two decades is Andrew Gordon's *The Rules
of the Game*. Most heed has been paid to the doctrinal points that the
author raises and it is possible that less interest has been shown to
Appendixes I–IV, a mere 17 pages in more than 600.[21] But they are of
great importance to the work in which they appear, this current
volume and to an understanding of operational naval history generally.[22] Further, they have rarely been stated and this is likely to mean
one of two things: either that they are so well understood that Gordon
is merely stating the obvious or else that they are neither understood
widely nor taken into account sufficiently.

In these pages, Gordon's theme is the inadequacy of primary record
material covering the Battle of Jutland in 1916. This, the largest clash
ever of British and German Dreadnought-era battleships and their supporting squadrons of lesser vessels, was conducted over a day of poor
visibility and a dark night in the North Sea. The problems not so much
of geographical position determination as of relative navigation, both
between the two sides and among the British large ships, are particularly described. The problems of attempting to reconcile different plots,
manuscript records and times are exposed with great clarity. Some of
these stem from the incidence of error, hardly surprising in the twin
lights of the anticipation of action and its sometimes grim, sometimes
exhilarating, reality. Some come from the requirements for making
such records being pressed either on to those who were already
burdened with other onerous responsibilities, or in some instances
insufficiently experienced to do the work well. It is also evident that
there was a degree of post-event record reconstruction. As Gordon
makes clear, there need not be any suspicion of conspiracy here:
merely the foibles of human nature. In particular, Gordon makes the
point that the recording of times is especially susceptible to problems.
It is difficult to avoid the conclusion that all these features have been
taken insufficient account of in previous analyses of the Battle of
Jutland.

But what, it might be asked, does this mean for the series of campaigns
conducted over 20 years later by different types of ships (and aircraft) in
the broad Atlantic? There are both similarities and differences. Both sets
of people were under the stress of battle and both were required to keep
certain records of their activities. The men of Jutland probably had more
naval experience but their activities were probably subject to less immediate post-battle scrutiny than those of those involved in anti-submarine
action. The means of assistance for navigation away from land were

little better in 1943 than in 1916 and the Battle of the Atlantic units were more involved in true oceanic war than were the battleships at Jutland. It is therefore fair to conclude that the same types of systematic difficulty existed with the keeping of operational records in both conflicts.

Does this mean, therefore, that the same degree of mistrust should be applied to the analyses based on primary material emanating from the Battle of the Atlantic as that from Jutland? At one level, the answer has to be yes. There cannot possibly be confidence in micro-analyses conducted without a full understanding of the limitations of the data used in conducting it. Further, it has to be suspected that at least some of the work carried out in the past has suffered from Jutland recorditis, that is, lacking an understanding of the data from which it has been based. This does not mean that it is all useless or that it serves no purpose at all. What it does suggest, however, are two things. Firstly, that without re-working all such previous material it is difficult to know what is sound and what is not. Secondly, there are always going to be limits – even if it is not always clear exactly what they are at the outset – to the amount and quality of the work that can be done at the tactical and perhaps operational levels.

Such a conclusion might seem a rather gloomy one and put paid to any possibility of constructing a full history of operations from the bottom up for the Battle of the Atlantic. This may be true but it does not necessarily rule out useful conclusions for the present study. These may spring from negative judgements – Ultra was of very little utility to an escort force commander once hot battle had been started and, in any case, he would have had no direct knowledge of it – is an example of such a finding. Further, carefully researched studies having full regard for the limitations of the data can produce useful material contributing to an understanding of the campaigns as a whole.[23]

There are two different traps which yawn here. One (to use a term little noted by twentieth-century naval historians) is antiquarianism as defined by G. R. Elton.[24] This is described as detail for its own sake and is properly identified as a sterile pursuit, standing between the facts and an understanding of their significance. The other problem is one of precision and accuracy. Most dictionaries and thesauri give these as mutual synonyms, which confuses the issue further. Here the distinction which should be drawn is between information expressed *precisely* and absolute *accuracy*. The relevant leading examples are geographical positions expressed in latitude and longitude. A fairly normal practice of the period would be to render these thus:

50°06′ North 42°23′ West.

This in words would be:

50 degrees 6 minutes North, 42 degrees 23 minutes West.

At such latitudes, and indeed any likely to be used during the Battle of the Atlantic, this precise form of expression would imply an order of accuracy of better than one nautical mile. Under certain conditions, such as being in sight of land, or recently having obtained a good stellar fix, this might be possible but for the rest of the time – which was by far the longest period – it was not.[25] Nevertheless, the precise form conceals the inaccurate reality and this is a difficulty which stands in the way of complete and reliable reconstruction of operations with confidence.

It should thus be obvious that there must be limits to historical analysis, brought about by deficiencies in both data and method. If numerate analysis is attempted, then the data should not only exist but it should also be of good enough quality to support the subsequent work. A lack of data, either quantitatively or qualitatively, is likely to be an absolute bar to subsequent work. But even if the data is adequate, this does not automatically endow a subsequent analysis with merit. The methods used must also be sound. These factors have been very much borne in mind in the analyses presented in the following chapters, most especially the two case studies. Gaps and areas for further work have been highlighted where appropriate.

Having now, and at some length, dealt with the general problems of the historical analysis of the Battle of the Atlantic, the general objectives of what follows should now be set out. These are:

- To clarify confused pictures
- To make the whole understandable
- To show underlying trends and causes.

3
The Economic Context

Why, it might be asked, in a book largely concerned with naval and intelligence history, is there a chapter with the word 'economic' in its title? This is an important and germane question which deserves a proper answer.

There are some who would suggest that the worlds of mid-Atlantic convoy battles and the intellectual struggles of Bletchley Park have no conceivable connection with economics. Although such a subject was probably rarely at the forefront of the thoughts of those two very different sets of practitioners, it is almost impossible – and certainly very unsound – to attempt to comprehend the Battle of the Atlantic without understanding the economic aspects of both the war as a whole, the role of shipping more specifically and the importance of the Atlantic in particular. But this does not come easily to the traditional practitioner of either naval or intelligence history, steeped in the arcana of their own craft. This was well expressed by Philip Pugh:

> Probably the main deterrent to more rigorous analysis of such matters is that they take the historian into the field of economics ✓✓ where conflicting theories abound and today's holy writ becomes tomorrow's bad joke. In truth, things are far from as bad as that; but it is understandable if most naval historians are reluctant to sail very far out on such turbulent seas with so few navigational aids.[1]

There can be few parts of the Second World War which can have been so intimately connected with economics as the Battle of the Atlantic, which was largely a series of campaigns to do with shipping and the transfer of material over long distances, clearly matters not only of economic significance but also amenable to econometric techniques as a measure of success or failure. However, apart from some fairly customary payment of lip-service to 'keeping sea-lanes open' or 'ensuring the flow of supplies', such factors have been largely ignored in the historical literature. Even among some of the more responsible schools of writing which have rightly rejected monocausal explanations of outcomes, the economic dimension has often been neglected, or at best, under-emphasised.

However, it is not only that this dimension is missing from many accounts but also that it did not just exist in some important but separate box; the struggle at sea, intelligence and economics are all best perceived in the context of each other. But economic calculation was also part of the fabric of the decision-making on both sides – certainly at the strategic and to some extent at the operational level of warfare. These are all aspects which need further exploration. A useful way of doing this is to examine a number of relevant topics from an economic perspective: national economies, strategy and shipping, anti-shipping campaigns, shipping stocks and cargo flows, German strategic aims and lastly the economics of antisubmarine warfare.

National economies and the Battle of the Atlantic

There were facets of the world economy in 1939 that were intercontinental, if not global, but the economic aspects of the world war – or at least its Euro-Atlantic theatre – are probably best perceived through a consideration of national economies both in general and particular terms. There were supra-national factors at work, too; most notably in the alliance of the United States of America and the United Kingdom, and the German exploitation of conquered Europe.[2] However, the most important determinants were almost certainly the national economies themselves. These were at once the enablers and limiters of grand strategy; they provided, or failed to deliver, the resources with which campaigns were fought. Some general factors in this (as can be applied to naval matters) are suggested by Philip Pugh.[3] More specific to the Allied conduct of the Battle of the Atlantic are some of Geoffrey Till's concluding remarks in a conference volume on the Battle of the Atlantic. Here he notes the following economic factors:

- A drastic reduction in British import requirements from 60 to 26 million tons annually, greatly reducing the calls on shipping[4]

- The effective management of shipping creating, in effect, sufficient additional capacity[5]
- The enormous merchant-shipbuilding capacity of the USA.[6]

Some of these points will be returned to later.

By contrast, the German war economy, potentially in a much better position, with great assets in the conquered lands and with a command politico-economic system in place at the outset of war, was unable to mobilise these effectively until after the American machine was fully in gear; by then it was too late for Germany. This makes an important point about the strength of national economies: they are complex, drawing on resources, manufacturing capacity, transport and – most importantly – planning of at least an adequate standard.[7]

For any nation or alliance, at peace or war, strategico-economic choices are constantly being presented. In war, these tend to be both more acute and vital, and cover a wide range of activities, both directly related to warfighting and to the maintenance of the domestic base. In the context of the Battle of the Atlantic, it may be useful to look at that of the ship-construction industry and the type of decisions that faced the UK. This is not intended as a chronicle, but rather an examination of factors, in order to demonstrate the complexities of the problems faced by planners and those charged with their execution.

A war on a global scale clearly generates a considerable demand for shipping for subsistence, and for residual trade activity as well as the support of military operations. Even in peacetime, changing patterns of trade and the replacement of time-expired vessels generate a demand for new ships. In war, this is unlikely to recede significantly. Nevertheless certain demand-led priorities have to be resolved in a reasonable degree of correspondence with that of supply. The resolution of such priorities are likely to be concerned with such choices as:

- *Merchant ships or warships.* There is likely to be high demand for both and although some yards may either be unable to build one of these or have expertise in one area, choices still have to be made.
- *Types of ships.* Within both warship and merchant vessel categories, there is considerable variety of ship type. The traditional decision mechanism for warships (naval policy) or merchant ships (commercial demand) is distorted at best by war or, more probably, altered radically.
- *Construction or repair.* Although normal peacetime operation generates a certain requirement for repair, this is liable to be higher in wartime. Further, there is likely to be an overlap between building and repair

facilities and some balancing may be necessary. Beyond a certain level of damage it may make more sense to build a new ship rather than repair a damaged one but this point, too, needs addressing.

Lastly, it is necessary to make the point that at any time it may be difficult to implement radical changes in these policies. The infrastructure required for shipbuilding is among the largest and least flexible of any in industry and has special requirements for access to water.[8] Very little of the lengthy coastline of the UK really qualifies once other considerations are taken into account. There were thus very few greenfield options available. In any case the diversion of facilities to produce radically new yards would have in itself the effect of tying up scarce resources of both materials and manpower for considerable periods of time.[9]

In this context it is worth noting the contrast with the case of the USA. Here merchant shipbuilding which, for the period 1939–41, had barely exceeded a maximum of one million deadweight tons in its best year, leapt more than tenfold over the next two years.[10] It is true that spare capacity of both plant and people existed, but access to a large, previously untapped source of labour, a willingness to build new yards and adopt production line techniques were also useful, as was the adoption of more type-standardisation.

A different aspect of national economies that was also relevant to the Battle of the Atlantic was the matter of joining the commodities at sea to the factories and warehouses on shore; even in the case of the UK, often some distance inland. This path started at unloading docks which, after the German advance to the Channel within the first year of war, had to be largely transferred to the hitherto lesser-utilised western ports such as the Clyde, Bristol and, above all, Liverpool.[11] This could be palliated to some extent by then running coastal convoys north round Scotland but, of course, this added even further to voyage times and some ports, especially those of the Thames estuary, remained awkward and worked at well under their potential capacity. The efficiency of turning ships round, that is unloading them and then filling them with ballast, if nothing else, before releasing them for another voyage, could vary greatly.[12] Although attempts were made to minimise this, they were not always successful.[13] One estimate suggests an additional 50 per cent might be added to turnround time.[14] Such calculations suggest that, to some extent, what is now being examined is not so much shipping as material flows, very much an economic study.

Nor did the process or problems end on the dockside. As is recognised by the *Official History* of merchant shipping, another considerable problem lay beyond that point with the infrastructure and organisation of the inland transport system.[15] It is clear that both rail and, especially, road transport had difficulties in rising to the challenge.[16] This should hardly be surprising, especially in the case of the railways, which were run down in any case, expected to improvise flows for which they were not equipped and, once the war started to absorb large numbers of working-age men, largely under-resourced with people. Beyond this point the matter of manufacturing efficiency is also relevant. Affecting all these further, especially in the first years after the German over-running of western Europe, was the disruption wrought by the Luftwaffe on the UK. The popular and contemporary impression of this attack was that it was devastating and efficiently ruthless. However, either in terms of the magnitude of the later Allied bombing offensive against Germany or its effects on the war economy, it cannot be considered to have had a decisively destructive effect. It is perhaps of interest that in the comparable Allied campaigns against Germany, the most successful Allied bombing actions may well have been the late-war ones against transport systems and oil production.

Strategy and shipping

The relationship between strategy and shipping – a mutual one – was a link which impinged on most participants in the Second World War to some extent but was probably greatest in both scale and significance for the Allies.[17] By the time this Alliance became formal in December 1941, it was no longer a game that could be played only by individual nations and although all the United Nations (used in its wartime sense) were involved, it was principally the concern of the United States and the United Kingdom. Thus an important element in the whole field was that specific bi-national relationship. It could hardly be otherwise with the distances in both Atlantic and Pacific and the large demands of sea-lift for cargoes – raw materials, goods, military stores, equipment and fighting men themselves. The modalities of these exchanges themselves are important, if under-studied.[18] From Kevin Smith's subtitle the term 'logistics diplomacy' can be drawn, although it is clear from his text that some of the exchanges fell some way short of what would now be described as diplomatic. Shipping was at once both a strategic asset and a constraint on military strategy. Operations in both European and Pacific theatres were absolutely dependent on shipping and the balances that had to be struck were multiple ones. Ships could not be readily transferred between theatres; the proportions devoted to imports and the support of military operations had to be balanced and, even within theatres, it was not always possible to carry out the desired military operations because the necessary shipping might be detained elsewhere.[19] Nor was it the simple case that once one operation was executed, say a landing in Italy, then all shipping involved could instantly be released. As one example, the Normandy landings took place at the beginning of June 1944. Late in the autumn shipping was still using Normandy to support armies who had advanced well into northwest Europe: such operations demanded considerable shipping. Were a system of information to have existed during the Second World War comparable to that now attainable, at least in theory, then it might have been possible to have made better use of the available shipping, but this is a thesis which posits the anachronistic existence of advanced information systems. It has been claimed that the heavy and early pressure on the UK led to a more quickly realised and thorough use of shipping, but this is difficult to measure, far less prove.[20]

Perhaps the other strategic–economic aspect of shipping is the account of gain by building (and other means) and loss, largely by enemy action. The economics of the world shipping market were complex even in peacetime; in war, they tended to follow a Clausewitzian path, becoming perhaps simpler in theory but more difficult to execute. From a shipping perspective, the British appeared to benefit from the German conquests of 1940. Not only were a number of vessels from these overrun nations already on charter to the British but many others, not in European ports at the time of their nations' capitulations, joined the British, more or less voluntarily. For this, German ineptitude was as much to blame as anything. The net result was that Britain received an accession of shipping, in the order of half a million deadweight tons.[21] This was quite insufficient for the years of war ahead but it went a long way to mitigate the losses of the next 18 months when German submarines were relatively productive, but fortunately fairly small in numbers, and before the USA entered the war.[22] On the debit side, the situation is complex. As well as direct enemy action, there was a considerable loss for other reasons. One estimate suggests that this may have been about 5 per cent by tonnage and 13 per cent by number.[23] Sometimes, this is referred to as marine accidents and it is probable that a proportion of these were attributable to war-related causes such as the extinguishing of lights both on ships at sea and of coastal navigation marks, together with the discouragement of the peacetime scale of radio-use. It is also probable that the Allied war demand for tonnage led to some rather ancient and decrepit ships either being re-employed or else kept in service beyond a normal prudent life, further increasing the accident rate. Nevertheless enemy action remained the greatest cause of loss of shipping and, of the methods open to the Axis, the submarine dominated these figures as did the North Atlantic theatre. Thus, what Dönitz's submarines achieved was important economically as well as strategically. Why this was so and the German calculations associated with it are described later in this chapter.

The other important area of this is the numerical balance itself of gain and loss. There are some methodological problems of comparison of statistics on this subject. They concern available data being expressed in different forms of tonnages; various national inclusions or exclusions with time, the imposition of a lower tonnage limit (often 1600 gross tons) for inclusion in data and the fact that figures for oil tankers were sometimes separately compiled.[24] However, looking broadly at these figures,some generalised but useful statements can be made:

- On entering the war, the British Empire had the single biggest merchant marine comprising around 20 million tons of shipping.[25]
- During the war, the British non-tanker stock fluctuated by about two million tons either side of a total of 20 million tons. It was at its lowest at the beginning of the war and again in 1942–43.[26] After the middle of 1940, an additional two to four million tons was also time-chartered to the British after the middle of 1940.
- By far the greatest merchant shipbuilding achievement was by the Americans, but this got off to a slow start, barely touching one million tons annually before 1942. After 1942 (nearly eight million tons) annual building did not go below 10 million tons and, in 1942 and 1943, the figure was in the high teens.[27]
- This building performance was sufficient to convert the net loss figure that had obtained generally since the outbreak of war into a net gain by the third quarter of 1943.[28]

This was a very important outcome, indicating that the successes at tactical and operational level of mid-1943 had also been matched by the strategic (some might say, grand strategic) result in shipbuilding. This indicated that, subject to the availability of trained manpower, that it would be very difficult for the Germans to effect any significant reduction of Allied shipping capacity, unless they achieved not just an improvement but also a very much greater one than they had previously shown themselves capable of achieving. Some numerical aspects of this are discussed in the next section.

This also serves to demonstrate that there is a connection between intelligence and the economies of the Alliance, at least when they are, in broad terms, striving for similar goals – in this instance the passage of materials across the Atlantic. In a theoretical construct, it might have been possible to balance the Battle of the Atlantic with either poorer operational/tactical performance (in which intelligence plays an important part) or less good shipbuilding achievements. It might even have worked with a minor degradation of both at the same time. Such ideas are, of course, counterfactual but nevertheless reasonably supportable. What would be less easy to put forward with confidence is a projection of any of these hypothetical scenarios which actually attributes figures of loss with any precision. Thus despite these uncertainties it can be seen that Rosie the Riveter working at a brand-new shipyard on the Pacific coast and Ivor the Intellectual in a hut at Bletchley were the human faces of two large and complementary Alliance assets.

Anti-shipping campaigns – an economic perspective

In a sense, the anti-shipping campaigns conducted by Dönitz had a different target from their obvious ones: ships and their cargoes. What, in effect, they were trying to do was to deal a mortal strategic blow by preventing both military buildup and economic activity. Nor was attack on shipping at sea the only conceivable way of carrying out such a way of warfare. It was, however, for the Germans in that period probably the means most likely to produce some form of desired outcome. In any case, it is arguable that either the cessation or even large-scale disruption of national activity is a difficult problem for any enemy to solve. An analogy here might be drawn in terms of purpose with the Allied bombing effort against Germany, which might be said to have had similar aims and, ultimately, reaching its greatest strategic utility when it turned to the effective attack against oil and transport. Such campaigns, however, have two important prerequisites, sufficient knowledge and the means of effective weapon-delivery. Both need to be of a reasonable standard although deficiencies in one may be compensated for by the high quality of the other. It is arguable that the Germans never had the capability of inflicting such damage on the British, far less the American economy. This would have best been done from the air with attacks, say, on ports, railway-lines and manufacturing facilities. But a combination of lack of knowledge (or the ability to choose targets correctly) together with difficulty in delivery made sure that the blows they did deal were well short of mortal. The knowledge would have been difficult to acquire not least because at the outset the flow of materials was not fully comprehended by the British themselves.[29] Even later on, when the new weapons such as the V-1 and V-2, came on line, their precision was quite inadequate to effect significant economic damage.[30] By such standards the U-boat pitted against a convoy was a well-directed system capable of effective weapon-delivery. The reality, of course, was that it was rare for individual U-boat captains, far less Dönitz, to be able to be truly knowing and highly selective – they shot at what they saw. But compared to anything else of the period, this was highly intelligent warfare.

Approached from a strategico-economic angle, there are several ways in which this submarine campaign against shipping might have been carried forward. At such a level of warfare there might even be confusion in the supporting thinking and selection of such ways without necessarily affecting the clarity of purpose at both operational and tactical levels, although ideally there should be some form of consistency. Here several non-exclusive and sometimes overlapping options might be examined:

- Complete annihilation
- Severe disruption
- Attrition
- Targeting specific types of cargo flows or shipping.

Complete annihilation. This has the merit of simplicity of aim set alongside difficulty of attainment. It has often been seen as the aim of military action and the history of warfare has many examples of this, or at least attempts at attaining it. Examples might be the Battle of the Nile (1798), Taranto (1940), Pearl Harbor (1941) and, some would argue, a part of the age of nuclear weapons. In the context of a war against shipping it is generally considered to be unlikely of attainment unless there is virtually complete command of the sea and, in this century, the air too. Taking a longer perspective than that open to Dönitz during the Second World War, this would never have seemed a particularly realistic proposition. Some commentators have argued that if a narrow index of performance is used, then annihilation might have been possible.[31] This would appear unlikely, as the business of finding and sinking targets is more complex than it would first appear, and projections based on considering single factors in isolation can mislead rather than illuminate. There have been instances of annihilation, or

near-annihilation, but these are rare: the only example that seems
apposite is that of the reduction of the Japanese merchant marine
under conditions of near-to-total air and sea superiority on the part of
the Americans. Even so, the campaign was protracted and American
success was aided by Japanese errors.

Severe disruption. It is, of course, possible to effect a strategico-
economic result by means not of sinking all of an enemy's shipping
but merely by imposing such losses that the economic activity either
ceases or else is reduced to such low levels of activity or efficiency that
other activities may be severely curtailed. German submarines brought
about such an outcome in early 1917 in the coal trade between southwest England and France.[32] Although some independently routed ships
were sunk – generally speaking, by surfaced submarines using gunfire –
the greater outcome from the German viewpoint was obtained not by
these sinkings themselves but by the threat of submarine activity.
When such warnings were in force, ships stayed in port, thus reducing
the flow of cargo to France. It was against such disruption that one of
the first – and most successful – convoy systems of the First World War
was organised.[33] This was certainly an example of severe disruption,
but it also hints at one aspect of this phenomenon; the fact that the
disruption has to be in the mind of the victim, not just the intention
of the aggressor. In other words, it is easy to recognise severe disruption in hindsight, but much more difficult to plan and execute operations which guarantee this outcome. Similarly, it can be very easy to
argue with full hindsight that disruption was never likely in the light
of coarse-grained statistics. Two examples of this approach are given by
John Ellis and Clive Ponting.[34] But such conclusions, although they
may help in establishing a perspective missing from the all-action
school of literature do not help in that they omit the great swings in
fortune of the two sides, remove the undoubted contemporary concerns of the participants and, most importantly, present the information out of the various contexts, one of which is certainly the
economic one, which in responsible history should be presented simultaneously. Disruption is liable to be the result in two circumstances – a
sudden change in fortune or a more gradual erosion of shipping. It is
to the latter, sometimes known as attrition, to which the discussion
now turns.

Attrition. If a sudden coup against shipping could not be attained, then
a strategic outcome might still be obtained over time by the erosion of
the shipping base by serial attacks, perhaps extending over months or
even years. To be totally successful, this would work gradually towards

the aim of annihilation but would probably produce worthwhile results well before that point was reached. At its very worst, from the aggressor's perspective, irritation and effort would be expended. Better still, would be the widespread diversion of effort to protect the threatened shipping. Beyond this would be a point where the losses resulted in changes of strategy or, at the very least limits on military operation brought about by the absence of ships which had been lost to the assault. Arguably, in the Second World War this is what happened and this paucity became in Sir Alan Brooke's words, 'a stranglehold on all offensive operations'.[35] It is arguable that losses in the Battle of the Atlantic were only part of the problem, but such sinkings could hardly be ignored. In arithmetical terms they were only effective if they resulted in a diminution of the shipping stock, or at least a significant constraint on growth.

As Figure 3.1 shows, even the momentary shipping stock situation is complex and no account is taken in such an exposition of the further complexities of the demands of certain cargoes. The interaction between requirements and efficiency of usage is especially complicated and can only be hinted at in such a limited exposition. In broad terms, shorter-term distant operations may make disproportionate demands on available shipping in terms of tonnage, time, the necessity for specialised hulls and – in most cases – on the quality of shipping requested. Such demands may be proper and indeed necessary for the conduct of military operations but they also tend to be fairly inefficient in their utilisation of such shipping, not least because of the tendency to make use of degraded or even non-existent conventional port facilities.[36] Even the more regular supply routes across the Atlantic could only be as good as their loading and unloading facilities together with the administrative backup to put ships into convoy with the minimum of delay.

Shipping stocks and cargo flows

When looking at Allied shipping as a whole, it is difficult to tease out some of the details such as a meaningful index of the efficiency of its utilisation. For that reason, an analysis of the relative weights of inefficiency and enemy action as shapers of the overall shipping balance is difficult to approach, far less complete. As Marc Milner says:

> The tonnage-shipping-cargo availability shell game points to the difficulty of attempting to define what was decisive about the Atlantic war and what decided it. In the process one moves a long way from the conning towers and bridges of the shooting war.[37]

45

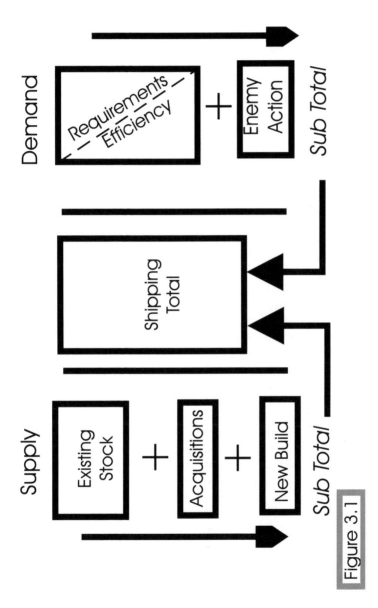

Figure 3.1   Simplified shipping model

To which, he could have added, '... or the huts of Bletchley and the cellars of Whitehall'.[38] Perhaps all that can be essayed is that there was considerably more to the shipping balance than convoy warfare in the narrow sense. The more measurable parts of this complex series of equations are the total stock of shipping, the Allied building perform-ance (which in effect means the USA) and the known performance of Dönitz's submarines. This is clearly analytically unsatisfactory, but does suggest that performance at sea cannot be considered the sole arbiter of Allied progress, far less success or failure. In other words, there is a further dimension to the Battle of the Atlantic, other than the one which dominates the literature. It is also difficult to argue that intelligence of any form, and certainly not Ultra, played any significant part in that other outcome.

If retrospective monitoring of the shipping stock is difficult, then it is arguable that any useful analysis of cargo-flows is probably even more elusive. The only exception to this is in terms of aggregate ton-nages imported into the United Kingdom. But although this conveys one element of Allied performance, it is more difficult to put together a comprehensive picture in other ways. It is less clear exactly how well the flow of cargo went in more particular ways. General statements to the effect that Britain did not starve, nor did its factories stop work due to lack of materials, and that forces despatched from both the USA and UK were reasonably well equipped can be made but other than that, and the consideration of a great quantity of low-level statistics, the quality of the system of cargo flow is very difficult to assess.[39] The nearest approach probably comes through the monographs on the econ-omic aspects of the war but, as far as is known, there is little or no higher-level synthesis of these works, or their subjects.[40]

There is clearly a difficulty for any historian in attempting to make sense of this economic and logistical puzzle. This may be the reason why it has received such little attention over the five decades since these events took place. It certainly presented problems for contempo-rary policymakers. One example of this lies in a British Cabinet com-mittee, the Battle of the Atlantic Committee, which met mainly between March and October 1941.[41] Despite its grand title, the body tended to owe more for its subjects to its predecessor, the Import Executive. While at one end of the scale there was close monitoring of gross monthly cargo flows into the UK, at the other end, there seemed few limits to the degree of detail that was grist to that body's mill. It is possible to marvel at the command of detail which Churchill, as its Chairman, had, but was it really apposite for such an entity to be considering power supplies at Avonmouth, gangways in Hull and the supply of pneumatic riveters in Bristol?[42]

It would therefore appear supportable, if not capable of proof beyond all possible doubt, that the Allies never had total understanding, far less control, of their own economic, production and transport systems. This should come as no great surprise. Looking into the present day, such tools of logistic efficiency as just-in-time delivery depend for their operation on detailed knowledge and fast communication of it, as well as a thorough understanding of the accompanying logistic system. All these facets were either absent or in such rudimentary form in the 1940s that degrees of both ignorance and inefficiency should, in full hindsight, be expected, not deplored. However, there is a far more important point to make about the contemporary understanding of these economic systems. Although Allied self-knowledge was far from complete, it did very well in comparison with German knowledge of the whole system that it was up against.

It is true that Dönitz and BdU together were able from time to time, at the tactical and operational levels, to understand the convoy system and its cycles. However, not even a sufficient – far less full – picture of the whole system was ever closely approached by the Germans. To have done so would have demanded a knowledge-level and under-standing of complex systems denied to their owners. It is thus fanciful to suggest, as some commentators have, that a strategically sensitive targeting policy by Dönitz would have led them to an Eldorado of economic warfare.[43] Thus one of the failures of the *U-Bootwaffe* had economic roots as well as tactical, operational and strategic ones. Again it is difficult to suggest that intelligence (except in the sense of German lack of an unattainable degree of knowledge) had any significant part in reaching this outcome.

German strategic aims – the economic dimension

Until the end of May 1943, it is fairly easy to see one abiding German doctrinal principle but less easy to distinguish its strategic purpose – annihilation, disruption or attrition. It would probably be fair to note that Dönitz never really contemplated annihilation as a reasonable aim; but distinguishing between disruption and attrition is less easy. The best summation would probably be that Dönitz aimed at attrition but would obviously have accepted large-scale disruption as an acceptable conse-quence of sufficient attrition. Tonnage warfare had attrition as its object-ive, but obviously the key to its success or failure lay in numbers. Thus

Dönitz's absolute success or failure depended on his ability to sink a certain tonnage. This would, over a given period, have at the very least to keep pace with the replacement-rate and preferably make sufficient inroads into the tonnage levels of the existing stock. Even if neither of these desiderata were obtained, it might still be possible to be of use to the German war-effort by inflicting sufficient attrition to frustrate planned future Allied operations through lack of shipping. This last, however, was a difficult outcome to plan for two reasons: lack of knowledge of specific Allied plans (and thus their requirements for shipping) and not comprehending what levels of loss would cause postponement, far less cancellation. In fact, the reasons given above for the difficulties in aiming for the vulnerable nodes of the import, transport and production facets of the Allied war economy, point to the very unlikely possibility of achieving such aims, as very similar factors apply.

Once a figure for sinking-requirements was calculated, an important further problem remained – establishing how much tonnage was actually sunk. This was at its easiest early in the war when the large number of ships sailing independently allowed both the clearest identification of the victim and the greatest certainty as to its fate. Thus, a reasonably certain understanding of overall tonnage sunk could be compiled. As the war moved on, changes in submarine warfare threw several layers of uncertainty over what had been a fairly easy piece of information-gathering. Attacks were often made at night, increasingly from submerged positions and both the outcome of the action and identity of a victim could be in considerable doubt. As convoy warfare became ever more difficult and the FAT and LUT torpedoes were introduced to take account of the difficulties of aiming at a single target, establishment of target identity became even more uncertain. Some assistance in some circumstances might come from radio intelligence but this was not always available. Another complicating factor was introduced as the war went on and submarine-sinkings rose, denying U-boat command both post-operation records and debriefing and sometimes even fairly timely post-firing information. Lastly, there were problems brought about by over-claiming by individual submarine commanding officers. To some extent this is a phenomenon inherent in human nature. It is also likely to occur when information is fragmentary and observation opportunities are limited. In this period a 2000-ton ship at one mile looked very much like an 8000-tonner at two miles. It is also likely that the Germans were somewhat less sceptical about claims than were their Allied counterparts. In any case, the German system of awarding grades of decorations virtually to a

tonnage tariff was likely to have been an encouragement to over-claiming. Some individuals were also likely to be more generous in their
own claims.[44] The importance of this is that there was a permanent
bias in the contemporary German view of their own successes, difficult
to quantify exactly but probably running in the order of 10–20 per
cent and this must be borne in mind when considering their performances, perceived and real.

Turning now to the German requirement for tonnage to be sunk per
month, it is interesting that there only ever seems to have been one
statement of this. This was made in June 1941 by the German Naval
Staff and cited a figure of 800 000 tons per month.[45] In approximate
terms, this would have amounted to some 10 million tons per year in a
period when replacement-building was in the order of 2 million tons
annually and thus would have suggested a first-year net depletion of
British shipping of some 8 million tons or about 40 per cent of the total
stock. Extrapolated, this would have resulted in complete annihilation
by the beginning of 1944. As a calculation, it is difficult to fault. But in
the event of actual, as opposed to wished-for, results there were two
significant flaws. The first of these was that this figure was only
approached once, in June 1942.[46] The second was that it made no
allowance for the enormous American achievement in the production of
merchant ships when that nation was fully engaged. The previous aim,
realistic as it had been as an aspiration, was completely outflanked not in
mid-Atlantic but in the building-yards of the USA. Assuming that the
entire prodigious output had been allocated to the Atlantic (which it was
not, but it could have been in case of strategic necessity), then the
German target would need to have been increased significantly not to
stand still in terms of attrition but merely to balance the American
output.[47] Thus the aim went the same way as its execution: failure. The
complementary Allied success was mainly attributable to economic
strength and the nearly coincident tactical, operational and strategic
victory has to be seen as to be running partly in a parallel track to it, and
partly as a consequence of the Alliance's industrial muscle. However,
important and welcome as the increasing numbers of merchant ships,
escorts and aircraft were, these were one of the necessary conditions of
the victory, not a sufficient cause in themselves.[48]

The economics of antisubmarine warfare

Another strategico-economic aspect that bears examination is allied
antisubmarine warfare (ASW). There are a number of approaches that

could be taken to this subject, but here it is intended to limit it to one – examining it in the light of the German rationale for the continuation of submarine warfare after the middle of 1943. This decision itself, together with its soundness and ramifications, are considered towards the end of this section. First, however, it is helpful to examine an entire and significant area of warfare activity using some basic economic tools.

Initially, there is a problem of definition. What is meant by ASW? There are some activities which clearly fall into this category, such as acquiring and running convoy escorts; others, too, suggest themselves such as specialist antisubmarine aircraft. However, even here there are difficulties. Very few ships were exclusively engaged in ASW for the whole of their wartime life, so there is a problem of attribution of costs. In any case, how can the costs of ownership of a warship be accurately assessed? One approach is that of Life Cycle Cost, but this is complex, considering all possible heads of cost. The illustration given by Philip Pugh in *The Cost of Seapower* actually applies to aircraft but there are likely to be few, if any, differences of method. Even here, there are two high-order divisions, acquisition and ownership, as well as seven at the next level down and no less than 63 at lower level.[49] What this suggests very strongly is that attempting to cost even a single warship would be a lengthy and complex exercise, even assuming the survival of appropriate data. Factoring in the partial employment in ASW that most units experienced would also involve some quite broad assumptions. But the problem is in many ways worse than that.

Some supporting technologies, especially sonar (or asdic) and antisubmarine weapons are clearly entirely ASW-attributable but what about those such as radar (which is at least likely to have one other significant application) or even the gun which saw some anti-submarine action? HF DF was largely, but not entirely, applied to ASW, but communications equipment was used across a wide spectrum of warfare activities. Moving ashore, some headquarters, such as CinCWA were heavily ASW-oriented but others were less so. Was any serious attempt ever made to cost Bletchley Park or to say what was the cost of any of its activities, related to warfare areas such as ASW? In the Admiralty or the Office of the Chief of Naval Operations some directorates were obviously ASW-related, some had some involvement and others virtually none – how to cost these?

Moving into other somewhat less obvious areas, are attempts to destroy or disrupt submarine base or building facilities through bombing, ASW or not? Were the fighter aircraft that escorted these large aircraft in the latter part of the war also engaged in ASW? The doctrinal view in Soviet military thought during the currency of that empire is that they were, and this is a point on which this writer would agree.[50] Two important considerations flow from this.

First, that any attempt to put certain units of warfare into a single category is difficult. Second, that the ease with which such units can be moved from one type of task to another is an important matter when considering both financial and other costing. What all these considerations point to is that any attempt at financial costing of warfare areas is at best complex and difficult in methodology, involving the acquisition of data and its manipulation (in the benevolent sense of the word): it would be a lifetime of labour for a workaholic accountant.[51] It can also be argued with conviction that such an exercise would be futile.

Another attempt to make economic sense of the Allied ASW policy, which emphasised the primacy of the integrity of shipping, would be to explore briefly the concept of opportunity cost. In this, the notion of direct monetary comparison is abandoned in favour of considering what alternatives might have been pursued or pursuable had the resources sunk in ASW not been deployed there, but instead used for other purposes. It is perhaps apt that a good historical illustration of this is the apparent dichotomy between guns and butter highlighted by a leading politician of Hitlerian Germany.[52] Such choices were a matter of national strategy, and some in the field of shipbuilding and repairing have been suggested earlier in this chapter. Although this is perhaps a more helpful economic concept, it is essentially counterfactual and depends for credibility on reasonable equivalence and convertibility. An example which deals in human capital rather than pieces of equipment is the U-boat arm itself. Throughout the war, it employed about 40 000 men at sea. Even if these had been instantaneously available for other purposes, they could only have manned two to four divisions of troops.[53] It is difficult to comprehend how such a force could ever have constituted the 'first charge on all Allied resources' that ASW was declared to be at the Casablanca Conference of January 1943.[54] Similarly, there is the issue of convertibility. Some military units are inherently flexible, capable without significant conversion or crew re-training of carrying out a wide range of tasks: a destroyer may be involved in ASW one day, surface action against warships the next day and take part in a shore bombardment or shore evacuation a week later (or even all three on the same day). Others are potentially so and, with a certain degree of effort and time, may move from one role to another: an example here is pointed to by the debate concerning the allocation of four-engined aircraft either to bombing Germany or carrying out long-range operations over the sea. Aircraft such as B-24 Liberators were basically capable of both but equipping them for either role and training crews to perform adequately in the task allotted was a process of at least weeks and often months. Stepping back further from the battlefield to the industrial front, decisions about the production of different sorts of military machines were rarely switchable rapidly. In any case, large redirections of military procurement would have been difficult to manage, would have incurred a significant cost in lost production during re-orientation and would have taken substantial amounts of time. Although the Americans, with advantages over the British in production techniques, engineering technology and spare capacity, were probably more capable of doing this, even they could not carry this out instantaneously. Thus, the Allies might well be outflanked in terms of fitting industrial production to the needs of the war, simply because of the difficulty of forecasting the exact tempo of a spectrum of widely different military operations anything up to a year ahead. However, the concept of opportunity cost was not entirely absent from German strategico-economic calculations, at least as far as the U-boat war was concerned.

One special use of the theory of opportunity cost was by the Germans as they applied it to the Allies and their ASW effort. In May 1943, despite their recent tactical and operational-level defeat in their assault on convoys, a high-level command decision was taken to attempt to continue with the submarine efforts against shipping, not as it was thought that it would succeed in its own right, but because of its potential to tie down Allied naval and air units. A strategic perspective is given on this elsewhere.[55] This section will consider the economic aspect of the decision and its apparent rationale. This important path was taken on 31 May 1943 committing the *U-Bootwaffe* to the war at sea until its end two years later. Its rationale at the time, a soundly based theory vaguely expressed, was that the large forces devoted by the Allies to ASW meant that a considerable proportion of British and American efforts would be deflected away from targets nearer to home. In isolation, this concept passes at least initial scrutiny. Forces used for ASW far outnumbered the relatively small number of submarines deployed. However, whatever justification there might be at what could be termed the operational–economic level, there were strategic flaws in the German argument. Firstly, the safe and reliable transit of shipping was a vital Allied interest whereas its destruction would have been a useful one for the Germans but it would not have resulted in the certain and immediate overrun of the homeland territories of Germany's two principal maritime opponents. Secondly, such was the scale of the resources available to the Allies in the last two years of the war that the relative inefficiency of Allied effort implied by Hitler and Dönitz was something that could be tolerated by the USA and UK in a manner unimaginable to the Germans.

It will have been noticed by the alert reader that no numbers whatsoever have been applied to the arguments in the preceding paragraph. This does not reflect sloppy thinking, but it draws attention to the somewhat strange circumstance that the Germans themselves were to take more than a year to produce a numerate rationale for the 'tying-down' philosophy, an early example of reverse operational research.[56] But not only was this timing somewhat odd, so too were some of the figures used. A total of 3440 ships from the Arctic to the Mediterranean together with 1450 aircraft in Coastal Command were claimed as being absorbed in the Battle of the Atlantic. The former figure falls into the trap of assuming that vessels *capable* of ASW were *engaged* in ASW, perhaps an understandable, if mistaken, assumption. The figure for aircraft, however, exaggerates their numbers by a factor of about two. The reasons for this are perhaps made clearer in the accompanying text.[57] The bulk of this concentrates on the idea that aircraft not used against submarines would be concentrated against the land territory of the Reich. Such a strategic turn-round might be feasible in the medium term for those aircraft which were derived from bombers such as the B-24 and in the longer term by the re-tooling of production lines. However, there is a definite atmosphere in the whole justification of appealing to an audience both domestic and political rather than the production of a fully numerate economic and strategic argument. Dönitz was demonstrating his growing adeptness in the political sphere, culminating in his brief leadership of the dying remnant of the Third Reich. The state and navy which spawned the tie-down strategy disappeared in 1945 but the idea outlasted them. The long-time leader of the Soviet Navy, Admiral Sergei Gorshkov, repeated the concept as a tenet of Soviet maritime doctrine some decades later, claiming that each U-Boat claimed the attention of 25 surface ships and 100 aircraft, in other words repeating Dönitz's apparent numerical errors.[58] Like his German mentor, he too was engaged in an act of special pleading.

Economics and the Battle of the Atlantic

It is hoped that the points brought out in this chapter have indicated clearly that there is not just added value in looking at the Battle of the Atlantic through an economic lens – it is an essential perspective. This comes about not only because the Battle of the Atlantic was an assault against Allied shipping – among the most important, if not the predominant, strategic asset – but also because it lends a greater understanding of what happened in attempting to comprehend the difficult problem of the big picture. It is only by means of statistical data and economic analysis that much sense can be made of a very confused and tangled story. But such thinking can be applied not only to events but also to intended strategies and declared policies. For example, the German naval staff's requirements for tonnages sunk demonstrate both temporary realism and later a measure of the failure of *Tonnageschlacht* once the Americans had formally joined the war. Similarly a combination of economic and strategic analysis tools demonstrate the policy flaws of the 'tying-down' rationale. Obviously there are limits to the applicability of economic analysis to warfare: in general terms, the smaller the military scale and the shorter the time-period, the less utility there is in the deployment of such tools.

Lastly, a word about intelligence and economics. It might be argued that these two fields of study are, to a large extent, antipathetic but this judgement would also ignore a subtle but distinct connection between the two disciplines. A negative demonstration of this was the deployment of submarines post mid-1943 against central Atlantic convoy routes, about which the Germans knew little. More positively, the Allied attack against fuel, transportation and submarine assembly targets, all of which were essentially economic, in 1944–45 was heavily informed by several intelligence sources. Thus the two subjects, intelligence and economics, were conjoined, surely if not intimately.

4
A German Perspective

In any form of military operations and history it is wise to look at the enemy: in a history looking at intelligence, this is essential. There is, however, a distinct problem of method here. The only true measure of how an intelligence system performed against an enemy should take into account not only performance in the combat area but also that enemy's perception of its own performance, what it wanted to do before a recent operation and what it wanted to do next. This may be further complicated by any side in a military conflict thinking that it has achieved more than it actually has or alternatively not realising that it has achieved a great deal: the former is fairly common, the latter less so.[1]

A further problem is introduced by the absorption of decisionmakers with current problems and thus their not being able to fully comprehend the environment in which they find themselves. Even when subsequent contemplation occurs, they have either moved on to a new set of problems or else retired from the fray. In either case, *post facto* recollection will almost certainly be distorted in one way or another. Yet another difficulty is the one related to quantity of material, the return of the concept of the maze – perhaps the central difficulty of the history of the Battle of the Atlantic.[2] Lastly, and by no means the most trivial difficulty is that of language, both in the sense of another tongue and that of specialist sub- and sub-sub-vocabularies. All this suggests that even a life long study of this topic may not be long enough Do these important difficulties mean that the search for any form of perspective should be abandoned? No. As long as the limitations described above are realised and the consequent risks accepted, then the dangers of ignoring a German perspective are much greater than the imperfections of an inadequate essay at this essential topic. Of course, this subject will not receive the treatment that it deserves; to do so would take at least a book to itself. This chapter will consider such a perspective in terms of organisations, methods and perceptions. Even within these broad headings, there are multiple interactions both with each other and with external entities and factors. Not all of these can be described fully, but some will be sketched. By such means, it is intended to arrive at a broad German perspective of the Battle of the Atlantic which can then be used to inform subsequent chapters, especially the two case-studies.

Organisations – leadership and structures

The quality of any organisation comes fundamentally from two factors – structure and the quality and qualities of those forming it, not least at the top.[3] Space precludes a full study of leadership generally in either the submarine arm or Nazi Germany but there is benefit in looking at the upper echelons of the leadership not least because of the emphasis laid on this factor in the politics of wartime Germany. In doing so, many important qualities of the organisations these figures inhabited emerge. There are perhaps three key figures: Hitler, Raeder and Dönitz.

The personality, philosophy and war-leadership of Adolf Hitler has exercised an almost uncanny fascination on the world in the late twentieth century: what is less chronicled is his understanding of, interest in and exercise of seapower.[4] It is very evident that he did not consider himself to be nearly as adept in this realm as he did in the sphere of land warfare. In the latter, having served himself at the front with distinction, albeit at a low level, during the First World War, he considered that his experience made him at the very least the equal of his generals during the Second World War.[5] His strategic instincts, leading to sweeping victories until the Russian reverses, reinforced this attitude. He never claimed any such authority for the naval sphere, considering himself daring on land and timid at sea. Certainly after the early blows to the German surface fleet during the Norwegian campaign and a subsequent period of commerce-raiding, more than a degree of caution was applied to that surface fleet and, in general, the bigger the ship the greater the reluctance to commit it to any significant risk. The submarine fleet was, however, seen in a different light as aggressive and decisive to the war. This opinion never seemed to waver significantly even when, from mid-1943 onwards, the achievements of this arm grew ever less. For Hitler, however, either the reality of the outfought Type VIIs and IXs or the promise of the new-generation submarines never seemed to dim. Nevertheless there were times when the same sort of caution that he applied to the operations of the capital ships impinged on submarines, especially on the restrict- 7, ions imposed on them in the latter part of 1941 on the western side of the Atlantic.

The other important impact Hitler made was through his conduct of business; this might be called, depending on the background and choice of the narrator or reader as leadership, organisation or management. Hitler's dealings with the *Kriegsmarine*, as with all bodies were conducted on a series of bilateral meetings, rather than on any form of committee system. Hitler, who might well have borrowed from Napoleon and described the English as a nation of committeemen is never known to have done so and although it could be argued that this particular organisational technique was carried to – and, according to some, beyond – its peak by the Anglophone Alliance, it was quite alien to the Third Reich. As a result subjects such as operations, strategy, the allocation of resources and policy were nearly always determined in a very inefficient manner. The features of the system were poor communications, overlapping and competing responsibilities and a tendency to arrive at decisions out of a context of wider repercussions. As a result many issues apparently decided were undermined by subsequent ones made in other forums, of which the original audience had no knowledge. This led to under-performance and confusion together with much wasted time and effort.[6] Such was the *Führerprinzip* in action and reality.[7]

Grandadmiral Erich Raeder had been at the head of the *Kriegsmarine* for over 10 years when Germany invaded Poland in 1939 and was to stay in that post until January 1943 when succeeded by Dönitz. This suggests more than a bare minimum of acceptability of Raeder by Hitler who became Chancellor in 1933. This may, however, have resulted from a compound of relatively low naval saliency and professional respect for the naval mysteries. Latterly, there was little sympathy and a loss of confidence. Raeder was conscious both of the attributes of seapower and also of German limitations at the outbreak of war. Despite it being clear that what he then had to fight a maritime war fell a long way short of the Z-plan which promised a much larger and better-balanced fleet by the mid-1940s, he intended to make the best of what Germany had, whilst recognising its severe limitations.[8] Under Raeder, the *Kriegsmarine* made a success of the Norwegian campaign, albeit at a price; went on to lend the planning of Operation

Seelöwe, the invasion of England, an otherwise absent air of realism and conducting a war on commerce by means of heavy warships, disguised raiders and submarines. Initial German naval involvement in the Mediterranean was successful in itself but the only sizable warships which could realistically reach there, thanks to the continued British tenure of Gibraltar, were submarines.[9]

The policy of sending submarines there provoked disagreements between Raeder and Dönitz, the latter seeing this and other diversions as an unacceptable distraction from the war on shipping. Such disputes were to continue until Raeder's departure from office. Nevertheless, Raeder appreciated the worth of the submarines. His downfall came through attempting to keep a residual flame burning for the balanced fleet, his long-term aim. It is possible that this emphasis on fleet-building was at the expense of both a balanced view of operations generally and an emphasis on advancing technology.[10]

Grossadmiral (as he became) Karl Dönitz spent the first part of the war as the operational commander of Atlantic submarines.[11] He succeeded Raeder in January 1943, while retaining both an interest in and responsibility for his submarines.[12] Although claiming little appetite for politics, he was unexpectedly named by Hitler as his successor and spent a few days as the last titular head of the Third Reich.[13] It is Dönitz who has become in Allied eyes most associated with the U-boat arm, and rightly so. The strategy, operational-level skills and tactics of the force owe much to him, especially the innovation and development of the *Rudeltaktik*. This is described more fully elsewhere but it is important to note that this apparently aggressive gambit owed much to Dönitz's perceptions of the weaknesses of both Allies and, more especially, his own submarines. Thus his perception from his own First World War experiences of the vulnerability of a single submarine attacking a convoy and the Second World War difficulties of reconnaissance were strong drivers of the *Rudeltaktik* and these were responses to shortfalls, not exploitations of strength.

But Dönitz brought far more than just a keen interest in the conduct of submarine operations to the war. As well as being an enthusiast for the submarine and in particular for its suitability for a war against shipping, he was responsible for a strong spirit which pervaded the *U-Bootwaffe*. Even when due allowance is made for propaganda, it is obvious that few, if any, of the 40 000 men who were part of it were unaware of this. Some of this came from an earlier period when, in command of the cruiser *Emden*, he was involved in the early training of several groups of naval officers.[14]

Dönitz did occupy a genuinely central position for the German sub- ✓
marine arm in a way which had absolutely no Allied parallel. In some
Battle of the Atlantic historiography it has been a commonplace to
present the conflict in terms of an almost personal duel between
Dönitz and Sir Max Horton on the British side: this is quite wrong for
two reasons – one chronological, the other qualitative. Horton did not
become CinCWA until November 1942 when Dönitz was only six
months away from *de facto* withdrawal from the Atlantic. At that point
Dönitz himself was only two months short of command of the whole
navy and a further two months from moving the submarine operations
staff to Berlin.[15] Perhaps more importantly it was not comparing like
with like. The Allied ASW effort was on a very large scale compared to
the tiny staff of the comparable German effort. However, in the Allied
case it compensated for at least some of the disadvantages of size by
being reasonably well coordinated. Such a *post facto* personalisation of
the conflict denies the Allied nature of it with both Americans and ✓
Canadians being very much in evidence. The same could not be said
for the German effort, far less any pretence at a united Axis performance. Perhaps this indicates the point that the German effort might
have been better-run had it not owed so much to one man and the
small team supporting him. This is not a problem exclusive to this
time and place:

> [I]t will be because Microsoft has a flaw at its heart. Bill Gates has an
> ability to visualise and implement a business strategy that is almost
> unmatched. But the clarity of vision is too often accompanied
> by blinkers. The flip side of flawless execution is a ruthlessness
> that takes Microsoft to the edge of – and perhaps beyond – the law.
> Mr Gates dominates his company as few men do. The reporting
> structure is flat, he controls every detail. For the bright, aggressive,
> relentlessly striving people who work for him 'face-time' with Bill is
> everything.[16]

It would be very apt to substitute 'BdU' for 'Microsoft' and 'Admiral
Dönitz' for 'Bill Gates'. Small and taut is not always beautiful.

The BdU organisation

The *Befehlshaber der U-Boote* (BdU – U-boat Command) – the system set
up by Dönitz – was compact, using a small number of relatively junior ✓
officers.[17] They were known colloquially as the staff without pot-bellies ✓

and this was probably a reflection of two things – relative youth and being kept very busy. They were also, except where very specialist knowledge was required, all officers with submarine experience, particularly in command. Thus they could not be accused of issuing orders without at least some appreciation of the practical implications at sea. However, this itself went through various phases and the experience they brought to the Battle was not always directly relevant to the situations with which they had to deal as staff officers. Thus those who had experienced submarine warfare in the period 1939–42 in which long spells were dominated either by the attack on independent shipping or relatively weakly escorted convoys might have some difficulty understanding the intensity of Allied activity during the months from mid-1942 to mid-1943.

Dönitz himself would take charge of anti-convoy operations or, in his absence, his Chief of Staff, Rear Admiral Eberhardt Godt, would assume this function. After Dönitz became Commander-in-Chief of the *Kriegsmarine*, Godt was more likely to be in operational charge. But after May 1943, there were to be few attempts at convoy operations at all, far less any on the scale that had taken place in the first months of that year.

Intelligence in support of the operations came from a variety of places, but predominantly from codebreaking and other Sigint sources. As the locus of the Battle moved westward into mid-Atlantic, the limitations of the German shore direction-finding system became more evident and thus the importance of being able to read Allied signal traffic was probably more important, both in itself and in comparison with the Allies. There is a guide to the importance of various forms of intelligence to the Germans in the listing of available intelligence in the daily summaries given in BdU's KTB but this is only detailed in the latter part of the war. However, it does enable a grasp of the utility of different sources of intelligence to be made, in a way that is generally missing from the surviving British OIC records. The same strictures that apply to the use of intelligence for the Allies to a large extent are relevant for the Germans as well. Tactical intelligence to be useful has also to be timely and *xB-Dienst* could have problems, in the same way as Bletchley. One leading German historian of the subject has concluded, for instance, that complications led to only some 10 per cent of material being decoded in time to be useful during the important period from November 1942.[18] Further, it can be argued that the German general exploitation of intelligence was not remotely in the same league as that of the Allies.

The BdU organisation itself has been described by Graham Rhys-Jones, among others, noting its small size and large sphere of responsibilities.[19] This carried two concomitant problems; a tendency to overload individuals and the inability to take longer-term analytical views. The first problem was hardly uncommon in wartime, so much so that it is difficult to suggest that by itself it was responsible for much reduction in the efficiency of BdU; the latter was a more serious difficulty. It is doubtful whether the staff of BdU were any harder worked than their opposite number in, say, the Admiralty's Trade Division or at CinCWA, although a more apt comparison might be with seagoing personnel. But whereas the British equivalents were backed up by professional second-guessers in such organisations as the Western Approaches Tactical Unit at one level and the operational research community at another, BdU had no such support. As more pressure was applied to the German organisation, the significance of such deficiencies became more evident, at least in retrospect.

Tactical support of U-boats at sea was carried out by a number of means other than intelligence. Ideally Dönitz would have liked to have made more use of aircraft for reconnaissance purposes but these were denied him in any appreciable quantities because of the non-coopera-tive relations between *Kriegsmarine* and *Luftwaffe*, especially at the higher command levels. Manpower, too, could prove problematical, especially towards the end of the war. But it was not just crewing the submarines that was a problem but also finding sufficient people to build them, then maintain them in service. The Allies, too, had difficulties in managing the strategic allocation of people to the war effort but their problems were probably more capable of fundamental solution because of the larger demographic base on which they might draw. The *U-Bootwaffe*, too placed a premium on forward manpower planning by its insistence on a lengthy training period, either at basic level or in the working-up of submarines as whole crews but this also worked against them, as the training regime tended to lengthen the period between arrival of the man and his playing an effective part in an operational crew. In general terms, logistics became more difficult as the war progressed, although there is no known full-length study of this subject. The outcome, however, was plain enough – diminishing availability of submarines for operational deployments.

Methods

Specific tactics are described in later chapters but it is appropriate to say something in general about the methods employed by BdU at the operational level. There was one over-riding philosophy running through these: the maximisation of damage to the enemy at the minimum cost to the Germans. This is probably the aim of any operational commander but, for the first part of the war at least, Dönitz had an unusual amount of choice in how he could go about doing this and a rare degree of autonomy for the relatively junior commander that he was at the time. Further, he turned an unusual degree of numerate analysis into the relatively narrow field of submarine performance.[20] This informed the decisions he made in at least two ways:

- Choice of operating areas in broad terms, for example, North American coast versus mid-Atlantic
- Types of operations, that is, single submarine operations against independent shipping or group attacks on convoys.

Such choices, or the balance between them, tended to be driven by two things – relative success together with the degree of effectiveness of enemy reaction to them. Initially at least, Allied deficiencies in two fields, inadequate numbers of ASW units and limited knowledge of major German re-deployments of effort, introduced a further element of choice to Dönitz – the switching of submarines between activities at the operational level. However, just as with the tactical level in the struggles against convoys, options were narrowed before being cut off altogether; the same thing tended to happen at the operational level too and choice was slowly denied to Dönitz.[21] Sometimes the two were connected. Thus the cumulative effect of a number of Allied tactical measures in mid-1943 led to at least an operational-level reredeployment away from mid-Atlantic convoy warfare. Indeed as, is argued elsewhere, this amounted to even more and was, in fact, a strategic reverse.[22] This contrasts markedly with the situation of some 18 months before when the choice had been Dönitz's to switch from convoy warfare to targeting shipping on the North American littoral.

But such operational level decisions were supported by doctrines operating at the higher end of the operational level and the lower end of the strategic. Two themes dominated in this which changed from one to the other, almost instantly in mid-1943, together with a subsidiary one which was present virtually throughout until late in the war when strategic reverses removed virtually all options. The dominant themes were tonnage warfare succeeded by a philosophy of 'tying-down'. The statistical and economic dimensions of these are addressed in the previous chapter, but it is appropriate to make some further remarks about them here.[23] These two policies did not appear to have any mutual overlap; one succeeded the other. Outside the economic context, tonnage warfare was a worthwhile German doctrine for a navy which did not possess a balanced capability. Further it went straight to the heart of one of the Alliance's weakest points: its shipping. This represented what would now be called the centre of gravity and it was a, if not the, key Allied vulnerability.[24] As an aim, it would be difficult to fault this tenet of German doctrine, but strategies must, in historical hindsight, be judged not merely by their aims but also by their performance.[25] A further complication is introduced by the process of carrying out contemporary measurement and whether such a system is adequate to monitor the progress of the strategy. When dealing with a land campaign, such measurement is relatively easy. If the aim is, for instance, to take Stalingrad by a particular date, then both date and location are readily measurable. There may have been some doubt as to what degree of control was being exerted over an enemy city, but time and place can hardly be in doubt. A long campaign against shipping is much more difficult to monitor. These are points which will be returned to later in this chapter. This 'tying-down' doctrine espoused in late May 1943 would appear to have its origins in a Führer conference:

> *Dönitz*: In 1940 a submarine was able to sink an average of 1,000 tons per day at sea; towards the end of 1942, approximately 200 tons. This shows clearly the growing effectiveness of anti-submarine defence, and the diminishing effectiveness of submarines. Nevertheless, I am convinced that submarine warfare must be carried on, even if great successes are no longer possible. The forces tied up through submarine warfare were considerable even during the [First] World War.

> The *Führer* interrupts at this point with the following remark: There can be no talk of a let-up in submarine warfare. The Atlantic is my first line of defence in the West, and even if I have to fight a defensive battle there, that is preferable to waiting to defend myself on the coast of Europe. The enemy forces tied up by our submarine warfare are tremendous, even though the actual losses inflicted by us are no longer great. I cannot afford to release these forces by discontinuing submarine warfare.[26]

This provides both a pure strategic and an economic–strategic policy for the final two years' work of Dönitz and the *U-Bootwaffe*. It is interesting to note that the previous strong reliance on figures has been abandoned: 'considerable' and 'tremendous' are hardly numerate terms. But setting aside the economic factors for the moment, the strategy alone bears examination.[27] Faced with the parlous situation that should have been becoming ever clearer to the Germans at that point, there was certainly some worth in continuing the Atlantic campaign as their other options were very limited indeed. This was especially so for the *Kriegsmarine* whose fundamental lack of balance was even more evident now than it had been at the beginning of the war. Any technological developments that might have allowed some alternative deployment of the submarine fleet were some time away from being in place and thus, it might be argued, the only true alternative facing the navy was either the fundamentally unproductive continuation of the Atlantic campaigns or else dissolution. Nothing in Dönitz's or, for that matter, Hitler's characters suggested that this might have been considered by them. Thus they jointly presided over a strategy that took the U-boats from losing a campaign to utter rout.

The minor theme that was present throughout most of the war, except very early on, was that of marginal exploitation. In this a relatively small number of submarines would be used well away from the main cross-Atlantic routes. There were a number of potential advantages to such deployments. Firstly, there was surprise for its own sake, hoping to achieve an unbalancing of the Allies. Secondly, once there submarines might well enjoy a period of relatively easy operating from anything ranging from a few days to a few months. It might be argued that the early 1942 operations off the east coast of the USA fell into this category but both plans and actual events suggest that it was rather more than this. However, as the war progressed, the balance of advantage of these ever-further-flung operations tended to decrease. They became even more marginal than they had been, both in terms of geography and results. Perhaps their last flowering was in Indian Ocean operations in the second half of 1943 when sinkings there exceeded those in the Atlantic by a significant margin. But this relative salience was as much a reflection of Allied dominance of the Atlantic as any intrinsic worth in using the distant areas. These operations, too, tended to be limited throughout by logistic factors. Before mid-1941, there was no suitable base and few submarines with the range to attempt remote operations. Latterly supplies were the constraining factor and, in the end, dreams of German U-boats supported by Japanese bases in the Far East were largely frustrated by a less than perfect alliance. Thus the marginal sub-strategy became exactly that: banished to the geographical margins and having but little effect on the outcome of the anti-shipping campaign, far less the war.

Viewing the Battle

The German conduct of the Battle of the Atlantic was limited by their
resources and guided by their various doctrines and, of course, determined too by Allied actions. However, the outcome also depended to
some extent on their own reading of what was going on, together with
their interpretations of the trends of the conflict, as this had a significant
effect on its future conduct. As the USA became ever more engaged and
German material superiority came to be overtaken then completely out-
matched, the importance of correct readings of the situation became
more, rather than less, important. How did they do in this respect? In
terms of historical writing, it is relatively easy to retrieve one aspect of
the German experience, that from the sea. The literature dealing with
the experiences of individual submarines, their crews and individuals
within them is reasonably well documented.[28] What is perhaps less well
covered directly is the higher direction of the war. This is hardly surprising, in the light of early memoirs probably having more reason to be
self-serving than ones by those at the lower levels and the relatively early
demise of some of the participants. This makes it more difficult to reach
back into contemporary thought. The task is rendered more difficult by
many of the contemporary records concentrating on events rather than
interpretation.[29] Perhaps the best compromise exists in the Hessler
volumes.[30] Although not strictly primary material, they do give a reasonably concise and accurate portrayal of the Battle of the Atlantic as
perceived through German eyes at command level. Hessler himself commanded more than one submarine and served on BdU's staff, as well as
being Dönitz's son-in-law. In addition to providing a wealth of statistical
data on submarine deployments and results, they also give an insight
into the way of thinking at BdU headquarters.

The three volumes fairly neatly cover three time-periods and, to
some extent, the same number of phases of the conflict, with divisions
at the turn of the year 1941/42 and at the end of May 1943. The first
period deals with the process of learning and development. There are
setbacks but usually of relatively short duration and these phases are
succeeded by greater achievements in other ways. The tone is thus realistic but optimistic. The only slightly false note in terms of historical
hindsight deals with the events of 1941 when the submarines are
pushed evermore westwards into the middle of the Atlantic, beyond all
possible hope of German air reconnaissance. This is described in terms
of responding to problems rather than suffering a significant loss of
effectiveness, which is now known to be the case.[31] Thus the reason

ascribed for the move westwards as early as the spring of 1941 is one of looking for areas in which groups can operate without hindrance as well as being unable to function in the areas immediately west and northwest of the UK and Ireland; there is little or no suggestion that such operations were less fruitful overall, but such was the case.[32] Here perhaps was an early hint of problems in reading the picture. It matters little for a German perspective, whether the contemporary one of 1941 or Hessler's more considered one post-war; it also barely signifies that there was a hidden factor in operation for some of this time – Ultra. What is important is that here perhaps is the first evidence of not facing up to the reality of loss of effectiveness; in effect, denial.

The following period from January 1942 through to May 1943 saw a return to reality, and that reality was a very rosy one indeed for BdU with the attacks on shipping on the east coast of the USA producing very good results despite the long passages there and back. This was succeeded by the gradual then complete return to mid-Atlantic operations, initially reasonably successfully (although nowhere near as productive as the American operations). The German reading of these was initially good but as these convoy battles became harder, there was a tendency to understand that all was not going as well it might, but not necessarily why this might be so. Here again, Ultra was a hidden factor although, once more with hindsight, few would claim it being as effective as in 1941. Both Allied aircraft and radar were correctly recognised as problems but there was no appreciation at this stage of the very considerable ASW menace of HF DF, both in itself and as a multiplier of the problems caused by the two recognised factors.[33] Indeed, the failure to appreciate the existence of HF DF led to a tendency to grossly overestimate the capability of radar and to consider whether other (and quite non-existent) devices might have been invented and deployed. This quest for the secret sensor was to continue into the last period of Hessler's chronicle.

The general tone of Hessler's last volume, covering the final two years of the war, is one of continuing hope, but also of mounting pessimism. It is also one of unfulfilled aspirations and several delusory ideas. The hope and aspirations were largely tied to promises of the new-technology submarine and it would be wrong to consider that this view was misplaced, merely that time in ordinary course and positive Allied action stood between the intention and the act.[34] In that sense there was no self-deception. However, this was not true about certain other aspects of the Battle of the Atlantic. Two important matters come to mind: the continuing puzzle of submarine detection by the Allies and conjectures about mis-assessed or even totally illusory devices. In the former category comes the view that Allied aircraft homed on radio signals emitted by the submarines' own radar detector, Metox.[35] Into the other category, that of the totally illusory, came noise-boxes and other ASW devices. Hessler devotes over a page describing devices which had little existence in fact, accompanied by laconic footnotes inserted by the British editor pointing out that these were 'mostly imaginary' and 'generally inaccurate'.[36]

It can thus be seen that the German ability both to understand the situation they were in at any given time and to look ahead varied greatly during the war. At its best it was realistic and appropriate; but it did not always serve them well. Some of this might be attributed to a simple lack of information. However, even making some allowance for the inevitable effect of mistaken assessments that occur in wartime, there were periods when it can only be considered that there was insufficient analytical effort put into the subject. In the latter part of the Battle of the Atlantic, too, it can be argued that there was a move from occasional error to a positive state of delusion; in more ways than one, the end was close.[37]

A view of Germany

The German war against shipping has been looked at from a number of different viewpoints: how can these be summed up? As a preliminary it is necessary to make the rather obvious point that any comments can only be made in the context of what actually happened – the problem with counterfactual hypotheses is that they cannot really be considered as the only factor that changed among the many that were significant. It is clear that, in two senses of the term, there was a marked German focus on the submarine as a sinker of merchant ships. Although it might be argued that there was little choice for them with an undersized surface fleet, no naval aviation to speak of and poor relations with the Luftwaffe, there was also a clear preference and aptitude for both the submarine and this form of warfare. The second form of focus dealt with the application to that warfare which was intense and professional. But at the same time, it was also perhaps, over-concentrated. German performance, too, was at its best at the tactical and lower reaches of the operational levels of warfare. As the ladder was ascended into strategy and grand strategy, the Germans' touch was less sure. Two defining conditions have to be made clear: these remarks are confined to naval warfare and there were changes with the passage of time.

For the Germans, naval warfare was never to produce the same level of success or spectacle as their lightning advances on land. There was no naval equivalent of the fall of whole nations in times which could only have been dreamed of in the previous European conflict; nothing comparable to the fall of Poland or France and no occupation of a large part of European Russia. The Battle of the Atlantic was certainly important and sometimes dangerous to the Allies but it lacked the apparent scale of the continental operations. Possibly, too, it was asking rather much of one leader, Dönitz, to operate at levels from grand strategic to tactical at the same time and with equal and considerable competence.

It can also be argued that it was in the middle part of the Battle of the Atlantic, from the middle of 1942 until the end of May 1943, that the Germans' grip on even operational and tactical competence crumbled, then disappeared. This was never to go completely and the decline did not come about through lack of either high-level will or effort. It would be easy to attribute this entirely to Allied superiority, both quantitative and qualitative, but this would be falling into an analytical trap. There is an obverse to this in such situations as the fall of Singapore in February 1942, which many British writers have perceived largely in terms of blunders, tending to deny by omission the capability of the Japanese. Returning to the Atlantic, and the rarely disproved aphorism of war that victory goes to the side making the fewest, least significant mistakes, not only did the Allies do most things right but the Germans did at least some things wrong.

The greatest (and very much linked) failures were a growing inability to recognise the situation in which they were and a failure to analyse their problems sufficiently well to allow effective remedial action. Thus the growing lack of understanding of enemy performance went hand in hand with declining results from the *U-Bootwaffe*, and tactical failure at sea was echoed in the inability at strategic level to deploy the new-technology submarines from which so much was expected. In the end, Dönitz and his submarines were outbuilt and outfought, but they were outthought, too. Over the first, they had ultimately virtually no control, at least after the USA was engaged; the second was perhaps more evenly balanced until the last two years of the war, but the last was largely attributable to deep-seated and inherent flaws in them and in their system.

5
Convoy Warfare

The convoy lay at the heart of the war on shipping: it was at once the principal countermeasure to the German attack on shipping and, for much of the war, the main target of German naval forces, especially submarines. However, its centrality has led to it being taken for granted to some extent on one hand and on the other derided as outdated. It is therefore helpful to look again at the convoy, both in theory and practice, to see what its merits and drawbacks are in general and how these worked out practically in the harsh arena of the Battle of the Atlantic.

Before beginning this, it is important to dispose of one important distinction that is sometimes made in warfare because it has often shaped perceptions of the worth or otherwise of convoy systems – that of offensive and defensive strategy and tactics. There is an inherent bias in military thinking and literature generally in favour of positive, often aggressive, action.[1] This is understandable, and to some extent, sanctioned by the history of military operations but does not tell the whole story. It is, of course, important to take the initiative in war but there are few things that play into an enemy's hand more than unstructured or unreasoned violence, unless of course, there is a gross imbalance of force in the first place. It is also important to note that what is apparently offensive or defensive at one level of warfare can be categorised differently at another. Thus it is arguable that the tactically 'defensive' measure of convoy was strategically 'offensive', permitting as it undoubtedly did the main thrust of renewed Allied operations in Europe in the summer of 1944.[2] Further, it can be argued that the so-called 'defensive' tactic of convoy actually accounted for most of the submarines sunk by the Allies.[3] Analytically, therefore, care should be taken in not confusing the proper invocation of an aggressive spirit in the practitioners of warfare with the appropriate selection of measures

69

to attain an aim. No one could cite lack of aggression in a Gretton or Heineman, yet their greatest achievements were on what many would define as defensive operations. Further, the convoy escort, be it on the surface or in the air, was the greatest sinker of submarines.[4]

The theory of convoy

Barley and Waters go to some pains to establish that there are two elements to the definition of convoy, the first being the collection together of more than one merchant vessel proceeding together and the second point being that this aggregation is under some form of warship escort.[5] Although this definition is reflected here it is important to note that some analyses of the properties of convoy do not necessarily depend on the second element of the definition. Clearly, both in practice and logic, warships cannot escort if they have nothing to protect but the concept of grouped merchant vessels proceeding together but without protection might be logically sustainable, if not tactically prudent.[6]

The first property of convoy which aids the protection of shipping is bestowed on it merely by grouping ships. In an era when the visual sensor was still the most important one, then sighting distances were the determining factor in open-ocean reconnaissance.[7] Thus the measure of grouping ships just by itself made the U-boats' task much more difficult. This results from the fact that the distance at which a convoy can be sighted is not a simple product of the sighting distance for a single ship multiplied by the number of ships in the convoy. This is because their sighting circles overlap and effectively cancel out any such potential enhancement.[8] The property is well demonstrated graphically (see Fig. 5.1).

There are, of course, a few potential qualifications that might be introduced. If a few means exist to limit the search area, known in some of the search literature as cueing, then the effect may not be so pronounced. This may be true in theory but the practice suggests that the benefit to the searcher is a little diminished. Looking at three examples of this are instructive: intelligence, geographical limitations and stragglers.

The Germans did have Sigint support for a considerable period of the war and sometimes it worked well to enable them to close convoys. However, it was not always timely or accurate enough to allow them to intercept convoys – especially when comparable Allied intelligence allowed evasive routing. Examples are the failed operations west of the UK in early 1941.[9] Perhaps this became less of a problem in the first

71

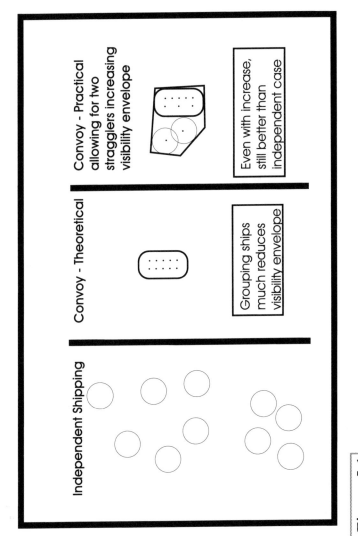

Figure 5.1   Theory of convoy I – reconnaissance and grouping

half of 1943, but by then the packs – and thus reconnaissance lines – were so long that intelligence became less significant in any case.[10] There were two broad instances of geographical limitations: choke points, such as the North Channel approach to the Irish Sea, and coastlines, of which the leading example must be the United States east coast. In the first instance, although the submarine reconnaissance problem was solved, these areas were relatively easy to defend and thus not really suitable for submarine operations.[11] The latter case is also interesting as the introduction here of a convoy system in the second quarter of 1942 led to a significant drop in sightings of shipping by submarines and, consequently, sinkings.[12] Lastly, stragglers. As the figure indicates, despite these increasing the visibility envelope quite significantly, it still does not increase this to anything like the same size as the independent case. In any case, grouping is the key to understanding the first property of convoy: the confounding, or at very least, making more difficult the problem of reconnaissance for an enemy.

The other great advantage that convoy has, however, is intimately connected with the second part of the Barley and Waters definition: the presence of escorting warships. What this then means is that these forces are concentrated at the only real place where these submarines can do any real damage, assuming that the U-boats are committed to an anti-trade strategy. The submarines are in other places at different times, but this is their most dangerous location, in the close vicinity of a convoy.[13] Assuming a submarine force to be capable of doing its job, this is also the one place they can be guaranteed to be aiming for. At a stroke, therefore, much is accomplished provided that there are suitable sensors and weapons, together with a reasonable degree of proficiency on the escorts' part; the side protecting shipping is in a reasonably advantageous position. If no submarine makes contact with the convoy, then the shipping is safely delivered to its destination and a victory has been won. Should this not occur, then at best there are opportunities to engage submarines.

These points may seem self-evident but it is worth remembering that the outbreak of the Second World War was barely a generation away from a wilful rejection of these principles by the British and failures by two other nations to observe them were to occur, at least for a while, with two other participants – the Americans and the Japanese – in the 1940s. The British First World War experience had flown in the face of much previous history when both the defence of trade in general and the adoption of convoy as a principal means of achieving this, had been considered as a valid and successful tactic over a number of centuries. This was evidenced in the activities of a number of maritime nations including the English, Spanish and Dutch.[14]

Knowledge of such success seems to have departed naval doctrine some time after the introduction of steam, although the full circumstances and reasons for this departure from the canon of accepted wisdom are obscure.[15] The worst result of this was the belated British response to German unrestricted submarine warfare in 1917, when a general convoy system was only adopted after large, almost catastrophic, losses of merchant shipping.[16]

Convoy in practice

Whatever the theoretical advantages conferred by convoy, its practice involved a great many more considerations and significant organisational effort. Further, it is necessary to realise that the convoy system as practised by the Allies was not a static system but one which was constantly changing in response to perceptions of enemy threat, Allied strategic priorities and the availability of resources. In addition, although some parts of the system were run by single countries, the most significant areas tended to be bi- or multi-national efforts adding, potentially at least, to the complications.[17] There are a number of ways in which the system as a whole can be looked at; these include routes and classification, cycles and size and control.

It is not intended here to look at the main routes in detail; that is covered elsewhere.[18] However, it helps to realise that high-level decisions had to be made in the first instance as to which routes shipping would run and that this situation changed largely with the changing line-up of nations committed to the war and as each of these underwent the transition from peacetime trading to wartime transport: the development in the nature of submarine operations was also germane. This picture – and its projection into the middle term – provided the basis on which the requirement for convoying was founded. Initially the remote areas were reckoned reasonably safe, although this perception was quickly changed, at least for the Atlantic, not so much by submarines as the activities of German surface raiders, either true warships or merchant vessels converted to auxiliary cruisers.[19] As a result of all this German activity, there was action from the Allies, with the geographical extension of the convoy system and a connected German reaction by moving to areas still uncovered. Consequently, on the western side of the Atlantic the convoy system was continuous from

Greenland in the north to Rio de Janeiro in the south. There was always an element of pragmatism in the Allied approach, with a proper reluctance to initiate convoys unless these were seen as necessary. This was entirely justifiable for reasons set out later in this chapter.[20] It was also necessary sometimes to take account of a number of other general factors such as specific commodity flows such as oil, sometimes resulting in specific routes or convoys comprised of specialist ships such as tankers. The other great realm of classification was that of ship-speed. This tended to effect the decision on whether ships were included or excluded from the convoy system. At one end of the range, this resulted in the 'Monsters', the large fast liners, often employed as troopships which generally sailed out of convoy, taking advantage of their speed as their best protection.[21] At the other end of the scale were ships whose advertised speed was below 7 knots. These would have slowed convoys unnecessarily and were excluded from the system. For most of the war, the normal speed range for convoyed ships was 7–15 knots with the majority tending to the lower end of this band.[22] What this tended to mean is that many convoys had within them ships not using their full speed potential. A further complication was introduced by stragglers, those ships which were nominally capable of convoy speeds but in practice were unable to maintain them. By dropping out of convoy, these were clearly at more risk of attack, not least when submarines were attempting to close a convoy.[23]

Once a route was decided on and a system established, two important considerations on any high-traffic route were convoy cycles and size which were related aspects. These factors would only come into play once a certain density was established. Thus WS convoys were to some extent *ad hoc* and the OG/HG series to and from Gibraltar were not entirely regular because of relatively low volumes, harbour capacity at Gibraltar and threat-assessment levels. It was on the main cross-Atlantic routes that the major discussions of cycles occurred. Clearly, the more often a particular type of convoy was run, the fewer ships it would be likely to have and the greater would be the demand for escorts. There would also be the disadvantage of providing more but smaller submarine targets – considering the convoy and not the ship as the target. At the other end of the consideration was a reluctance for most of the war to have convoys that were considered too large for the operational authorities. Their concerns were physical control of large bodies of ships and a perception that bigger convoys meant greater risks. Returning to the discussion of cycles, in the spring of 1943 the increasing cargo flow requirement, predicated by Allied strategic plans,

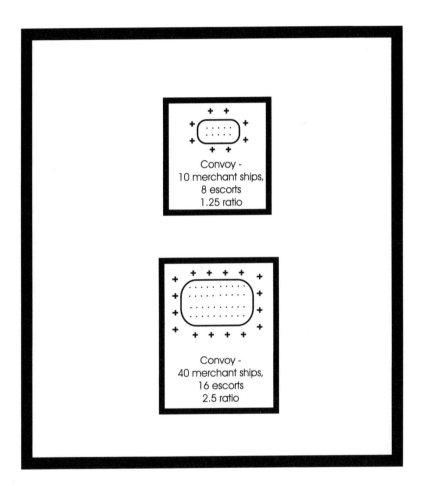

Figure 5.2

Figure 5.2 Theory of convoy II – convoy size and escort requirement

led to consideration of decreasing the existing eight-day cycle to six in
April, then five in May. This was resisted successfully by Horton,
CinCWA, on the dual grounds of thinning out of the escort force and
disruption of the sophisticated plan of their deployment.[24] At the same
meeting, a reluctant Admiralty accepted the other alternative and
allowed for exceptional convoys of up to 60 ships.[25] Eventually this too
was to be greatly exceeded. The Admiralty's worst fear on this never
came to be realised because, as pointed out at the time by Professor
Blackett, the leading exponent of operational research, larger convoys
were actually safer as well as being more economical in the use of
escorts.[26]

Convoys were controlled in a number of ways. Within the formation
itself, the media of flag and sound signals, together with signal lights,
were the normal method, supplemented from time to time by the
expedient of sending an escort to pass messages either by handline or
megaphone. Radio was not resorted to except where strictly necessary.
The lower frequencies tended to carry much further than the area of
the convoy and were thus insecure, while the useful development of
very high frequency (VHF) radio telephone was not generally available
until late in the war and was generally confined to warships. However,
VHF radio, known to the Americans as Talk Between Ships (TBS), was
of great tactical utility to the escort groups. There were two foci of
command in a convoy: the convoy commodore in one of the merchant ships and the escort force commander in one of the escorts. The
former was usually a retired Royal Navy or RNR senior officer; excep-
tionally, experienced merchant ship masters were used. All did well.
The escort force commander was a relatively junior officer, a commander or lieutenant-commander, even. These relative positions called for
tact on the part of the junior; tolerance from the commodore. This was
especially so, as the escort force commander directed the whole,
passing his requests and advice to the commodore. This continued to
apply, even when a second group was allocated to the convoy in
support, notwithstanding relative seniorities. In British escort groups,
the senior officer also commanded a ship, whereas in American groups,
he did not have this extra responsibility, he and his staff being borne
additional to ship's officers.[27] A great number of the British officers and
ratings were in service only because of the war, many of the officers
rising to ship command by the middle of the war, and some even
receiving group command.

At a higher level, control was exercised from such headquarters as
that of CinCWA in Liverpool whose task was the monitoring of the

progress of all convoys in the Atlantic and the allocation of assets
under its command to strengthen threatened convoys. For this
purpose, the headquarters had access to a picture which was a dupli-
cate of that in the Admiralty. This was done partly as a necessary pre-
requisite to sound decision-making and partly as a redundant measure,
should anything happen to the London plots. A small number of
people on the CinCWA staff were privy to a full intelligence picture;
that is, they had access to Ultra. Another innovation was the integration of No. 15 Group of Coastal Command into this headquarters. This
was an important asset for the Allies and served as a model for some
postwar command structures. At a higher level still, in the Admiralty, a
number of directorates were involved, principally the operations and
trade directorates, and the OIC of the NID.[28] Here, too, the system of
maritime air force and naval coordination was repeated with Coastal
Command of the RAF being under Admiralty operational control, a
generally harmonious arrangement. The general level of involvement
in operational-level decisions from Admiralty to CinCWA was properly
restrained, as it was from CinCWA to sea commanders, although this
had not always been so.[29] One possible difficulty, however, was that
commanders at sea in relatively small ships were not allowed to receive
Ultra information directly although the flow of information and, less
commonly, orders had been informed by this source. At sea, escort
group commanders had some discretion in varying the convoy's
progress. This could be in terms of an agreed number of miles either
side of the planned track, or a number of hours early or late on the
schedule.

Convoy participants

There were many different types of ships that might be part of an
ocean convoy, normally from about 1000 GRT and upwards. These
could carry anything from bulk, fairly inert cargoes such as grain,
through mixed general cargo to the more dangerous loads such as oil
and especially its refined and therefore more volatile derivatives and
most of all explosives. Ships were of varied age, condition and ability
of crew. This alone could provide difficulty for the management of the
convoy, particularly in terms of the ship's ability to maintain convoy
speed. Older ships which had, over the years, been maintained with
more attention to cost than reliability, and whose theoretical service
speed was at or only slightly above that laid down for the convoy, were
likely to be the most troublesome and were thus a constant worry to

convoy commodores and escort force commanders. Allied to such problems of material origin was the matter of comprehension and willingness to understand the organisation of convoy. Although most masters, even when English was not their first language, had a rudimentary understanding sufficient for the essentials of seagoing, this did not always extend to a thorough knowledge of convoy instructions, both the standing ones and those issued specifically before each convoy and during its progress. Much too depended upon the competence or otherwise of the officers actually on watch at any given time. As a result, much of the work of the commodore and escort commander was taken up with the business of keeping the convoy together, a problem made worse in poor visibility or foul weather, even without the further complication of the presence of the enemy. In that sense, there was probably no such thing as an uneventful convoy. Weather was a constant concern and with such a mix of ships, there was always an awkward series of compromises to be considered as it worsened. Convoy speed might have to be reduced several times as weather worsened, with each occasion being an opportunity for confusion and dispersion and, in the worst case, heaving-to might be necessary.[30]

The escort groups themselves tended to evolve as the war went on, undergoing a marked transformation from being a very mixed bag of ship-types, with no experience of having worked together, to more homogenous groups. Although these would normally have more than one ship-type in them, such as destroyers or sloops and corvettes, they became much more stable as to composition. Later, the British in particular tended to keep the same specific ships together in groups, although this only became possible as escort numbers grew and the necessity for sudden transfers declined. The benefits of working together in this way made the groups much more efficient than they had been and it was to maintain this that Horton fought so hard to retain the system as told earlier in this chapter.[31] Obviously, some groups had more relevant experience than others and not all rose to the challenge of convoy battles as well as others, but the system as a whole, combined with a heavy emphasis on training – both at the outset and in continuation – ensured that even the lowest capability group was at least adequate. These two factors – organisation and training combining symbiotically – went a long way to dealing with the problems which ensued when intelligence was unable to ensure avoidance of German submarines, either because of a blackout or else when so many submarines were deployed that their total avoidance was impractical.

The disadvantages of convoy

It would be wrong to conduct a worthwhile discussion of convoy without noting that it did have disadvantages as well as benefits. Whilst undoubtedly safer in terms of the submarine problem, it has to be recognised that it was not the optimum way of delivering cargo except under these extreme wartime circumstances. Ships whose service speed was markedly greater than that of the convoy took much longer to make voyages and the time taken to assemble ships into convoy was also a significant factor. Routes, too, were often changed and not just in a minor way. For a while at least, shipping from the Caribbean and even South America had to make the longer journey up the American coast to New York or Halifax before moving eastwards across the Atlantic. Perhaps the greatest long way round was caused by the closure of the Mediterranean for most of the period 1940–43 and the resultant necessity to supply the Middle East via the Cape of Good Hope route. This not only added enormously to the voyage time but also exposed shipping to Atlantic submarine depredations for much longer. The management of convoys and their escorts, both at sea and in the terminal points, absorbed a major amount of administrative effort.

Convoy's record of success

Despite all these disadvantages, it is clear that the convoy system generally was a success. It maximised the delivery of necessary cargoes and minimised losses. It is difficult to make this point statistically, not because there is a lack of data, but rather because there is a very great deal of it and it is very complicated. Overall figures suggest that it was at least twice as dangerous for a ship to sail independently as in convoy.[32] There were certainly large-scale disasters to convoys, such as SC42, TM1, HX229/SC122 and (outside the Battle of the Atlantic arena) PQ17 but these must be considered as very rare as against a total figure of over 25 000 convoys run.[33]

Environmental factors

Running a convoy on one side and attacking it on the other were very much affected by a number of interlinked environmental factors: the seasons, day and night, and the weather.[34] The changing seasons played an important part in the nature of operations. Winter conditions meant short days and, often, heavy weather. From the Allied viewpoint, this tended to increase strain on crews and meant keeping convoys together more difficult. The weather factor often meant too that it was difficult to allow much diversion from the direct, that is, Great Circle route across the Atlantic. This, in conjunction with fears about fuel consumption, could limit the scope for planners to take convoys in more radical directions and also inhibit evasive routing superimposed on these direct transits. Sometimes the winter weather factor predicated more southern routing in an attempt to avoid the worst conditions, even accepting the fuel penalty involved. There was another price to pay, as for much of the war, going further south meant even less chance of the air-cover that might be provided from the UK, Iceland and Canada. Bad weather affected crews of all types of ship and although submarines could dive to give some respite from the very worst conditions, this was a remedy only really suited to times when the tactical tempo was low. Weather, too, could have an effect on ships' geographic positions which were not always readily ascertainable by the navigational methods then in use.

The winter feature of long hours of darkness generally worked to the advantage of the submarine as, until radar was widely fitted, it allowed the maximum use of the surface for closing a convoy, manoeuvring into attacking position and firing torpedoes, as well as subsequent escape. More generally, the division of night and day was an important one, escorts often adopting different postures and formations for each. By day, escorts tended to be more distantly spaced and an escort commander was probably more likely to permit longer detachments in daylight. The change between the two conditions was also seen by some escort commanders as a good opportunity to confound an unseen shadower's task by conducting a fairly radical convoy course alteration at about this time. The state of the moon combined, of course, with cloud cover was also often important. A bright moon could do very little to help the convoy but it was often of benefit to attacking submarines who preferred to attack from the dark side with the moon silhouetting their targets if at all possible. Lastly, the state of the weather could be an important factor for an escort commander to take into account when dealing with the problem of a ship damaged by a submarine: should salvage be attempted or should it be sunk by the escort? The scarcity of escorts normally dictated the latter course.

Navigation in the 1940s

At the end of the twentieth century when very precise satellite navigation is available to virtually every mariner and can be accessed by

almost anyone who wants to use it, thinking oneself back into the navigational problems of the period of the Battle of the Atlantic can be
very difficult. It is also worth making the point that there are problems,
too, for the historian.

Looking first at the contemporary problems, there were only a
limited number of methods available once out of sight of land. These
limitations applied to all of the participants, under, on and over the
sea. In essence, there were two: radio aids and astronavigation. The
main radio aid which was likely to be used was MF DF. Transmissions
made from shore for navigational purposes were readily detectable on
ships, the equipment was widely fitted and cross-bearings could establish position to an extent. There were, however, some difficulties.
Similar constraints applied to those discussed in detail later on shore
HF DF, that is, the angle of intersection of two or more bearings
obtained, and this was made worse by the accuracy of shipborne equipment obviously being less than that which was deployed ashore. Of
course, it was possible to play the system in reverse, so to speak, by
having the ship at sea transmit and the shore stations take bearings on
it, then transmitting the derived position back to the ship, but this was
generally and properly considered to be insecure and therefore not
allowed.

Astronavigation on the other hand entailed no such risks.
Opportunities for this tended to be of two sorts: solar observations
during the day and star sights at morning and evening twilights.[35] Sun
sights generally involved at least two observations, spaced some hours
apart and even then produced an answer which was probably better
suited to a peacetime merchant ship on passage from A to B, rather
than a manoeuvring escort. Star sights did not need the several hours'
run between observations but took some time to calculate. Because
under good conditions they generated more position lines, they could
be more accurate in themselves, possibly to within a mile or two.
However, sun and star observations were both subject to the same limitation: cloud cover. The realistic pattern of Atlantic weather often
meant that sights might be some days out of date and the resultant
accumulation of errors might be quite significant.

Such inaccuracies created difficulties for all participants in the battle.
Submarines might make for positions some tens of miles distant from
where their command wanted them to be, with the neat-looking search-
lines on plotting boards in shore headquarters having in reality no
resemblance to the actual search-pattern achieved. This might result in
considerable overlaps and yawning gaps. Furthermore, the difference in

actual and perceived positions when reporting sightings might not result in the desired outcome, a group of submarines making contact with a convoy, if forced to rely solely on reported positional information. This was the main reason why a contact-keeping submarine was supposed to make repeated homing signals on MF.[36]

Aircraft, too, experienced difficulties especially in meeting convoys, and the problem worsened the further out from their base they had to go. This was an early problem tackled by the Operational Research Section of Coastal Command, and their studies have revealed some interesting data. It should be remembered, of course, that in any encounter problem there are two sides to consider and there seems little evidence that the surface side was studied to the same extent.[37] Two particularly interesting items produced when aircraft are attempting convoy contact with the aim of augmenting their escorts are the initial 'not met' rate of $8\frac{1}{2}$ per cent per 100 miles from base and the average error in a convoy's reported position of 35 miles along the course and 15 miles across it.[38]

For the historian, there is a further problem which lies with the form in which navigational information is shown. Typically this is presented in records as being to within one minute of both latitude and longitude, this apparent precision suggesting an accuracy of about one mile.[39] As the preceding discussion has indicated, this is indicative at best and fanciful at worst. Obviously, once contact is made, either between surface escort and aircraft or between submarine and convoy or any other possible combination, then geographic accuracy is a matter of less importance. But when discussing such topics as evasive routing, it is important to remember the serial and parallel inaccuracies; the sometimes self-cancelling, sometimes cumulative pool of errors between decoded convoy routing instructions transmitted by BdU to submarines at sea, their own perceptions of their positions, the intended and actual tracks followed by convoys, the subsequent reporting of sightings and the reactions engendered by them.

Attacking a convoy

The process of attacking a convoy can be considered in a number of different ways, but it is suggested that there are four distinct phases in the process, all relevant in different ways to the problems which the Germans had to confront. Thinking about the attack in this way is a useful analytical tool in realising the difficulties faced by the submarines and the methods open to the Allies in opposing them. The ability to do anything about submarine activities varied greatly during the war and breaking down the process makes it easier to realise the true effects of any given measure.

Not long after the war P. M. S. Blackett used a threefold division in looking at the problem of large versus small convoy size and the method below has some similarities to this, although arrived at independently.[40] It is suggested now that there are four phases to the process, which can be conveniently be referred to by the acronym ORCA:

- *Outer*: Before organised reconnaissance is started. Normally, this would mean before the formation of submarines into groups. It is worth noting that it was not unusual for submarines in this state to make convoy sightings.
- *Reconnaissance*: Organised search until one submarine gains contact.
- *Closure*: This takes the process through two sub-phases: the remainder of the group closing until initial convoy-sighting and each submarine moving from sighting to starting its attack run.
- *Attack*: The final phase of the attack process, involving weapon-firing.

These are illustrated by means of a simple diagram (see Fig. 5.3)

This has both the virtue and vice of simplicity. It will be noted that no specific ranges from a convoy, which lies at the centre, are given. The suggestion, too, is that these activities are equal in either space or time. This is not true either, but their extent in either of these dimensional senses can vary so greatly that it stands in the way not of understanding one given attack but rather that of having a clear idea of what is involved in attack more generally. In general these activities will have to be entered into sequentially from outside in for the U-boat, whereas the perspective of a convoy escort commander is largely from the inside out. From now on, when reference is made to any of the components of ORCA it will be with the initial letter capitalised, e.g. Reconnaissance.

The submariner's tasks and methods of operation might have to change radically depending on which phase he was in. The first, the Outer, was likely to be concerned with safe passage, while keeping a sharp look-out, either for chance convoys or independent shipping targets. Above all, there was a strong emphasis placed on survival, aircraft while within range of Allied air bases being a particular concern. During the period of Reconnaissance, it was important to cover the assigned area thoroughly whilst maximising the water swept. This could be limited by visibility and the hours of daylight.[41] Like the

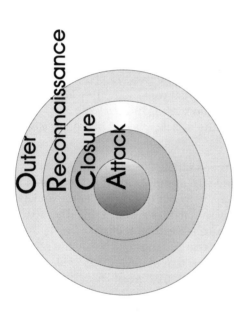

Outer
Reconnaissance
Closure
Attack

Outer   before packs formed for search
Reconnaissance   search until one U-boat gains contact
Closure   rest of pack in contact to start of attack run
Attack   self-explanatory

Figure 5.3

Figure 5.3   Submarine attack – the ORCA concept

previous activity, there was liable to be a fairly high ratio of tedium to activity.

The first two phases tended to be much the same for all submarines: the third was sharply different. Once one submarine detected a convoy, its task was to remain in contact, letting both BdU and fellow-members of its group know that it was continuing in contact and reporting the convoy's position. During this process, the others of the group had to close the convoy as fast as they were able. The process posed two difficulties: it took time and it could be disrupted. Properly speaking, there were two sub-phases here for submarines other than the contact-keeper. One consisted of finding the convoy itself, based on the information being broadcast by BdU and the MF homing signals made by the contact-keeper.[42] The other was moving from the first visual indications of the convoy to a position from which an attack run could begin. There was often a considerable difference between these two as a convoy might be sighted at ranges well in excess of 10 miles and a potential firing-run began from very much closer. The dynamics of submarine group and convoy movement, too, often meant the initial approach was from astern of the convoy but the ideal position to be in as darkness fell, prior to an attack, was ahead of it. This involved working ahead at relatively high speeds, on the surface but planning to be beyond visual sighting distance from the convoy. All these processes are relatively simple to describe but, in practice, a considerable premium was put on both skill and training. There were various different ways in which these processes might be frustrated, as will be described. Lastly, the attack itself. The word 'wolfpack' has conjured up the image of attacks being coordinated precisely in space and time, rather as the zoological analogy suggests. But wolves attacking their prey can nearly always see their fellow-members of the pack (as well as the prey) and, even if they do not use verbal communication are capable of exacting considerable damage on their adversary by a combination of shock and coordination. In this sense, the term is a poor analogy for the submarine operation as such coordination did not occur. This may not have seemed the case to the victims but attack was very much of an individual effort with neither communications nor available systems of information available to the Germans allowing much else.

Countermeasures to submarine attack

Turning to the escort group commander, he would have tended to see from the inside out; thus he would have had to concern himself greatly with submarines about to fire torpedoes (although he may not have known this was about to happen) but there was little if anything that could have been done about submarines assembling for reconnaissance some hundreds of miles distant. Such is a brief, and fairly obvious overview of his concerns. Clearly, the task was to thwart the submarines' purpose; sinking them might have been a useful way of achieving this, but it was a bonus and should always have taken second place to the aim of safe and timely arrival of the convoy.[43]

But it is one thing to understand what an enemy is trying to do – and quite another to prevent it. It is dubious if any British escort group commander who had been exposed to the initial training at Tobermory, the inter-operation refresher work by Western Approaches staff and the rigorous process of post-operation analysis and enquiry that went on in Liverpool after each convoy arrived, would be in any doubt at all about this.[44] However, it is one thing to understand what has to be done: quite another to be able to do it. To a large extent this was limited by the performance of sensors and weapons, especially early in the Battle. Throughout, however, there was a marked disparity between the situation above and underwater. The only sensor that could operate in the latter environment had a relatively short range and this was matched by the appropriate weapon, the depth-charge. Fortunately this was well suited to the operational characteristics of the submarine which, despite its name, operated largely on the surface. The greatest equipment problem faced by the early war escort group commander, however, was the problem of locating submarines on the surface by night before the fitting of radar was widespread and because illuminants could not be used constantly. This was a constraint of both logistics and tactical prudence. Thus, illuminants only tended to be used in response to a detection by other means, most especially after a successful torpedo attack. It can thus be seen that the scope for ASW early in the Battle was very limited and this constraint was made worse by the comparative paucity of escorts, resulting both in holes in screens and the inability to detach escorts to prosecute contacts. When the latter happened at all, it was to the disadvantage of the convoy as a whole and could rarely be done for long enough for maximum effectiveness. For these reasons, and because there was no suitable sensor, it was beyond the ability of an escort group commander to do anything much to counter submarines in the Closure phase, other than with such passive measures as radical turns at critical times.[45]

Nor was it possible in the early years for any other authority or asset to do very much about the situation once a submarine had sighted a

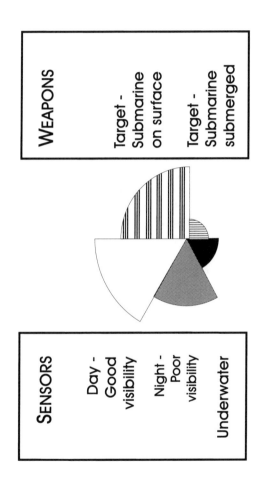

Figure 5.4   ASW in 1939 – comparatives ranges

Notes: Ranges are comparative, not to strict scale

Ranges are for a surface escort – a similar diagram for an aircraft would show greater day visibility, none at night or underwater and very limited weapon capability

convoy. Even when Ultra became available in the second half of 1941, even when it was at its best in terms of timeliness, it was by its nature not timely enough to deal with the problem. Moving back out into the Reconnaissance phase, the escort was even less able to influence events but at least Ultra and other intelligence might have enough space – both literally and in the modern colloquial sense – in which to operate.

The situation which has been described is broadly that which obtained in the early war years, say until the end of 1941, although Allied quantitative and qualitative improvements did occur, making the German task harder. Nevertheless, as is discussed in Chapter 8, at the end of this period the fundamental picture remained the same. For the Germans, a successful Reconnaissance led in almost all cases to a successful *Rudeltaktik* operation. By the time that convoy warfare in the mid-Atlantic was resumed in the summer of 1942, the situation had changed greatly in the Allied favour.

There were a number of reasons for this, all of which can best be explained in terms of ORCA and the Allied responses to its phases.[46] Hardly any of these had been entirely absent from the earlier period but then they were neither well developed nor widely deployed. Again working outwards, it is useful to note those things first which have not changed. Neither sensors nor weapons which might be deployed in good daytime visibility against a surfaced submarine had altered significantly. But by 1943 this was even less of a desired submarine operating area in any case than it had been previously.

There had been gains in both sonar and weapons which effectively increased the underwater effectiveness of surface escorts, making submerged operations in the vicinity of a screen much more hazardous for a submarine. This was further compounded by greater numbers of escorts. These were useful, but on the whole incremental improvements over the previous situation. On the other hand, the changes made to above-water sensors were of a different order of advantage. Radar, by now of increasing quality and more widely fitted, did much to make the surface untenable by night and at all times in poor visibility, greatly complicating the Attack and latter parts of the Closure process for the submarines. This resulted in decreasing results for submarines even after contact had been made with convoys and latterly in the period ending in May 1943, increasing sinkings of U-boats.

But it was in the outer part of the Closure area that perhaps the best improvement was made. This was due to two particular innovations, high-frequency direction-finding (HF DF) and airborne radar. These

ASW IN 1943 - COMPARATIVE RANGES

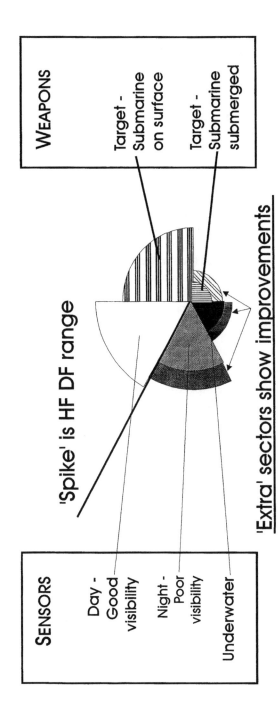

Figure 5.5   ASW in 1943 – comparatives ranges
Notes: Ranges are comparative, not to strict scale
Ranges are for a surface escort – a similar diagram for an aircraft would show greater day visibility, better at night (radar), still no underwater sensor but improved weapon capability

two sensors made it possible to locate and take relatively quick action against not only those submarines that were trying to move from visual contact to firing positions, those attempting to home on convoys but – and most importantly – the contact-keeping submarine itself. The German submarine of the period – which, it has to be remembered, was not a true submarine and had to operate mostly on the surface, at least if it <u>was</u> to be effective – was thus largely neut- *[were]* ralised in two out of the four phases of the attack.

The Reconnaissance phase, too, was under some pressure, although the sheer size of the deployed submarine force went quite a long way to compensate for the availability of Ultra to support evasive routing. Airborne radar allowed the possibility of being able to exact attrition on such U-boats but such was the general paucity of either VLR and carrier-borne aircraft that such operations did not tend to occur until after the crisis of May 1943. Similarly a radar set fitted to an aircraft provided such vast coverage compared to ships that operations such as those against U-boats transiting the relatively restricted area of the Bay of Biscay were feasible, certainly as a deterrent and, at times, also serving to sink submarines.

The centrality of convoy

These measures, viewed together and within the context of attacking convoys, make it very clear why the German attack on shipping failed. ✓ Successive advances in appropriate weapons and especially sensor applied technology, combined with the growing professionalism of the men using such systems were able to counter the imperfect tool that was the German submarine of the period. These findings not only re-establish the convoy as the principal tool for the protection of ship-ping but also make it clear that it was also convoy that was an important reason for the rapid decline in German submarine fortunes from the middle of 1943 onwards. Ultra played a part in this process ✓ but was at its most effective before active warfare between submarine and convoy. Although it can be both difficult and invidious to attempt to attribute relative weights to the performance of different factors operating at different parts of a process, there seems to be little doubt that the contribution to the defeat of German submarines made by the ✓✓ convoy system in both theory and practice was considerable.

6
Technology on Both Sides

The relationship between technology and operational innovation is complex and obscure even in modern times. The type of information used by historians to explain the relationship in the twentieth century is largely unavailable for earlier centuries. Many records of the growing naval administration have survived, but contemporary records of the process of innovation are not clear or substantial. Even the battle, the centre piece of military activity, is difficult to understand clearly. Unlike land battles, which can be pieced together from circumstantial evidence provided by the prevailing topography, sometimes by civilian observers as well as by the participants, sea battles take place in a featureless environment, away from the eyes of observers and are riddled with a terminology and craft that did not translate well into diplomatic or political despatches. Even the basic information is sometimes missing, such as the line of bearing of a fleet in action or the wind direction at critical points. Consequently, in some of these battles crucial movements are guesswork or supposition. The less dramatic aspects of naval warfare are even more obscure.[1]

Richard Harding's remarks, largely intended to refer to earlier centuries, bring out rather well some of the salient features of attempting to plumb the history of the Battle of the Atlantic. In particular, his comments on the problems of understanding naval battle and the obscurity of 'lesser aspects' should be noted. Not least, his comments on technological matters are both helpful and welcome.

The Battle of the Atlantic was, among other things, a technological struggle and this is important in the context of the full assessment of Ultra in the battle. There are two reasons for this. Firstly, the technologies deployed by both sides form part of the general and especially the tactical environment in which Ultra operated; secondly Ultra played a part in formulating the Allied response to German technologies. There are a number of different ways in which this aspect of the world war can be viewed – chronological or thematic. Here it is intended to take the latter approach, examining in each case the tools with which both sides attempted to achieve their aims and the ways in which these developed as the war went on.

German technology – the U-boat

When looking at the German side, there is only one real point of focus – the submarine itself, as virtually everything that happened concerns the boat proper, its sensors and weapons. A certain amount can be said about supporting measures but the majority of these, too, were concentrated in the submarine itself. This stands in distinction to the Allied case where there were a number of different types of anti-submarine units. A good starting point is the German submarine itself as it began in the Second World War. It is important to understand the nature of this animal so that its development can be best comprehended and also to realise not only what it could do but, just as importantly, what it could not.

At the end of August 1939, there were 46 submarines disposed in three different areas, the Baltic and North Seas, and the Atlantic.[2] But more than half of these were the small 250-ton Type II boats, adequate if somewhat cramped and constrained for use in the first two areas but not suitable for the Atlantic. The remainder were largely the 500-ton Type VII and the 700-ton Type IX. The Type II disappeared relatively rapidly from operational inventories but the other two types, albeit much modified and improved in detail, were still to be the staple of the U-boat command through until May 1945.[3] Here lies one of the most significant differences in the technology of the two sides, as the Allies produced new platforms, sensors and weapons in abundance.

The Germans did recognise the inadequacies of the submarines they had in service although, to some extent, only after these had been rudely emphasised to them by the Allies. A further factor delaying the incentive to progress, too, was early success and thus they failed to comprehend how quickly events might turn against them. It would be easy to blame Dönitz in particular, the German Navy more generally and the higher leadership too, but it took some time for the potential of the U-boat arm to be recognised. In the early war period, say until

the spring of 1941, there were some stunning successes, such as the
sinking of the British battleship *Royal Oak* in Scapa Flow by U-47 and
these tended to obscure the problems. But even then, there was a
difficulty with the actuation of torpedoes.[4]

The Type VII submarine, on diesel engines, had a maximum sustained surface speed of 16 knots, which was more than sufficient to
overhaul all but a tiny fraction of merchant ships, although slower
than most warships.[5] Submerged, however, on electric motors, it was
not only much slower (eight knots) but it was also limited to the capacity of its rechargeable battery. Assuming this to be fully charged when
it submerged, there was then a complex trade-off of speed and
endurance. This maximum submerged speed of eight knots could only
be sustained for one hour. At half this speed, however, progress could
be made for 18 hours, and if speed was halved again, then the theoretical endurance was 65 hours. In practice, however, it was not always
possible to maintain a full charge and general considerations of habitability limited the longer submerged periods.

In tactical terms, this meant that some at least of the approach to the
target had to be made on the surface.[6] This was feasible and acceptable
in the early part of the war when targets were either independents or
else weakly escorted convoys, but not so as the conflict progressed. In
fact, the realistic tactical situations encountered by mid-war demonstrated that the Type VIIs and Type IXs were not so much submarines
as part-time, submersible torpedo-boats.

The solution, as far as propulsion was concerned, was a very much
better underwater performance. The Germans tried several approaches
to this problem. The one which took up much of their efforts was the
Walter boat, using a system of a turbine and hydrogen peroxide fuel:
there were also attempts at closed-cycle propulsion, allowing a diesel
engine to be used underwater.[7] These suffered from a number of problems, principally engineering complexity and the hazardous nature of
the fuel. The research and development time was inordinately long.
Walter had started his work in the early 1930s but no operational submarine using his methods was ever put to sea by the Germans.[8]
However, the work on these experimental submarines was not entirely
wasted, as there were to be quite a few features of their design which
saw realisation in a different form. The principal legacies of the Walter
submarine were twofold: a more hydrodynamic hull form and
increased electrical storage capacity.

Submarines of the Types VII/IX generation were designed as much for
surface speed and seakeeping as anything else, a perfectly reasonable

design philosophy in the light of their likely tactical employment. But, as a result, their underwater performance was far from being as good as it might be. Partly as a result of the Walter submarine work, new hull shapes were evolved, more suited to an underwater boat. This was one of the ways in which revolutionary change was approached. The other was by means of greatly improved battery capacity, which held out the prospect of much greater underwater endurance and thus approaching, if not quite achieving, the true submarine. By late 1942, it was becoming obvious that the true Walter boat, despite its enormous promise, was unlikely to enter service quickly enough to be decisive. Accordingly, a decision was made in 1943 to build submarines using much of the technology thus explored, with the exception of the propulsion system, which would follow more conventional lines. These were to be known as Types XXI and XXIII – also referred to by the Germans as Electro-boats.[9]

The XXI was a large boat of 1600 tons whose surface speed was comparable with her predecessors, but which could also reach similar speeds underwater. More importantly, underwater endurance was much improved; at 10 knots the submarine could run for some 11 hours and at lower speeds, very long submerged periods were possible. This opened up the possibility of closing a convoy and attacking one or more targets before withdrawing to safety, all without coming to the surface. These capabilities were complemented by a very much improved underwater sensor system and rapid torpedo reloading to allow attacking several targets in succession.[10] The Type XXIII was a smaller (250 tons) submarine, incorporating some of the same features but of lower overall capabilities and clearly less suitable for oceanic warfare.

There can be little doubt that the Type XXI especially represented a potent threat to the Allied dominance established in mid-1943. However, it was never to be deployed significantly and it is thus difficult to judge how it would have done if large numbers of them had been available. It clearly exploited an Allied weakness inasmuch as underwater detection as a whole was less sure than above water; tracking, far less attacking, a fast underwater target was also problematical. Such matters will be addressed later in this chapter. But avoiding attack and regaining productivity are two quite separate things: the first must be considered as highly likely and the second unproven. There was clearly considerable disquiet felt in high Allied circles about these submarines and the paucity of means of combating them.[11] Another view which has been aired more recently considers the threat much over played, largely on account of poor material standards of submarines in American hands after the end of the war.[12] But even were this to be totally true, the problem remained for Allied intelligence staffs and strategic decision-makers towards the end of the Second World War: could they afford to ignore this problem? Obviously, they would be failing in their duty were they to do so, because unless and until a horde of Type XXIs were unleashed on the Atlantic no sure proof could be available. Surely it would be better by far to postpone and reduce the plague rather than waiting to see what it could achieve. In broad terms, this was what was done.

The means of achieving this were many and included the bombing of component manufacturers and assembly yards, as well as the transport systems that connected the two types of facilities.[13] A further measure was the continued pressure put on the submarine trials and training facilities in the central Baltic.[14] But such actions were not conceived in a vacuum and were informed by several sources of intelligence. Perhaps the most useful and powerful of these was codebreaking from an un-expected area: the communications of the Japanese ambassador and attachés to Tokyo which gave accounts of German briefings on both capabilities and building programmes.[15] This alerted the Allies to the Electro-boat problem. Further intelligence on assembly was to come from photo-reconnaissance, and the combination was extremely thorough, providing sound intelligence at the strategic level. Later this was to be supplemented by documents captured by Assault Unit 30 when a German factory at Strasburg was overrun.[16] This provided information on both the sources of components and the general schedule for completion of submarines.

There was one significant feature which the Electro-boats did have in common with some of their less sophisticated predecessors: the schnorkel or, as it was often called by the Allies, the snort. This device, originally Dutch, was quite simply a breathing tube which allowed a sub-merged submarine to continue to run its main propulsion system while remaining otherwise submerged. It was, of course, not so simple in practice. For a start two tubes were required; one for induction, one for exhaust.[17] Further, this meant two large and additional piercings of the hull, thus rendering it more vulnerable to damage. Yet another complication was caused by practical running in anything of a seaway, where a simple open-ended tube would either have to have been extended so far above the water as to reduce much of the point of having the system in the first place or, as happened, a system of valves was necessary to close the tube should it become temporarily submerged. The schnorkel was

also fitted into the existing fleet as fast as it could be. In itself, the equipment was very successful, again making the submarine more difficult to
detect, both by eye and radar. Indeed, it virtually removed the submarine's susceptibility to aircraft at a stroke. However, there were many disadvantages: unskilled operation could lead to serious flooding or the
creation of a partial vacuum within the submarine, and living conditions, never good previously, became extremely poor indeed. But
perhaps the most important points were tactical ones. Although the U-
boat's underwater endurance was much increased, its underwater speed
whilst schnorkelling was not in practice improved. Mechanical weakness
represented an absolute upper limit to schnorkelling speed but usually
before this factor came into play the mast would betray its presence by a
distinct plume of white water in all but the roughest seas. Thus there was
a tactical limit of about six knots. Perhaps more importantly, the submarine, even when surfaced was a poor reconnaissance platform, and
became a markedly worse one with only one man able to use a periscope
only a few feet at most above sea level. Thus the schnorkel should be
seen principally as a survival aid rather than as a means of improving
tactical performance. Nevertheless, it proved of concern to the Allies
although they were well informed of its development and fitting within
the submarine fleet.[18]

Submarine sensors

In order to find and attack targets, they first of all had to be detected
using one or more sensors with which U-boats were equipped. From
the beginning to the end of the war, the most important of these was
undoubtedly the human eye, either unassisted or else enhanced with
either binoculars or the periscope. It is very difficult to suggest that
there might have been any realistic alternative to this in the technological and tactical era and environment in which the German submarines operated. Although not normally considered a technological
factor, as the eye was often pitched against more technical devices, it is
important to note some of its properties here, as they had a profound
effect on the conduct of submarine operations. The human eye is
compact, versatile and is a sensor of high performance. On the other
hand, even when enhanced, it is subject to limitations. In the U-boat
case it was at its best when the submarine was on the surface and
several lookouts could be employed, each with an allotted expanse of
sea or sky to scan. German optical devices of the period were probably
the best in the world and convoys could be detected at 20 miles or

even more in clear weather often with at least one unintentionally cooperative member of the convoy producing copious smoke. On the other hand, night and poor visibility diminished performance, as might poor weather due to its adverse effect on lookouts.

Some radars were fitted to submarines, largely as an aircraft-detection measure, but little faith was put in them by U-boat crews. Further, it was felt that having a sensor which emitted actively was inconsistent with the submarine's stealthy method of operating and they were little used. This stands in distinction to the American submarine technique of making copious use of radar by night to position themselves to advantage against, then attack, Japanese shipping.[19]

Radar detection, on the other hand, was a strong and growing interest in the U-boat fleet. The main concern was not the radars fitted in surface ships because, although these limited tactical options, they rarely posed a threat to the submarine of the immediacy of that other radar-fitted opponent, the aircraft. This became apparent in the middle period of the war and the German response was to produce a detector capable of picking up centimetric radar transmissions. This makeshift, known generally from the name of the French company manufacturing it as *Metox* was an aerial that had to be conveyed to the fin on surfacing and there was an electrical cable connecting it to electronic equipment below. It was introduced to the fleet in August 1942. Not really robust enough for this treatment, it often failed in service. However, it was capable of producing good results, adequate enough to allow the submarine to dive before the aircraft was close enough to sight it. However, what *Metox* could not deal with in any way was the Allied innovation of the higher-frequency centimetric radar of whose existence the Germans were initially unaware. This realisation took some considerable time and allowed aircraft equipped with centimetric radar to detect and close submarines without warning. Further it led to a German loss of confidence in *Metox*, in the belief that it was itself an aid to enemy aircraft homing.[20] Improved German devices followed, such as *Wanze, Fliege* and *Mücke* and these were generally effective.[21]

Submarine weapons

German U-boats used three fundamental types of weapons against Allied shipping; torpedoes, guns and mines. Of these, the first was by far the most important. This was principally due to its heavy explosive payload, actuated underwater where the effects of shock were most disruptive, combined with a generally effective delivery system and the difficulty of detecting it, far less taking useful countermeasures against it, once launched. The torpedo generally, and however launched – be it from surface ship, aircraft or submarine – was one of the most significant ship-killers of the war. The submarine's combination of lethality and stealth rendered it especially effective.

The German torpedo has to be considered together with its target and the likely tactical circumstances of delivery. Targets, considered as single ships, fall into two broad categories: merchant and warships. The former is generally easier being bigger, deeper in the water and less prone to disconcerting alterations of course. If filled with a hazardous cargo, such as petroleum or explosives, then a single torpedo explosion is probably sufficient to ensure not just sinking but disintegration.[22] Warships tended to be smaller, faster and more difficult as targets. The ideal firing-range for a straight-running torpedo is at or under 1000 metres and this was quite practical and reasonably safe for the submarine in the early part of the war. But as the war progressed, such short firing-ranges became virtually suicidal and the ranges had to increase often beyond the screening escorts. This carried two penalties; the possibility of some torpedoes quite simply running out of endurance and, in any case, the increasing risk of not hitting a target. This also suggested returning to the problem of attacking escorts themselves.

There are four headings under which it is useful to look at German torpedo characteristics: propulsion, warhead actuation, pattern-running and homing weapons. Most of the German torpedoes used electrical propulsion, largely in the G7e model.[23] This had the advantage of virtually wakeless operation but both range and speed were limited, initially not of great significance. Later thermally propelled models, principally the G7a, were deployed, improving in-water performance but at the expense of both noise and creating a more visible track. The Germans considered that they started the war with a more advanced weapon than their opponents in the sense that the weapons had magnetic pistols. The theoretical advantage of these were that they could be aimed under their targets rather than to hit them, which was explosively superior. There were difficulties with magnetic actuation in practice. However, these pistols were extremely unreliable even when the problem had been perceived and reversion to contact-actuation had been made. Now inconsistencies in depth-keeping bedevilled the torpedo and the situation was not fully under control. Indeed torpedo-reliability problems of various types continued sporadically into 1941.[24] The deteriorating tactical situation for the U-boats, especially in mid-1942 when the attack on cross-Atlantic convoys was resumed, was responded to in two ways. The increasing ranges from which attacks on merchant shipping had to be carried out, usually from a submerged position, created tremendous problems of aiming. The longer weapon-run accentuated errors, made observation of accurate target movement more difficult and, in any case, made it more probable that a target manoeuvre might occur. One answer was to have a torpedo which did not so much aim at a point as cover an area of water, increasing the probability of hitting at least something. There were to be two such weapons: the FAT and the LUT.[25] These performed a series of turns so that their chance of contacting a target when fired from greater ranges was much improved. LUT was more complex than FAT and only introduced in the latter months of the war. Their importance lay in their firing-submarines no longer having to attain a very precise and often difficult firing-position. The other innovation was the T5 torpedo.[26] This was quite different from any of the others and was an acoustic homing weapon, specifically intended as an anti-escort torpedo. It worked by detecting the sound of an escort's propellers and was effective in the target speed range of approximately 10–18 knots. This enjoyed marked but relatively short-term success as Allied countermeasures were rapidly implemented, largely as a result of good intelligence, much of which came from non-Ultra sources.[27]

All ocean-going submarines had guns and these had two basic purposes: the attack of unescorted ships and anti-aircraft fire. In general terms, the first was only effective for some of the time in the early years of the war when such targets were reasonably plentiful. The growth of the convoy system effectively put paid to the gun as a significant means of sinking ships. In the more remote areas, where warships or aircraft were scarce, the gun might still be of use. In any instance where the submarine itself came under fire, the contest could swing either way. The submarine was a small target and its gunners might be quite well practised; on the other hand, the underwater environment was not the best one to keep a gun in and a submarine was not always the most stable weapons platform. But the expenditure of a number of gun rounds was almost certainly more economical than the use of one or two of the scarce outfit of torpedoes, especially on the longer and more distant deployments. The heyday of the anti-aircraft gun was in the middle of the war, especially during the phase when Dönitz determined that fightback and group tactics were the best answer to the aircraft problem. While there were several instances of submarines defending themselves doughtily against aircraft – even shooting down more than one or at least causing severe damage – the policy was flawed fundamentally in that it was, on the whole, easier for the Allies to increase the pressure. Perhaps, more importantly, the modification of submarines to be 'flak traps' merely resulted in resources being put into activities which did not assist the submarines materially in carrying out their main operational task, that of sinking merchant ships. As a result, submarines became less stable and the requirement for extra gunners rendered the boats even less habitable than before.

Mines, on the other hand, were directly related to the task of sinking ships. They were not as directed as torpedoes and tended to have a relatively low probability of success when compared to the torpedo. But being underwater weapons they were very effective when actuated. Minelaying, part of mine warfare, is a distinct naval art and science in itself. To be effective, minefields either need to be large or very cleverly placed. The numbers carried by a submarine and the length of time it takes to deploy do not make it the ideal minelaying vehicle, unless covertness is imperative. The largest specialist minelaying submarine, the type XB, could only carry 66 mines, a relatively small load for extensive laying. Most submarines could carry TMA and TMB moored and ground influence mines respectively, usually on a substitution basis for torpedoes. This meant that the load was far less even than with the specialist minelayers. Where these appeared to be particularly effective was on the more distant operations where it was possible to lay some mines off a port, say in southern Africa, before there were any other significant indications of a submarine's presence. Here the nuisance value of closing a port and arranging sweeping facilities, possibly from a place many miles and several days away, was considerable and probably justified the effort.

Measures to support the submarine offensive

There were a number of auxiliary measures and systems intended to support submarine operations which deserve note. Very few, if any, of these ended by making significant contributions to the U-boat effort but are worth mentioning because they indicate both the range of technology and the contribution, where appropriate, that Allied intelligence made to countering them. The subjects covered are *Sonne*, kites, U-boat tankers, decoys, *Alberich*, and *Kurier* (Squash).

Sonne was a radio navigation aid intended for the use of German forces in the Bay of Biscay and out into the Atlantic. The requirement for it was indicated by the discussion of navigation in Chapter 2. It was discovered by radio-monitoring, operated in the Low Frequency range and its parameters were ascertained largely by Sigint and photo-reconnaissance. It used a number of stations, including one in neutral Spain, to send out a series of signals. These interacted in such a way that pairs of stations would produce a dot-dash pattern that varied with the position of the receiving unit. With equipment no more elaborate than a radio receiver, suitably marked charts and a stopwatch, a position could be obtained by obtaining readings from two or more station-pairs. This was active from about mid-1943 and it was a useful system.[28]

Kites were a device intended to increase the reconnaissance range of submarines in distant waters.[29] Although they were at least useful in their intended role, they could only be used in such remote areas that their effect was very marginal at best. On the other hand, submarine tankers were a development that held out the promise of considerable operational advantage. They could either let submarines range even further afield than they already did, or else they could permit the prolonging of patrols by boats which had diminished fuel but retained a significant stock of weapons. As is discussed in Chapter 9, they could by doing so not only obviate a hazardous double passage of Biscay but also cut out the lengthening turnround times in the French bases. Their worth was recognised by the Germans and many of the operational plans in mid-1943 were critically dependent on tankers. Their systematic elimination – a policy largely made possible by Ultra – played a large part in limiting the Germans operationally from mid-1943 onwards.[30]

Decoys were used both above and below water. The above-water ones were intended to provide distractive radar targets. These were *Aphrodite*, a balloon-based device and *Thetis* which floated. Both were successful to some extent, but once Allied forces were alerted to them, their effectiveness diminished. Underwater, the most commonly used was *Bold* – known to the British as the Submarine Bubble Target (SBT) which chemically generated bubbles and could mask a sonar successfully, at least for a while.[31] 'Wreckage' was sometimes also ejected in an attempt to throw off pursuers. Intelligence was of little help with these as there were few external signs of these systems until they were put to use. A similar device was *Alberich*, an experimental rubber coating of a submarine hull in an attempt to reduce its sonar echo. This was not particularly effective, and tended to come loose from the hull, thus increasing the submarine's noise.

Perhaps the last piece of technology deserving mention is *Kurier* (known to the British as Squash). This was an attempt by the Germans to deny radio intercept to the Allies by using a compressed signal and relying on the very short transmission time as a safeguard.[32] Not only were countermeasures to this devised but its potential impact was thoroughly investigated.[33]

Allied antisubmarine technology

On the whole, the German technological effort is easier to survey than that of the Allies. As against one nation, one main platform (the submarine) one significant sensor and one variety of important weapon – the torpedo – there are three nations, two main types of platform – the surface ship and the aircraft – several sensors that mattered, a number of weapons that were of use in the ASW battle as well as a series of supporting measures that can only be regarded as of a much higher order than the corresponding German category. Thus it might be said colloquially that the Allied technological response to the submarine problem was one of width and depth and lots of them, too.

The approach taken here is to place the main emphasis on sensors and weapons before briefly considering the performance of the units that deployed these items and ending by taking a look at the supporting area. It is stressed that this is a very quick and necessarily superficial survey of these topics in themselves and concentrates on two things: their overall contribution to the ASW war and the part – if any – that Ultra played in their development. There are, however, suggestions made as to where further study can be made.

ASW sensors

The first sensor of significance was the same as for submarines, the eye. However, the Allies could consider this from a different perspective than the Germans. In general terms, a submarine was likely to see its target under most circumstances before the target could see it. Thus, for the U-boat, the priority was to stay invisible. This was not the case on the other side and thus a whole avenue of visibility enhancements, especially for night use, was opened up. These ranged from flares and starshell for use from aircraft and ships, and ships only, respectively, to aircraft systems such as the Leigh Light.[34,35] The latter was an excellent complement to aircraft radar at night as the more advanced sensor tended to lose contact in the sea return at shorter ranges and a visual contact was necessary for weapon delivery.[36] There were also some efforts made to reduce the ranges at which Allied units might be seen and camouflage was prob- ably the most obvious application. It is difficult, however, to devise a scheme for this which is effective over a wide range of meteorological and light conditions. Further, there is not a great deal of point in devising devilishly clever schemes for escorts when the targets of choice are a large number of big merchant vessels huddled together, most without any camouflage scheme and some helpfully emitting clouds of thick smoke visible at great ranges. Perhaps the one great success was the repainting of the undersides of aircraft white to reduce their contrast against the sky.[37] There is no evidence that Ultra made any significant contribution in this field.

Underwater detection – sonar

The most difficult detection problem was finding a submerged submarine. The only method likely to yield any chance of doing so for most of the war lay in underwater active sound detection – sonar to the Americans, asdic to the British.[38] The equipment that was in use during the entire war was capable at its best of detecting a submerged submarine at a typical range of about 2000 yards.[39] Often this was very much less, owing to water conditions or inexpert operation. It would be realistic to regard wartime sonar as a contact-keeping device rather than a true sensor. Nevertheless, it was often tactically useful as clues to submarine position were often available. Further it provided the only reasonably certain information on which to place underwater weapons. This might all suggest that sonar was a sensor which advanced but little during the war, but great efforts – largely rewarded – were put into making it easier to operate, more reliable and to give it capabilities it had lacked at the outset, such as target-depth determination.[40] Its importance, too, was increased as the war went on by two developments: the tendency of submarines to have to spend longer submerged than at the outset of the war and the formulation and practice of specific tactics which took account of the sensor's known weak areas. One of these was the Deep Creep attack developed by Captain F. J. Walker. As an escort going over the top of a submarine invariably lost contact, precise aiming of dropped weapons was very difficult. In the Deep Creep, one escort would stay in sonar contact from a distance, vectoring a second ship to the right place while it stayed sonar-silent. Intelligence, again, appears to have played little direct part in the improvement of sonar.

There were two other possible methods of detecting a submerged submarine – magnetic anomaly detection (MAD) and sonobuoys. With former, the disturbance created in the earth's magnetic field by a submarine was measured. This system could be deployed from aircraft only and had an effective range even less than that of sonar, typically about 1000 feet. Even the aircraft's greater speed could not compensate for this. Thus MAD could only really be regarded as a device for refining location already established by some other sensor.[41] Sonobuoys were developed in the USA, entering production from the autumn of 1942 onwards.[42] These gave the dropping aircraft the ability to monitor a submerged submarine and produce enough information to release a homing weapon.[43]

Above-water detection

For the majority of the war, U-boats tended to spend significant time on the surface. In daylight, they would probably see surface ships long before they were themselves seen, assuming good visibility. This advantage was even more marked at night, allowing the surfaced attack to be a viable tactic. However, the fitting of radar at sea firstly reduced the security of this ploy, before making it altogether hazardous to the submarine. The initial sets were relatively crude and unreliable, limited by both the fairly low frequency deployed and aerials which rotated neither fast nor automatically. Further limits might be imposed by weather and operator skills. The initial metric (less than 300 megaHertz in frequency) sets were replaced eventually by centimetric equipments (frequencies in the low gigaHertz range). This made detection of a surfaced submarine all but certain and effectively terminated the night surface-attack as a practical means of attack.[44] But this success was hard won and not all convoys enjoyed the protection of an adequate number of quality radar-fitted escorts for some time into the war. Further, there were difficulties with both manufacture and fitting. Perhaps the worst-off of the principal three allies were the Canadians, whose tribulations have been well chronicled.[45] However, by mid-1943 the type of escort force that could be mustered in support of a convoy was invariably well equipped enough to make surface attack very difficult, if not fatal for a submarine. For this tactical advantage, radar must be considered primarily responsible.

The other important application of radar was in the air. Here, technically speaking, it was even more difficult to fit the equipment than in a ship. Nevertheless, and despite the considerable problem of greater sea return problems from a higher aerial position, the advantages of putting a radar on board a vehicle which could sweep out a vastly greater arc than any surface ship were enormous. Aircraft, too, went through the same progression from the unwieldy metric sets to the relatively elegant and far better performing centimetric ones. It became possible, too, to fit ASV radar to fairly small single-engined aircraft such as the Swordfish.[46] But it was perhaps in the land-based aircraft of the principal Allies that radar was most effective and again by mid-war virtually all engaged on ASW operations had this powerful sensor available.[47]

But even this considerable asset was complemented by another powerful one. The technique of direction-finding on a submarine transmission using a shore station was well known and understood by both sides.[48] However, the employment of this by surface ships was less realised by the Germans; according to some sources, they never knew about seagoing High Frequency Direction Finding (HF DF – sometimes known as Huff Duff) at all.[49] But although this lack of appreciation affected the most critical part of the Battle of the Atlantic, there was certainly a clear understanding of the potential of Allied HF DF in the last year of the war. Further it is evident that Allied intelligence authorities knew that the Germans were then aware of this development.[50] The equipment was developed independently on both sides of the Atlantic, virtually simultaneously, the American effort owing much to that of French researchers who had escaped the Germans.[51] Perhaps the most important technical point about the equipment as developed by both nations was the adoption of cathode-ray tube displays, allowing not only detection but also bearing determination of the relatively short (under 30 seconds) transmissions often used by the Germans.[52,53]

It is perhaps, difficult, to over-stress the utility of shipborne HF DF. It provided, together with the aircraft, the only sensor capable of operating outside the limited horizon of the eye and radar. Further, although it relied on an enemy making a transmission, its range was in the order of tens of miles rather than miles. But unlike the aircraft, HF DF never slept; it could work all the time whereas aircraft might not always be present or readily available. It provided not only warning but often information good enough to allow the despatch of an aircraft or ships down the bearing which in turn might lead to submarine contact with a convoy being broken off. It was one of the most useful tools of the Battle of the Atlantic and until the advent of the Williams book, one of the least recognised.[54]

Weapons – submarine on the surface

Because of the superiority of the above-water sensors in terms of range, many antisubmarine engagements began at least with the submarine on the surface. Ironically, most of the weapons that could be used for engaging a surface target were relatively crude. There were fundamentally three: the gun, rockets and ramming.[55] The guns fitted to many of the escort vessels tended towards the unrefined end of the spectrum of gunnery. Relatively close range (which was not a great disadvantage at typical submarine engagement ranges), slow-firing and visually aimed, these were not examples of advanced technology. Nevertheless even these guns could be quite effective in a number of different ways. Firstly, if fortunate, they could sink a submarine; secondly, while not doing it this much damage, sufficient might be done to prevent prudent submergence by the submarine. A surface ship can tolerate a number of holes in its structure. Some of these may be well above water, not affecting immediate seaworthiness; even if below the waterline, the ingress may be controllable as the resultant water pressure is not high. A submarine, on the other hand, has to have a virtually intact pressure hull, otherwise the next dive might well be the last. Airborne guns, too, particularly of the larger calibres, could be very effective. Lastly gunfire, whether from relatively well-aimed main armament or from a machine-gun aimed with more enthusiasm than precision, can have a very unsettling affect against even a well-trained submarine crew suffering from the effect of several other blows. In this, the gun was as much a psychological disruption device as a structural damager. By the time a submarine tried to fight it out on the surface it was in considerable trouble, in any case.

The rocket was an aircraft-mounted system developed and deployed relatively late in the war, from about the summer of 1943. The weapon was its most effective not, as might be thought, when it hit the visible portion of the submarine, but rather when it was aimed to enter the water short of the U-boat, passing through its target underwater and thus causing the maximum damage. This weapon proved very effective.

Although the crudest possible tactic, ramming was attempted in a number of cases. In some it worked, although submarines could escape, particularly if they were in the act of submerging when rammed. On the other hand, this tactic also tended to damage the ramming unit. Loss of the sonar underwater fittings was usually the minimum price to pay for a successful ramming.

Weapons – submarine underwater

It is possible to divide these weapons into a number of categories but they all have certain characteristics in common. They all have a delivery system, an explosive charge and some system of actuating that charge. Some have further characteristics but it is in solving the challenges of the three main areas that the weapons are defined. One in particular slightly steps across the distinction made by these two sections – that of the location of the target, on the surface or underwater – and that is the depth-charge. There are two reasons for this. A depth-charge set to explode at shallow depths can damage a submarine on the surface and, in any case, especially where aerial delivery is concerned, an attack may well be started with the submarine on the surface but end with it wholly or partially submerged. In this section it is intended to examine weapons broadly by four types of delivery method: static, dropped, projected and propelled to target.

Other than obstructive devices such as nets, there was only one static weapon, the mine. Although an important device for the defence of ports and anchorages, it would appear on the face of it that this weapon played little direct part in the Battle of the Atlantic. However, mines accounted for over 4 per cent of submarines sunk during the war, marginally better than sinkings by Allied submarines.[56] Although none of these losses occurred in mid-Atlantic, the natural focus of the campaign, such sinkings were still significant. They might occur in peripheral areas such as the Mediterranean or Baltic but there were also some losses sustained during the inshore campaign around the United Kingdom in 1944–45. These were a result of very deliberately laid 'Deep Trap' fields.[57] Such mines were at depths such that they would not harm surface shipping but were a hazard to submarines.[58] In the Baltic some 10 submarines were lost to mines and a similar number damaged, but perhaps the true worth of the Baltic mining campaign lay not so much in ships sunk or damaged as the degree of disruption to German shipping movement in general, and submarine trials and training in particular.[59] Here, the hand of Ultra was very much involved, because the thorough knowledge of German routes and areas of activity gained by that means allowed the optimum placing of relatively small but effective fields.[60]

The next category of weapon was the dropped one, and this generally meant the depth charge. This was quite the crudest of the ASW weapons deployed, consisting of nothing more than an explosive charge, a case thick enough to prevent it being crushed either on meeting the water or at its normal working depths and some form of actuation.[61] The latter was normally selectable in theory but, in the case of aircraft, this had to be done prior to flight, much reducing the potential flexibility of the weapon.[62] In any case, even the largest and most powerful of these devices had a lethal range measured only in tens of feet, putting a considerable premium on accurate placement in both plan and depth. With both surface and air delivery, this caused problems. These tended to be overcome by two techniques, both fairly crude – pattern attacks and repeated applications of them. For a surface ship, this was relatively easy, as Atlantic escorts tended to carry quite large outfits of depth charges. For aircraft, this was difficult as they could carry a much smaller number of charges. The other problem with air-dropping lay in the dispersion of the pattern, a function of speed, height and, above all, timing between drops. Alfred Price has illustrated the advantage of a tight pattern but the efficacy of this procedure demands much more in the way of accuracy – not all pilots had this degree of skill.[63]

One other dropped weapon – of a sort – was the retro-bomb used in conjunction with MAD-fitted aircraft. The problem here was that the aircraft only knew of the submarine's location when passing over it. Any normally released weapon would thus enter the water well ahead of the submarine. The retro-bomb obviated this by use of a small propulsive charge which compensated both for reaction time and the aircraft's forward velocity by imparting backward movement to the bomb. As far as is known no submarine was sunk exclusively by such means, but the solution demonstrated the imaginative application of technology to new problems.

The next step on was to disperse the depth-charge or other explosive projectile some distance from a surface ship. This served more than one purpose. Firstly it could produce a much better pattern of charges than one which relied merely on a ship's movement along a single track, producing dispersion in one dimension only. Devices such as K- and Y-guns could lob charges to ranges of about 100 yards on either beam of an escort.[64] But although this was better than only dropping charges off the stern, a major problem remained. It was clearly imprudent and wasteful to drop weapons before going over the top of a submarine. This induced inaccuracy in the attack as sonar contact was invariably lost at, or slightly before, this point. A further difficulty was that the submarine was well aware of what was happening and could take advantage of this loss of contact to start a drastic manoeuvre, vitiating accuracy still further at best and escaping completely at worst as sonar invariably had difficulty in the highly turbulent water stirred up by the exploding depth charges. Now a second variation on the projected theme appeared, the ahead-thrown weapon.

This was to take several forms, but the basic principles were the same. Although it might have been desirable to have projected an explosive charge of the same weight as a depth-charge, there were practical problems in the way of such a solution. Thus a multiple-charge system was developed, using smaller projected charges; this was known as Hedgehog. It fired 24 projectiles, each of 65 pounds, to fall in a circle up to 200 yards ahead of the firing ship. The charges would only explode on contact, a measure intended to account for target-depth being unknown. Although introduced as early as 1941 and fitted in many ships of British, American and Canadian navies, it did not achieve its first kill until late 1942.[65] Because it did not always produce a reassuring bang, unlike a depth-charge pattern, it was not always well liked and did not attain its full potential until late in the war. A smaller application of the same weapon using only four-round launchers and deployed in light craft was the American Mousetrap.

Another approach to the problem was taken by the British Squid. This was a later development than Hedgehog and depended critically on a sonar device to measure target depth; in this respect, it might be considered the first true ASW weapon system as opposed to weapon. The weapon itself consisted of one or two three-barrelled mortars, each tube capable of firing a 200-pound charge ahead of the ship to a range of about 270 yards ahead of the ship. Depth-setting was achieved by a timing system.[66] Not available until late 1943, it had its first kill in mid-1944.

The last type of weapon was that which was propelled (as opposed to being thrown) at its target and there was only one successful example of this, the homing torpedo. This approach was clearly the right one to follow, as even the type of relatively undynamic submarine with which the Germans entered the war was a difficult enough target for dropped or projected weapons. This had multiple causes: inadequacy and inaccuracy of data, the time lag between the last information being available and the arrival of the explosive charge at the aimed point and the physics of explosives measured against the strength of a submarine's hull. The Gordian-knot solution of having a weapon which steered itself to its target took care of all these problems. However, much science, technology and sheer application was necessary to translate this idea into reality. The American Mark 24 torpedo was able to do this and was largely successful after its introduction in 1943.[67] It did depend on the target making enough noise on which to home and it was relatively slow, but it did work.

ASW ships and aircraft

It would be very easy to see ships and aircraft as mere mobile means of transporting sensors and weapons to the scene of action. This is, of course, one description of them but it hardly gives a sufficient account. The demands of the Battle of the Atlantic gave rise to a specific genus of ships which certainly influenced one strand of the postwar development of medium-sized warships. It is, however, one of the ironies of maritime historiography that while there is plenty of literature dealing with ships and aircraft in great detail when applied to individual classes and models, there is hardly any which deals with these as systems.[68]

Before looking in more detail at the development of Battle of the Atlantic ASW units, it may be worth considering the qualities which go to make up two types of ideal unit; one on the surface of the sea, one in the air. The surface unit characteristics should be as shown in Table 6.1. For an aircraft a similar list might be made up. Such methods allow a number of insights into the units that fought the Battle, their strengths and shortcomings.

For a start it shows very clearly the comparative advantages and disadvantages of ships and aircraft: the former score well on endurance, low on speed. For this reason alone, the two are ideal complements, not competitors at Second World War ASW. The other thing that it does is to provide an ideal against which to measure any given class of unit or member of the class. At the same time, however, it must be

Table 6.1   Surface-ship escort – desired characteristics

Characteristic	Description
Endurance	As much as possible, or alternatively an ability to refuel at sea
Speed	Enough to outrun a surfaced submarine, so at least 20 knots
Seakeeping	Good in rough conditions, avoiding damage to structure and crew
Sensors	A complete set to cover above and under water
Weapons	Adequate to exploit the sensors fitted
Communications	Tactical ones to permit full communication with convoys, fellow-escorts and aircraft. Longer haul to shore
Logistics	Sufficient to support operations around a convoy for at least part of its transit, preferably all

remembered that there were many different types of task to be performed and that the mid-Atlantic one was almost certainly the tough-
est and most demanding. The small American SC (Submarine Chasers)
and PC (Patrol Craft) were unsuitable for the mid-Atlantic, especially in
winter, but did valuable work elsewhere. British corvettes were uncomfortable in this area, not very well armed and slow, but they had two
great virtues: endurance and relative abundance. The same point could
be made about aircraft. The historiographical concentration on the
employment of the most capable of all – the long-range B-24 Liberator
– tends to obscure the fact that many much less capable aircraft had
tended to make less remote areas almost impossible operating areas for
submarines. Indeed it was that success which had forced the U-boats
into areas less amenable of aircraft access, thus accentuating the
'Air Gap' problem.

The Battle of the Atlantic gave rise to the development of specific
types of ships and aircraft, neither of which had been emphasised prior
to the war. On the surface, the British corvettes were quick and easy to
build but had a number of disadvantages, principally lack of speed,
equipment and habitability. Although a useful stopgap, this line of
development did not go very far. In early days too, there were several
types of improvisations. Fleet destroyers, although capable, tended to
be a little too precious for the broad Atlantic, with armament really
meant for other purposes and low endurance. To make matter worse,
there were many other demands for such ships. However, a degree of
adaptation was applied to some of these ships, increasing their fuel
capacity at the cost of some speed and adding to their outfit of depth-
charges.[69] There were two types of response to the ASW challenge on
the two sides of the Atlantic. One was the British evolution of the prewar type, the sloop, into an ASW specialist unit. The sloop's earlier
rationales had been mixed, including minesweeping, colonial cruising
and anti-aircraft roles as well as some antisubmarine input. The war
saw it develop into very much of a specialist ASW ship and the lineal
ancestor of the British postwar frigate. The American approach owed
more to the destroyer as a model and resulted in the destroyer escort
(DE). As American destroyers, intended for Pacific service, had greater
endurance than their British counterparts, this was a logical development and what tended to develop was essentially a small destroyer
with emphasis laid on antisubmarine weapons and sensors. Many of
these were built for both the USA and UK.

There were similar developments in the air, although almost no specific
model of land-based aircraft was designed from scratch as a maritime, far

less ASW aircraft – all were adapted from existing airframes. Clearly, the fighter type was too short-legged for any sensible ASW purpose but the bomber, especially the four-engined heavy type, promised useful range and endurance.[70] Many, but not all, of these were adapted from American airframes and the specific equipment changes for the ASW role meant that they were not readily usable in their original roles. Their combination of speed, good surface sensors and rapidly deliverable weapons made them potent for search, deterrence and first attacks. However, in the more remote Atlantic areas, there was inevitably a payoff, even with the VLR aircraft, of range from base and time on patrol.

The last main point worth noting is the emergence of sea-based aviation as an important factor in ASW operations. This did not really appear until mid-1943 and it represented not so much a technological innovation as the making of it accessible and reasonably economic. Aircraft such as the Swordfish had long had the ability to deploy a rudimentary ASW capability. The subsequent fitting of metric, then centimetric radar made it much more useful in this sphere. While such aircraft had nowhere near the speed, endurance or weapon-load of those based on land, their much greater availability compensated for these deficiencies. The economic part came from the innovation of the escort aircraft-carrier; small, cheap and quick to build compared to its larger sisters. These were built in the United States for both USN and RN. Their basic nature is summed up by their nicknames in the two nations – Jeeps and Woolworth carriers respectively. In general terms, their relatively limited load of aircraft meant that they had to concentrate on one role and ancillary facilities were limited. However, their very utility in so many aviation roles meant that they were often needed as a supplement to the larger fleet carriers and they were not much in evidence in the Battle of the Atlantic until the main point of crisis had been passed.[71]

Lastly, perhaps, it is worth mentioning that lighter-than-air craft, Blimps, were deployed by the United States Navy in a number of places, notably along the American eastern seaboard and from a number of more remote locations such as Morocco. Nobody would suggest that these were the ideal vehicles with which to engage a surfaced submarine, but their mere deterrent presence was often important in thwarting attack.[72]

Soft technologies – hard results

In the 1940s, 1950s and even 1960s the word technology would suggest to many the idea of equipment rather than other methods of studying or doing things. But most definitions have allowed for the concept of systematic study as part of technology and this is very much the subject matter of the last part of this chapter. It is perhaps a little ironical that the turn of the twentieth century into the twenty-first should see this sort of usage more accepted: what, for example, bearing in mind that neither concept nor reality were much in evidence during the Second World War, would have been made of the term 'software engineering'?

A number of such techniques were deployed in fighting the Battle of the Atlantic and one specifically merits being classed as a new discipline, although it drew on earlier threads of work dating back at least to the First World War. Others represented less obvious developments, sometimes drawing on observations from fields well outside the ones normally recognised by the disciplines of naval history, technology or science. Before dealing with the new discipline, operational research, it is best to deal with these other subjects briefly.

Four of these are considered: one technical, immediate in time and very close to the front-line of the Battle of the Atlantic, one an evolutionary development, a further item dealing with the production of *matériel* generally and lastly taking a broad look at organisations.

The submarine's main weapon was the torpedo and this was formidable indeed. The weapon's two most intractable features were unstoppability and explosive power. In a sense, nothing could be done about either of these but, providing that its presence was detected in time, then it might be avoided. The technique of 'combing' or turning the target ship parallel to the torpedo track, thus presenting the smallest possible target, was an old one dating back to the earliest days of torpedoes. It depended critically, however, on both detecting and knowing the angle of approach of the torpedo. At night, especially, and always when the Germans used electric torpedoes, this was not easy but might be possible if conditions were suitable and the target alert enough. For warships only, warning might come from the noise the torpedo made being detected on sonar. But even this fairly dubious escape-route from the well-aimed torpedo was closed completely once the Germans started using a homing weapon, the T5 torpedo.[73] However, largely due to intelligence information, which had given prior knowledge of the development of this weapon, a solution was rapidly put in hand which countered the torpedo within weeks.[74] This was a towed device known as Foxer which can simply be described as a number of rattling pipes and it made more noise than the towing ship.[75] Here simple (and what can be regarded as soft-kill in the sense that it did not itself destroy the German weapon) technology, aided by naval intelligence, overcame a more sophisticated and potentially very deadly threat.

The second item was the development of Action Information Organisations (British) and Combat Information Centers (American), from now on referred to as AIO/CIC. These reflected the changing face of naval warfare generally, not just ASW. Virtually every First World War naval action was fought from the bridge, where most internal and external communications were terminated, and the main sensor – the eye – could operate relatively well. The advent of such sensors as radar which might reveal the presence of enemies well beyond visual range made it necessary to have a place where the picture generated by these sensors might be displayed to the command. A particular driver of this solution was the complex and often dense air environment in such places as the Mediterranean and the Pacific. The problems of display and plot illumination meant that the bridge was unsuitable both by day and night. The ASW problem was relatively simple and thus both radar and sonar displays, together with a rudimentary plot might well be adjacent to the bridge, but not on it. It was also still the normal practice to con the ship for ASW action from the bridge, but it was from these sensor requirements that the modern complex AIO/CIC sprang. This, too, was a contemporary piece of technology.

One almost invisible form of technology is the way in which ideas are changed into practical pieces of equipment and in turn how one working prototype can achieve fleet-wide fitting in a relatively short period of time. Time and again this took place on both sides of the Atlantic with sensors, weapons and platforms generally being turned out rapidly and well. This is not an unduly rosy view; there were, of course, dark spots as well as bright ones but the general trend was one of being able to produce better quality and quantity than the Germans could. It is true that there are some who would argue that the British especially were industrially inefficient and the Canadians were much hampered by ideas of defence industrial autonomy.[76] On the other hand, one writer at least has seen the material superiority as not just marked but overwhelming:

> he demonstrates conclusively that Allied victory both against the Axis and Japan (*sic*), finally owed far more to the endless stream of tanks, artillery and military aircraft coming off Allied production lines than it did to the ability of their commanders.[77]

These two views probably represent the two extremes of the 'strategy making through industrial production school'. However, there would appear to be little doubt that Allied superiority in production engineer- ing was marked and that this was an important technological factor in winning the Battle of the Atlantic.[78]

Connected with this, though far less easy to quantify, was the relatively easy way in which organisations communicated and interacted. It might be argued that this point does not belong here at all, but it was an important factor in Allied success. Further it leads very well into the next section of this chapter. The point is that this general lessening of bureaucratic friction – this word being used in both its general and Clausewitzian sense – maximised Allied effort that might otherwise have been devoted to inter-agency squabbling. It was not that such disputes never arose; rather that they were not built into the structure of administration in quite the same way as they were in Hitlerian Germany. Historians have tended to distort a proper perspective on the period by stressing the disputes rather than the accords; the battle for VLR Liberators rather than the close accord between Western Approaches and Coastal Command; the recalcitrance of Admiral Ernest King USN (seen from a British perspective) rather than the unprecedented general degree of cooperation between the two nations; and Patton versus Montgomery, rather than Eisenhower and Ramsay working together. It echoes, if you like, the historiography of convoys. There are plenty of books about the incident-packed convoys, very few about the others. This may result in interesting literature but it also makes for poor history. This aspect of neglected history might be termed bureaucratic engineering or political technology – it deserves better.

The new science – operational research

Operational research, as it was practised in the Second World War, almost exclusively on the Allied side, was largely a child of studies which had accompanied the application of radar to air defence, starting in about 1938. It had a number of threads. One was the use of numbers as a means of studying warfare, where this was applicable. This was done on both sides.[79] However, operational research (OR) was very much more than just the application of statistics to warfare – a sort of accountancy of aggression. Rather it was the application of scientific investigation to all warfare activities in an attempt to make them work as best they could and, to some extent, to inform the development of both equipment and tactics that might succeed them.

To work, it depended critically on a number of conditions. Although it may seem a truism, first and most importantly, it was necessary to want to do it. Without high-level support at the outset and worthwhile results reasonably soon afterwards, then continuing throughout the war, OR would have been a very sickly infant with a short life-expectancy. Further, it needed unprecedented access, which cut across the strongly entrenched hierarchies of service life. OR practitioners might on one day have to observe a low-ranking operator in an escort or aircraft and the next have to argue a case for change with that man's commander-in-chief. Further there might be a cultural problem with scientists, no matter how brilliant, not automatically being accorded respect by uniformed forces. As well as culture, there was also the problem of specialisation. It is interesting looking at some of the leading practitioners to note that many came not from the sciences which might be thought applicable to warfare, such as physics and chemistry, but from the life sciences.[80] It would appear that scientific method was more important here than specific knowledge. This ability to absorb and exploit talents from somewhat unusual sources was a product of societies less absorbed in internal secrecy than that of Third Reich Germany.

It would be wrong to suggest that the success of OR was complete and lasting and that relations with military authorities were always totally harmonious. It can be suggested that such disputes had two sources: competing cultures and specific issues. An insight into this on the American side is given by the correspondence between Captain H. A. (Pat) Flanigan of the United States Naval Forces in Europe staff in London and Rear Admiral F. S. (Frog) Low, Chief of Staff 10th Fleet in Washington. On 3 June 1943, Flanigan wrote,

> Please don't be disturbed at certain reports or studies which we will send you from our Operational Research people. They work up a good many things which have some value and considerable interest, but their conclusions are not always correct because they don't know the practical and material difficulties which stand in your way, and sometimes these conclusions are phrased in such a way that they may be irritating ... I presume you have the same problem with your scientists and research people there, and, like us, don't wish to discourage them by refusing to let their studies get the utmost consideration.

On 12 June, Low responded,

> I send to you, sir, my complete understanding and sympathy as to
> the OR people. As you know, they are our ASWORGs and we have
> just designated Captain Haines as ComASWORGs.[81]

It is an interesting reflection on the military–scientific cultures of the
two nations that there was never quite the same attempt in Britain to
put a relatively low level of military control on to OR organisations, as
in the USA.

A good example of a dispute over a specific issue was that of convoy
size, which took place in 1943. The scientific conclusion was that
convoy losses tended to be independent of convoy size; thus it was
desirable for several reasons to opt for larger convoys. These included
lower theoretical losses and greater economy of escorts.[82] The battle
between the OR scientists and the Admiralty, whose instincts favoured
a 40-ship maximum convoy size, were fought out at cabinet committee
level.[83] Nevertheless, the formation in the UK of the Coastal Command
ORS, the office of the CAOR (later DNOR) at the Admiralty under
P. M. S. Blackett, both in the UK and the ASWORGs in the USA
were very positive contributions towards winning the Battle of the
Atlantic.[84]

Some further examples of their work give an indication of both
scope and worth. A good and relatively early example of this was the
study of the depth-settings of air-dropped depth-charges. It was evident
that very few such attacks resulted in significant damage, far less sinkings of submarines. Despite the relatively low lethal radius of depth-
charges, performance should have been better. Analysis of attacks
adduced the fact that most occurred either with the submarine on the
surface or having submerged only a few seconds before the attack.
However, then current doctrine dictated a depth-setting of some 100
feet as a notional average submarine operating depth. That it may have
been, but it did not apply in the circumstances of airborne attack. Thus
the OR staffs agitated for much shallower settings. These were in turn
reduced to 50, then 25, feet and lethality improved correspondingly.
OR staffs also did good work on the improvement of aim-points and
the recommendation for more powerful explosive fillings.[85]

But many other aspects were also looked at by Coastal Command,
Admiralty and American OR staffs. Mention has already been made of
the British work on convoy size but virtually no area of ASW operations went without study. Some matters might seem obvious like

search, screening, use of sensors and weapons, tactics, mining and independent shipping.[86] But there were other areas, too, which were not quite so obvious: for example, enemy actual or potential operations. It is noted, for example, from analysis that pack attacks took some 20 hours to develop, allowing a degree of reinforcement to occur.[87] The effect of the fitting of schnorkel on U-boats was also reported on.[88] Navigational studies were also made, these being of great importance by allowing the more efficient deployment of aircraft.[89] Where aircraft were concerned, the effect of weather on their bases was also studied, as was the optimisation of their maintenance.[90] In short, OR covered virtually all the activities of the Battle of the Atlantic and, despite the American reservations alluded to earlier in this chapter, it is probable that it made a considerable, if unquantifiable, difference to the Allied effort.[91]

Before leaving OR, it is necessary to touch on one difficult subject: the degree to which OR was informed by intelligence in general and Ultra in particular. This is an awkward matter about which to be absolutely sure, for there appears to be little, if any, surviving primary material to make the situation totally clear. On the British side, there was certainly some connection. Not only do we have the only slightly indirect evidence of Captain Pat Flanigan that two Admiralty and two Coastal Command OR men had access to Ultra but there were also certain OIC publications which were produced as SI reports but minuted as being produced by DNOR staff.[92] It is further suggested that one scientist may have been loaned to the OIC in 1943 from CAOR.[93] It is thus fairly evident that there was a British connection between Ultra intelligence and OR, and it is also possible that there may have been further drip-down in an *ad hoc* fashion.[94] On the basis of limited research, the American situation is less clear. The tone of the Flanigan correspondence suggests that although the British number of those in the Admiralty and Coastal Command privy to Ultra was limited, it was still large by American standards. This might suggest, no more, that the American OR community had no – or very little – access to Ultra.[95]

The Battle of the Atlantic, technology and Ultra

The bulk of this chapter has described technology, its impact on the Battle of the Atlantic and, where appropriate, the links between technology and Ultra. Two themes are evident: most technology is applied at the tactical level and the Ultra linkages, even at their most pronounced, are relatively weak. None of this should be particularly surprising. Once a submarine-attack develops beyond a particular point it is sensors, weapons, training and, to some extent, numbers of escorting units that are more important than knowledge of what an enemy may want to do next week. In the case of the first set of factors, technology supports sensors and weapons especially and it is evident that Allied technology was an especially important factor in first balancing, then overcoming, the natural advantages of the submarine. Ultra played virtually no direct part in this process. However, as well as looking at Allied technology, it is necessary to also consider that of the Germans, although this cannot be studied in detail here. Although often ingenious and technically advanced, it suffered from a number of defects. Bureaucratic fragmentation stood in the way of not only technical achievement but also production efficiency. Further, there was a tendency to persist with systems that were theoretically advanced but practical dead ends: the leading example of this must be the Walter and other advanced propulsion systems.

It is a fallacy in war to engage in direct technological comparison, except where direct combat between like types occur, such as fighter aircraft versus fighter aircraft combat. In the Battle of the Atlantic, it was a case of submarines versus warships, aircraft and merchant ships. The technological comparisons therefore have to be with this complex interaction and not with each other directly. In this the Allies started from behind and ended up well in front. What aided them greatly, however, after Ultra started to become more available was that they were in a position to monitor German technology in a way which was not mirrored by the German intelligence system. This, in effect, bestowed a double technological benefit. New German equipment was, generally speaking, countered shortly after its introduction into service. In the case of the Type XXI/XXIII submarines, action was taken which slowed their progress and effectively prevented operational deployment by means of attack on the methods of building, transport, trials and training. This last outcome was one of Ultra's greatest contributions to the Battle of the Atlantic and also one of the least mentioned, not because it was kept especially secret but because of its indirectness. It might be possible to produce a rather clumsy parody of Mahan which would read:

It was these far-distant, leafy-gladed huts in the Buckinghamshire countryside on which neither the North German shipyards nor the training staffs of the central Baltic ever gazed that stood between the new technology submarines and their domination of the Atlantic.

7

Signals Intelligence and the Battle of the Atlantic

In discussing Ultra and the part that it played in the Battle of the Atlantic, it is important to understand not only what it was and how it was obtained but also to realise how it fitted into a number of contexts, especially communications, the enemy's efforts in the same field and intelligence as a whole. Unless these are absorbed to some extent, then the tendency to mythologise Ultra becomes nearly irresistible, to the detriment both of appreciating its true worth and of understanding its part in the whole history of the Battle of the Atlantic.

Initially, it helps to define a number of commonly used terms. Sigint is properly speaking the exploitation by reception of any transmissions made by an enemy in the electromagnetic or acoustic spectra; it does not just refer to emissions in these media used for communications. To be correct, this is Comint. There are, of course, instances of radio emissions used for non-communications purposes which are of intelligence interest. Most notably, there are the German radio navigation systems such as the *Knickebein* air bombing aid and the *Sonne* oceanic navigation system.[1] While describing terms, it is appropriate to look at the language of the decryption process and its product. *Enigma* is the name for the cipher machine used by the Germans. It had many variations, both in the electro-mechanical machine itself and in the systems of use, by the various selection of wheels, plug connections and the settings of these components. The various systems were known by different codenames by the two sides. Thus the Atlantic U-boats for most of 1942 used a system known to the Germans as Triton and the Allies as Shark. Ultra is a term which has caused some difficulty. It has been contended that originally it referred to what was only a security caveat on signal messages carrying information derived from the decryption of Enigma-encoded materials and not to the product itself.[2] Whatever the truth of the matter, it is now fairly common to refer to the output itself by the name of Ultra and this could hardly have been avoided when the original work published in English on the subject bore the title that it did.[3] However, it is important to note that there were other terms in use such as 'Z', 'Special Intelligence (SI)' and 'Boniface'. But perhaps the most important thing to remember is that Ultra by whatever name it was known was only a part of Comint, in itself a subset of Sigint and even that was a component of the whole range of intelligence available to the Allies.[4] This will be expanded on later in this chapter. But before returning to Sigint, it is necessary to examine some aspects of radio and its use that Sigint exploits.

Radio – basic characteristics

Radio permits long-range communication. This is such a platitude simply because it has been taken for granted in an age when speech and images from the furthest part of the world and from outside it are transmitted either directly or via space into our homes; when it is possible to talk from almost anywhere to almost anywhere; where aircraft, ships and even weapons can navigate themselves with great precision to almost anywhere in the world. Under these circumstances it is easy to forget two things: the simplicity of the presentation now overlays considerable complexity and that it was not always quite so easy as it now seems to be. It is therefore useful to describe some fundamental properties of radio as they applied to submarine warfare in the 1940s.

The first point to note is that the selection of frequency band, that is the number of vibrations or cycles per second that were used was of critical importance for ensuring communication.[5] In broad terms the highest frequencies which are of use for communications have excellent characteristics but for one problem – their range. In practical terms their limit under most conditions is about 25 miles for two stations attempting communication when both are on the earth's surface.[6] Such technology was not generally available at the outset of the war in any case and its applicability to submarine warfare would have been dubious.[7] The most reliable frequencies for long-haul communications are those of the Low and Very Low Frequency (LF/VLF) bands which travel great distances. But these tend to be much more suitable for shore installations than for units at sea for two simple reasons: size and power requirements. A typical shore LF/VLF shore transmitter might easily occupy an area measurable in hundreds of yards or more. It would also use a great deal of power. What became

122

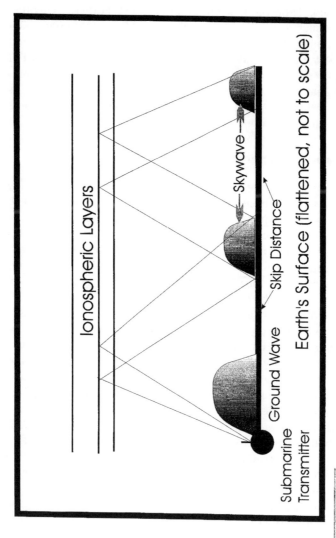

Figure 7.1

Figure 7.1 High frequency (HF) propagation

known as shortwave or High Frequency (HF) radio appeared to be much more attractive for submarine communication. It made no inordinate demands on aerial size for either reception or transmission and it only required relatively low power for long-range communication. Here, it would appear, was the answer to the passing of information to and from submarines at sea in the deep Atlantic from Europe and the passing of orders back to these U-boats.

But there was a problem, too. Whereas LF and other frequencies below HF worked by having a considerable groundwave, that is, a signal path which followed the curvature of the earth for very considerable distances, HF did not behave in this fashion. What it tended to do was to behave less uniformly. Firstly, there was a ground wave extending some tens of miles from the transmitter. Although this was to have important consequences for the Battle of the Atlantic, the groundwave is not described in this chapter.[8] Secondly, the signal would move upwards until it hit the layers of the ionosphere, which are found some 50–400 miles above the earth's surface. Then, in general, they would be bounced back to earth in a footprint of some size some hundreds or even thousands of miles from their originator. The first problem with this phenomenon is that there is a gap, often of considerable distance, between the outer limit of the groundwave and the first of the returning skywave or between the first and second or subsequent skywave footprints. None of this would be very troublesome were it not for the next difficulty, that of predicting the effect of ionospheric bouncing. The effect is also subject to variation with location, time of year, frequency selected and, most notably, time of day. Sometimes, too, transmitter power would be insufficient. As a result, although it would be desirable to exploit the effect by bouncing it to where a known and friendly receiver was stationed, this was quite simply not practicable and thus interception by unintended receivers was all but inevitable. The problem was most marked for units at sea whose transmission options were most limited. It was much easier to cover a range of options from shore transmitters by means of transmitting on more than one frequency within the HF band and also by use of the other long-haul bands. The net result of all this was that submarines often had difficulty in communication, resulting in the need to transmit messages more than once and thus giving more interception opportunities to the Allies. For the purposes of this book, and to a readership largely weaned on instantaneous and reliable communications, this is an important point to remember.

Radio communications – a two-edged sword

For much of the Battle of the Atlantic, radio communication was both
an essential part of the German submarine system and its greatest vulnerability. This rather bald statement needs both qualification and
explanation. The proviso is that, of course, for very considerable
periods submarines worked in effect as more or less independent units.
Under these circumstances, much of the rationale for copious signalling disappeared. This occurred at different times and for different
reasons. The first exclusion should perhaps be made for those submarines operating singly in distant waters. As they did not have to
coordinate their activities with any of their brothers, except in a very
general sense, there was no need for frequent signalling. Indeed, their
modus operandi militated against it.[9] Next, there were long periods even
in the main Atlantic battlegrounds when closely coordinated action
was neither desirable nor, latterly, possible. Such action related to the
early part of the war when the numbers of submarines were too low to
allow group operation and independent targets were both easy and
plentiful. A further period occurred in early 1942 when *Paukenschlag*
took submarines to the east coast of the United States and the ready
availability of targets meant that there was no necessity for group operations. A different rationale informed the decision in 1944 to engage in
inshore operations around the United Kingdom. Here it was the
impracticality and unprofitability of attempted anti-convoy operations
which predicated submarines being used singly.

However, for the group operations – the *Rudeltaktik* – which predom-
inated in several periods, largely from the autumn of 1940 through to
the end of 1941, and again from mid-1942 to mid-1943, plentiful radio
communication was not just desirable but essential to the conduct of
operations. This arose from a combination of Dönitz's own experiences
of submarine command in the First World War where he learned in the
hardest way possible that a single submarine opposed by a number of
escorts was at a disadvantage. It also took account of pre-Second World
War tactical exercises and trials when despite the promise of group
attack it became obvious that control would be a central problem of
this tactic.[10] Originally it had been thought that a seagoing senior officer
in a submarine himself could coordinate and control such attacks but
this quickly proved impractical. As a result a method of command
evolved in which this function was assumed by the BdU headquarters
ashore in Europe. Such a method, whilst it could be effective, put an
enormous premium on the flow of information from U-boats at sea and

thus created a very large demand for radio communication. There can be little doubt that the *Rudeltaktik* could be every effective at its best and that the Allies paid dear for those cases when it was working at peak efficiency, such as with the attacks on convoys SC42, TM1 and HX229/SC122.[11] But what is also clear is that all such operations – even when no convoy contact was made – generated a great deal of signal traffic in both directions. This was to be one of the submarine force's most vulnerable points.

Reaping the communications harvest I – direction-finding

Although the system of submarine communications used by the Germans was an integral part of their pattern of anti-shipping warfare, it also presented the Allies with a major potential source of information. A casual student of the Battle of the Atlantic might assume that all of this came from Ultra but even before and besides this, there were other useful products too. In the limited sense of what might be extracted from a single signal, clearly decryption represented not only the most difficult technical feat but also the most thorough exploitation too. Such a statement, however, tends to ignore the other Sigint products that were available. This is to some extent interrelated with hypotheses and, at best, knowledge about how an enemy is either conducting himself or would like to.

It should never be forgotten that the mere act of intercepting an enemy signal provides information in itself, however rudimentary. The existence of a number of broadcasts or other transmissions by a shore authority may suggest scale and type of activity. Clearly, without too much technical analysis, frequencies selected and power of transmission may suggest, for example, whether the intended recipient is likely to be close to the transmitter or further away. From sea, the very least that can be deduced is that some seagoing unit is there. At the next level it may well be possible, without any significant deep analysis, to count the number of units at sea. This may be made more difficult if either total or partial radio silence is enforced – a circumstance which rarely obtained during *Rudeltaktik* operations. A good example of the opposite is the surprise obtained by the Japanese carriers on their long transit to Pearl Harbor in conditions of almost total radio silence.[12] But even if total silence is not adopted then the composition of a group of ships, which may transmit only selectively, might well be difficult to deduce from mere intercept alone. Dönitz's semi-autonomous submarines, however, used radio a great deal.[13] Initial British facilities for this were adequate rather than luxurious but the advent of American participation improved the potential for interception.

Beyond doing little more than listening to German radio transmissions lay a series of techniques, the greatest of which in terms of both technical achievement and utility was almost certainly Ultra. But before discussing it, there are several other processes that are worth discussing. The foremost among these is almost certainly direction-finding of transmissions from ships and submarines at sea. Here the subsequent discussion is entirely concerned with this skill as practised on land; taking HF DF to sea took longer, was more limited and an account of its significance belongs elsewhere.[14] In the first few months of the war, the considerable geographical limitations of the British system – with its stations confined to the British Isles – was largely offset by the fact that many German operations were in any case restricted to the North Sea. However, once the Germans overran Norway, the Low Countries and France in 1940, the submarine genie was able to leave the bottle with ease and the inadequacies of the British direction-finding system were exposed. The Germans at this point correctly assessed this situation. However, what they failed to do was to keep pace with subsequent improvements in the system. These came about partly through physical extension of submarine operations into the Atlantic where direction-finding could be done, by better coordination of the product and eventually and most importantly, by the ability to use western hemisphere stations, not only in the USA but also in Canada.[15]

Although the interception and taking of rapid bearings eventually became commonplace and the collation of such information to produce locational information when the data supported it was a routine activity, there were elements of both science and art involved in getting the best out of the system. Perhaps the most important aspect was the simple one of the angle of intersection of the bearings.

Determining position depended in the first instance on obtaining at least two intercepts from at least two different stations. The greater the baseline distance the better, as this might permit improved triangulation. However, it was not just the distance between two intercepting stations that mattered but also their location relative to both each other and the signal source. Figure 7.2 illustrates this point. When the angle between the bearings is relatively narrow then the area of probability in which the target is likely to be is made much larger. This is, of course, partially a function of bearing accuracy. Were this parameter to be totally accurate and reliable then the angular orientation would not matter but, in practice, bearing measurement is subject to a number of

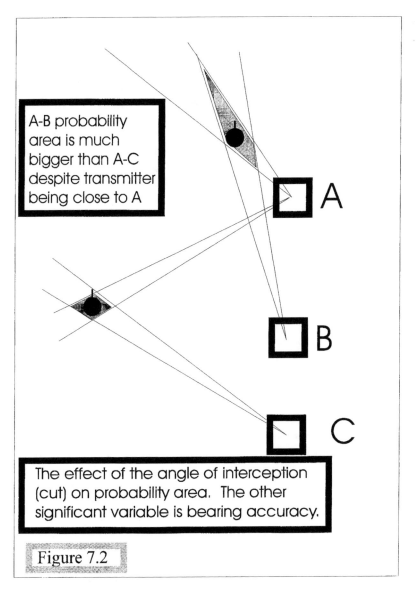

A-B probability area is much bigger than A-C despite transmitter being close to A

A

B

C

The effect of the angle of interception (cut) on probability area. The other significant variable is bearing accuracy.

Figure 7.2

Figure 7.2   Direction-finding accuracy

errors and any given bearing is likely to be correct within a tolerance of several degrees. The factors which affect this include environmental ones along the signal path, the characteristics of the receiving equipment and local factors related to the placement of the aerial system. A further problem was that, in general, signals tended to follow the shape of the earth and thus HF DF bearings could not easily be plotted directly on standard, that is Mercator, projection charts. That said, those whose business it was to work with HF DF regularly, at intercepting stations and within such places as the NID and American organisations, rapidly became adept in extracting the best information possible from imprecise data. It is difficult to say exactly how good HF DF was as a locating device, as it could vary very considerably with circumstances. A broad American study taking in two years' worth of data concluded that average accuracy was in excess of 100 miles with the median figure some distance below this.[16] This might suggest that HF DF was not particularly useful for intelligence purposes but that does not square with both experience of the correlation of imprecise information and the anecdotal evidence.

Even imprecise information may yield a far more accurate product if there is enough of it to permit correlation and smoothing of several data points. This is a technique which is routinely employed in many fields of signal processing and although perceived today as a matter of electronic techniques and computer algorithms, it is also amenable to human perception and calculation. A simple example would be the visual interpolation and placement of a trend line in an ordinary graph with either missing data points or a degree of scatter in order to extract best-fit or trend lines as is done elsewhere in this book. This is hardly either unduly mathematical or high-technology although the more advanced ways of doing this might be. In the context of HF DF during the Second World War, a number of individual HF DF positions which might be of only moderate accuracy singly could yield less imprecise and much more useful assessments when considered together. This is supported by the evidence of the OIC carrying out evasive routeing – often successful – for a considerable period before timely Ultra information became available.[17] Direction-finding was thus extremely valuable inasmuch as at its best it provided reasonable positional information and some trend of the movement of a submarine or a group of U-boats. Assuming that the particular movement continued to follow the pattern previously observed, this was obviously valuable. However, once the pattern was departed from, then such information was of lesser value until a new trend could be discerned.

Reaping the communications harvest II – other techniques

But direction-finding was not the only Sigint technique of value other than Ultra. There were a series of different exploitation methods, not every one of which was usable all of the time. Some of these complemented direction-finding directly; some did not. Similarly Ultra, too, derived support from or contributed to these at times. The idea that any of these three general fields – Ultra, HF DF and other Sigint techniques – existed in some form of hermetically separate compartments has to be dispelled. A distinction should be drawn between the handling of any sensitive material – especially intelligence – as it moves from place to place – and its processing. It is certainly true that many activities were by their specialised nature dealt with by a single organisation. But it was also important that there was adequate cross-fertilisation between these strands, otherwise important connections would not be made. It is unlikely that anyone who worked in intelligence organisations would ever claim that such communication always worked perfectly or that it was never so excessive as to endanger security. Such tensions will always exist in any intelligence system. This will be alluded to later in this chapter in the context of the two opponents' relative intelligence systems.[18] Conversely, if such communication is working properly it may create difficulties for the analysis of the effect of individual factors.[19] Although there were many other techniques used, it is intended to concentrate on three here: codebreaking short of Ultra, technical identification and traffic analysis (TA).

There can be no doubt that Ultra – the decryption of machine ciphers – was an achievement of the highest intellectual and technical order. However, it should not conceal the fact that it was not the only activity of its kind and that other systems were read consisting of codes and ciphers technically less secure than Enigma.[20] The German Navy probably made less use of such systems than did other German entities, but they did not avoid them all together. These were often much easier to read and their exploitation was, on the whole, much more reliable than Ultra. Their use was often for what would be regarded by many as irrelevant and mundane matters such as coastal waters information (such as shipping lanes cleared of mines), administration, merchant-ship movements and weather reports. Certainly such information in individual packets was rarely significant for its own sake; even when formed into a body of data it only provided a low level of background information. But it did have two great benefits, the provision of an insight into German organisation and methods, and as a window into the higher-grade ciphers.[21] The latter worked because of a German propensity for putting the same literal information into signal messages sent in both low- and high-grade systems. As a result the relatively routine decryption of a low-grade signal might produce the partial text of a high-grade one, thus providing an opportunity for a more general decryption at the higher level.

A shore radio station might have several radio transmitters at its disposal; a major warship too could deploy a number but the constraints of space in a submarine rendered such luxuries infeasible. In most boats, there was one main transmitter operating in the HF band.[22] Although these sets were manufactured to a high standard and German radio technology was as good as any other nation's, at least at the outset, there were small variations in the performance of sets, because of manufacturing tolerances being relatively wide by late-twentieth-century standards. To some extent these were measurable by an intercepting station using a technique known as Radio Finger Printing (RFP). This was done by photographing the signal and analysing its characteristics. However, this was probably only capable of indicating the broad type of submarine, i.e. the supply and minelaying craft.[23] A similar process to RFP was TINA.[24] In this the Morse 'fist' of individual operators was the characteristic studied. Although a submarine would carry more than one operator, the number was limited, especially when compared with a surface ship. This was even more marked as the latter only went to sea comparatively rarely. Both of these were useful supplementary techniques.

Moving on from there is Traffic Analysis (TA). In one sense this is a ragbag of techniques, disciplines and borrowings from other parts of the Sigint spectrum. In broad terms it is the study of an enemy's communications as a system and the conclusions which may be drawn from such an investigation. Although it might be argued that it includes decryption – and it can certainly benefit from it – it is normally taken to exclude that particular skill.[25] Traffic analysis looks at patterns of communication. If, for example, a particular form of shore broadcast has been associated with a certain type of operation then its re-activation may suggest the imminence of another such operation. From sea, it may be possible to recognise certain procedures, such as those used in enemy reporting to realise that an anti-convoy operation is in the process of being initiated. Such characteristics as the frequencies of these transmissions may also give more than an inkling of the intensity of operations. Sometimes, too, signals carried clear indications of the type of message they were and this too had significance for those intercepting, even if the full meaning of the enciphered text that followed was not rapidly made clear, if ever. This was especially so of the so-called E-Bar and B-Bar messages, whose prefix used the German Morse forms of these letters. These might indicate either a further signal book from which the body of the following message came or even the type of report being made. Thus in 1942 and 1943, the most common U-boat short signals (other than weather reports) used the *Kurzsignalheft* (Short Signal Book) and were called B-bars by the British (beta signals by the Germans). Although other subjects, such as fuel reports were sent in this format, their most frequent use was for convoy-sighting reports. Although these examples indicate the type of questions answered by TA, they do little to describe the skill as a whole. It is more than a little difficult to indicate more fully how TA was carried out. It depended much on not just observing radio signals but also of gaining the greatest possible understanding of the system that was being studied. It also suggested flexibility of thinking and of being prepared to abandon favourite hypotheses when new information came to hand. Further it paced a premium on developing the ability to discriminate between new developments in a communications system and understanding more of an unchanged system in which a large accession of knowledge has just been made. As a conceptual study, TA is probably the most difficult area of Sigint to grasp and certainly the most difficult to evaluate. In practical terms, however, it contributed greatly to assessments of U-boat numbers at sea, submarine casualties and realising that the enemy was experiencing problems of ambiguous orders or reports.[26] However, it would not be going too far to say that TA and Ultra enjoyed a symbiotic relationship.

Decryption – the Peak of Sigint

The decryption of the signals involved in the German attack on shipping by submarines represented one of the greatest achievements of the Second World War in a number of different ways. Whatever may be said elsewhere in this book that suggests that its reputation has been somewhat overdone in the last quarter of this century, there can be little doubt that it was an intelligence achievement of significance. Further its execution pioneered mathematical, electronic and computing techniques which have a considerable impact on the world we live in today. It is not too fanciful to see this undistinguished redbrick English country-house as an intellectual hothouse comparable to the

Massachusetts Institute of Technology or Silicon Valley. But this is looking ahead. To understand the business of Bletchley Park in the 1940s it is necessary to look instead at the fundamentals of codes and ciphers to gain some idea of what its inhabitants were trying to achieve. It may be helpful to dispose of one linguistic point initially – the difference between codes and ciphers. There are many different definitions of these, often overlapping. Perhaps that adopted by David Kahn in his book on the Battle of the Atlantic is most useful for clarifying the issue.[27] Here he talks of codes using words and ciphers letters. This is broadly correct and illustrates the point well. Code-names are widely used in military operations, either for clarity, brevity or as a means of obtaining a degree of secrecy, usually in the short term. This is usually best suited to spoken communication. Once important communications are entrusted to radio this method becomes not only relatively insecure but also cumbersome in operation. In this, the Second World War occupies an intermediate position between the cleft stick with a message in secret writing of some form and the late-twentieth-century secure communication which needs no or little operator intervention other than to pass a message.

In mid-twentieth century, the system normally employed was to use a cipher in which one character is substituted for another. Clearly if this was done on a simple basis, say always *a* for *b*, *b* for *c* and so on, there would be little difficulty in attempting to extract the meaning from the coded text; there is thus a necessity for a system which changes every coded letter each time it is used. This could be done by a variety of methods, such as randomly generated one-time pads in which the sequence is worked out by hand and both sender and receiver of the message have access to the same encrypt/decrypt pad which, as the name implies, is used only once. Assuming that the tables in the pad are truly random, that they have not been compromised by capture and that they are (as intended) only used once, then this is the most secure method possible. This comes about because the key is used just once, thus making it impossible to use cryptographic methods against it, since the key (that is, the one-time pad) never repeats, unlike some other code systems in which a high volume of traffic may use the same setting. But for all their considerable theoretical advantages, such systems suffer from a severe practical disadvantage. While they may be ideal for running a small espionage circle with a limited number of stations and infrequent transmissions, they are completely impractical for a complex military machine with hundreds of potential transmitters and the possibility of each one generating a significant signal traffic at any one time. In the case of submarines, which undertake relatively protracted operations, there are also difficulties of logistics to consider. These would be merely awkward but the problems of the reception station, too, have to be considered and the sheer scale would be a constant headache. One solution would be to use a similar system but to make continuing use of the same key or settings. This would have many disadvantages, not least security. A machine system on the other hand, such as Enigma, at least in theory, would appear to be the ideal solution.[28] Once set up, the scope for human error is greatly reduced and the machine's security is very high.

How was this achieved? It is difficult to give a short, thorough and correct account of the Enigma machine, but a simplified explanation can be given.[29] Cryptography did not begin with the Enigma machine; it has a history extending back over centuries. What, however, machines such as this did was to mechanise and automate the complex business of ciphering or deciphering a signal message. This was an important consideration, for the growing complexity of cipher systems resulted in two undesirable implications: time for the process and like-lihood of error, leading to messages rendered incomprehensible to the addressee. Once a machine such as the Enigma was set up, it was very simple in operation. Pressing a keyboard key for the plain language message lit up a letter for the coded version. By the standards of the late-twentieth century, this was clearly awkward because the resultant stream of letters still had to be transcribed before being sent by hand-keyed Morse, but for the 1930s and 1940s this was advanced techno-logy. But this was arguably not the most important implication of the Enigma machine.

Enigma's great utility lay initially in its ability to produce a cipher which was derived in a complex way and, without extraordinary aid, one which was very difficult to decrypt. Beyond this lay a system, or rather a series of subsystems, which gave Enigma such a large number of possible settings that even if an enemy had a complete working machine it would still be very difficult to work out the correct setting. Before moving on to see how this problem was solved, it is helpful to look at some of these complications. The Enigma was an electro-mechanical device whose heart was a number of rotor wheels. Described in its simplest form, their rotation produced the cipher text letter. But there was very much more to it than this. To begin with, the rotors themselves were not simple mechanical wheels; they carried internal wiring with different cross-connections between their elect-rical contacts to other parts of the machine. At the start of the war

German army and air force Enigma machines only used three rotors out of a total set of five, and the next level of complication was introduced by the selection of rotors and the order in which they were fitted into the machine. In the case of naval Enigma, a further cryptanalytical problem was caused by the main naval systems using four rotors out of a range of up to eight available rotors. Even had there only been three possible rotors, each always placed in the same position relative to each other, the probabilities for initial settings start to mount up suggesting around 17 500 possible combinations: with the possible choice being four from eight rotor types, and a free choice of rotor position relative to each other, the numbers mount further. But the rotor complications do not end there. Each rotor as well as having its fixed electrical connections also had a rotatable outer ring, which was set in position by the operator before inserting the rotor into the machine. It might be thought that this was sufficient to give a feeling of security to the users but there was a final complication. Many of what had been the internal electrical connections were instead broken and terminated in a series of sockets on the front of the machine. Obviously, these would have to be reconnected, but by using the socket system it became possible to reconnect them in a different order than the one they had been in originally, using a system of leads with plugs rather like the telephone exchanges of the period and in use for some decades after, and thereby introducing a further layer of probability to a system already with very many combinations. Setting up an Enigma machine for use involved setting all these variables plus one further step. This was to advance each rotor to a specified start position for each signal, thus producing a different set of coded text than had this start position been in a different place.

It was fully recognised by the Germans that it was possible, likely even, that at least one machine, possibly with a complete set of rotors, could fall into enemy hands. Their worst case would occur when it happened in such a way that the machine was captured with the day's current settings set on the machine and a list of the settings for the remainder of the month in question. But even this would not necessarily be a disaster in the medium and long-term. This was because, as a matter of routine, settings were changed daily. This introduces the subject of the administration of the system used by the Germans.

The Enigma machine was widely employed by the Germans, not just for submarines, not just by the Navy and it was widely used in the communications systems of organisations beyond the armed forces as normally perceived by the Allies. Thus the SS, the *Abwehr*, the police and even the railway system made use of it. From a cryptographic viewpoint the often simpler levels of its use being so widespread helped an understanding of the basics of the machine and its method of use. On the other hand the greater levels of complexity were sometimes even more difficult to fathom because of their relative rarity within the Enigma system as a whole.

However, any working cryptographic system has to adhere to certain schemes, rules and procedures in order both to function and to minimise its vulnerability to enemy attempts to penetrate it. The details of these may differ from system to system and from time to time but the basics are likely to remain the same. Ideally the system should be both secure and simple to operate, although these may be mutually exclusive aims. Clearly, if a completely different group of settings were to be employed for every signal message, then security would be enhanced. But it would also make life more difficult for those working under field conditions, be they in a Panzer division command vehicle or a submarine pitching in heavy North Atlantic weather.[30] So, certain facets such as the selection of rotors, their order, the ring setting and the plugboard connections were in force for one or two days at a time: this was known as the cipher key. It was obviously prudent to change these from time to time, perhaps at monthly intervals routinely, and if compromise of the settings was suspected. Deployed units, such as submarines, were likely to carry a number of reserve settings to cater for this and for operations extending over more than one setting period.[31] This was necessary because it would have been nugatory to have signalled new settings in a cipher known or suspected to be compromised. The change to a new group of settings might well, of course, have to be signalled using a setting, possibly compromised, but this would not specify what these settings actually were. For much of the war a relatively large number of participants might share the same settings, such as all submarines on North Atlantic operations and this conferred an advantage on the Allied decryption organisation, giving them more rather than less material on which to work. Indeed, when towards the end of the war the Germans changed both their method of submarine operations and gave each submarine an individual key then decryption became extremely difficult as there was relatively little material on which to work.

The more traffic that was decrypted by the Allies the better, but even a relatively small proportion might be of considerable value.[32] It has to be realised, though, that even if the ideal of total traffic decryption is attained, not everything necessarily became known to the Allied side.

There was still some information needed that might lie in standing information and instructions given to submarines and which was not available to the Allied side. An example of this was the geographic grid system used by the *Kriegsmarine*.[33] Although such supporting information might become known in time, its earlier absence might greatly reduce the value of an otherwise useful decrypt. As well as holes in knowledge, there could also be ambiguity. In May 1943 a debate took place between the British OIC and the American F-211 (otherwise known as Tenth Fleet's Secret Room) over the likely future area of operations for a submarine group, their assessments differing by some 1000 miles.[34] These denials of information and ambiguities of interpretation were also sometimes caused by the German technique of further concealing especially sensitive information.

Progress in reading submarine Enigma

This is a complete subject in its own right and it has received considerable attention.[35] But in order to position Ultra fully in the history of the Battle of the Atlantic, it is necessary to deal with this topic in a very abbreviated and simplified form; no attempt is made at this point to assess the significance of Ultra, either generally or in the context of specific times and situations.[36]

At the outset of the war, the German submarine signal traffic (like all German naval signals) was opaque to the Allies. The Government Code and Cipher School at Bletchley Park had access to an example of the machine very quickly, courtesy of the Poles who had also done a fair amount of cryptographic work, although none of this had been on the naval side. However, a lack of knowledge of both the specific systems used and of being relatively low down on the cryptographic learning curve – by comparison with what was to come later – meant that general solutions were to elude Bletchley for a long time. In a sense too, the Germans were unconsciously uncooperative by conducting the majority of their submarine operations on a single-boat basis, thus generating comparatively little signal traffic, accentuating the basic problem of a lack of signal cribs. Although progress was made in 1940, largely in terms of learning more about the general system rather than having a useful product, the important breakthroughs did not occur until 1941.

In the first part of the year, a number of factors came together to permit the breaking of submarine ciphers by the middle of the year in close to real time. The general knowledge of the Enigma system, combined with information gained from such sources as traffic analysis, was a useful background factor. Bombes, used in decryption, were British-built devices which represented an improvement on the original machines manufactured and donated by the Poles. Their purpose was to try out different potential rotor-settings in order to determine the actual one used. These electro-mechanical machines played an important part in the many achievements of Bletchley. They were large, sometimes temperamental, and in many ways very limited. Most importantly, for much of the time, they were a rare asset much in demand. They did not have the capacity to try every possible combination for every one of the keys in use by Germany. Significant, too, were a number of seizures of both equipment such as rotors or even the complete machine as well, sometimes, as supporting documentary material such as key settings. Some of these were planned 'pinches' such as from the trawler *Krebs* during the Lofoten raid; some came about fortuitously such as during the attack on the submarine U-110; but all contributed to the ability to read Enigma more or less currently, with occasional lapses.[37]

This happy situation obtained until February 1942 when the introduction of the four-rotor Enigma machine resulted in a blackout which was to last effectively for the rest of the year. This hit Bletchley hard, not only making many of the supporting tasks difficult but also outflanking the wonderful bombes which had been designed and manufactured on a three-rotor basis.[38] By the end of the year, however, the situation had been largely recovered, partly because of a growth in cryptanalytical equipment and partly because of the recovery of equipment from the submarine U-559 on 30 October 1942. Nevertheless an uncomfortable period had been endured as the Germans had changed their emphasis at the beginning of the year, from single submarines attacking shipping on the USA's eastern seaboard, back to the pack attacks on mid-Atlantic convoys from about the middle of the year onwards.

In cryptographic and operational terms the most unpleasant period after this occurred in March 1943 when a change in the short-signal code-book – which had provided a way into the Enigma key – caused a further short blackout. Fortunately this was measurable in days rather than weeks or months and reliable Ultra remained available until Dönitz's withdrawal from mainstream Atlantic operations at the end of May 1943.

After this point there were still failures as well as successes but these occurred in a different context: that of Allied dominance. In a communications sense, too, the U-boat world changed with less and less use being made of radio as it was correctly realised by the Germans that this was dangerous, even if deciphering was never blamed. Ultra had done its job.

Security failures – both sides of the fence

The dramatic revelation of Ultra in the middle of the 1970s and the subsequent greater accessibility – by reason of location and language – of British and American records to scholars writing principally in the English language has led to a skew in the general understanding of the significance of Sigint in the Battle of the Atlantic. What was either not realised or alternatively not stressed sufficiently were the many German successes in this field. The Germans had a fully functioning and equipped system – using an organisation called *xB-Dienst* – at the outbreak of the war and enjoyed many useful insights into British operations. What was probably their greatest sustained achievement was against Naval Cipher No. 3, a system in use for North Atlantic convoy traffic. This was introduced in June 1941 and it took the Germans some time to come to terms with it. At the beginning of the following year, *xB-Dienst* had made some progress with this cipher system.[39] By December of 1942 the Germans were reading the majority of the traffic, although it is not clear what the time-scales involved were. Their mastery of this system was to continue until mid-1943 despite some problems around the turn of the year 1942/43, brought about by changes in the cipher procedures.

Indeed, the Germans' efforts did not come down from the plateau on which they had established themselves until the summer of 1943, that is after the *de facto* withdrawal of the U-boats from the cross-Atlantic routes, due to the introduction of a new British system. This makes two further Sigint-related points. The first is that the German successes in cryptography were themselves betrayed by the growing Allied facility in Ultra. However, there was an inevitable and under-standable lag between the first realisation that No. 3 Cipher had been compromised and the putting into place of a new system, Naval Cipher No. 5.[40] This emphasises the principle that cryptographic success should not itself be compromised by over-enthusiastic and under-cautious use of the information obtained by such means. A further point is to illustrate the close relationship between crypto-graphy against an enemy's signal traffic and the security of one's own.[41,42] There is also an observation worth making from this case about the relationship between Sigint and operations. The Germans

did not lose their window on to convoy operations until after they had
been comprehensively defeated at sea in May 1943. So, despite having
a valuable intelligence asset, they were nevertheless defeated at both
tactical and operational levels. In other words, battles cannot be won
by intelligence alone, reinforcing David Kahn's characterisation of
intelligence as a secondary factor.[43]

Although the Allied failure to appreciate that their communications
had been compromised was significant, the German assessment of
complete security is probably a misjudgement of a much higher order.
It is very striking, reading the German postwar account of their submarine operations, to realise how close they seem to have been to making
the right assessment without ever quite reaching that point.[44] There
would appear to be two elements to this: allied discretion in
the exploitation of Ultra and what military psychologists call cognitive
dissonance.[45]

The first of these is to some extent a relative matter, there often
being either internal or inter-allied debates about the degree of
exploitation of Ultra. In general, the Americans tended to be more
aggressive in their plans to use Ultra, as evidenced by the CVE operations in the central Atlantic in mid-1943. But the British, too, were
sometimes quite bold in their use of this source of information.[46] Such
was a strategy which, with the benefit of full hindsight, was conducted
very close to the line of the Germans realising that their ciphers had
been compromised. On that side, there was the psychological effect
referred to above. Perhaps this is better explained in terms of a British
submarine aphorism, used in the context of considering a torpedo-
firing solution and cautioning against becoming fixated on a single-
target course of action – 'Don't get sold on one solution'. It refers,
therefore, to fixation to the exclusion of other possibilities. It is very
clear that the Germans more than once appreciated that all was not
well and that they should seek a reason for, in particular, their inability
to find convoys. It is fair to say that they started off by considering
almost all possibilities, not excluding decryption, but that they consist-
ently concentrated on the wrong explanations – some of which were,
quite literally, fabulous. Into this category came the attribution of
quite impossible ranges to airborne radar and the bestowal of tremendous accuracy to shore HF DF. But this tendency did not stop there and
even better was their idea that their own radar warning device *Metox*
itself produced a radiation that allowed Allied aircraft to home on
submarines.[47] On occasion, non-existent devices were imagined as
working against the U-boats, such as the noise boxes.[48]

It would be very easy to attribute all this purely to the psychology of Dönitz and the very small staff who supported him. But there were other factors at work too. Not only was the BdU staff small and very hard-worked; it also communicated little with other authorities which might have been of assistance – at least by comparison with analogous British and American bodies.[49] Moreover, the spirit of sceptical analysis was not prominent in the forming of decision and policy in the Third Reich and this lack of the ability to step back from a problem and look at it more widely was also a contributing factor to the misjudgements that were made.[50]

Successes and failures – two organisational systems

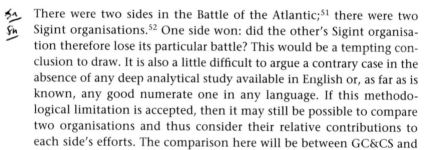

There were two sides in the Battle of the Atlantic;[51] there were two Sigint organisations.[52] One side won: did the other's Sigint organisation therefore lose its particular battle? This would be a tempting conclusion to draw. It is also a little difficult to argue a contrary case in the absence of any deep analytical study available in English or, as far as is known, any good numerate one in any language. If this methodological limitation is accepted, then it may still be possible to compare two organisations and thus consider their relative contributions to each side's efforts. The comparison here will be between GC&CS and *xB-Dienst*.[53]

Both produced relevant Sigint for a considerable period of the Battle, but by no means for all the time when it might have been useful. In very general terms BP was stronger later in the war and *xB-Dienst* was most successful in the earlier period. There were times for both organisations when blackouts occurred fortuitously; that is, when they were of less significance to the operational situation than they would have been at other times. One good example of this was in the early months of 1942 when the quasi-independent operations being carried out by U-boats off the US east coast required little in the way of communications. At other times, however, they were more critical such as the German loss of Cipher No. 3 in late 1942. In summary, there seems to have been a balance of these peaks and troughs. Qualitative comparison of product is very difficult indeed: although it may be possible to compile some general indicators such as decryption time and positional accuracy of information, these parameters by themselves do not necessarily answer the question of how the information helped commanders on shore and at sea. This can only be approached approximately by such analyses as those done by Syrett.[54] On the other side, the only known analysis of the value of *xB-Dienst* information was carried out by the American Operational Evaluation Group (OEG) – the main American OR organisation – postwar and its classification is binary – good or no good – which hardly lends itself to deep analysis.[55]

Looking at other aspects of the two organisations, there are, however, some striking differences which may go some way to understanding the progress – positive or negative – of each. The first point is that GC&CS was not fundamentally a military establishment in the way that the term would be understood then or now. Although employing a great number of service personnel – although many of these had never known service in peacetime – the fundamental tone of the place was not dominated by any one service or indeed a military ethos. Clearly, indeed, many of its most important people were not just civilians but a very particular type of person, drawn from universities and all professions. This implies two great strengths. Firstly, individual service cryptographic organisations did not compete for rare assets and secondly a very much deeper range of talents and disciplines was brought to bear on problems than was the case in Germany. The concentration in particular of the cryptographic skills and the machinery that was developed to greatly speed the penetration of ciphers had not only a mutual benefit for the breaking of different ciphers but also allowed the relatively easy redistribution of assets across vastly different operational fields. This was a major advantage enjoyed by Bletchley.

But similar considerations extended well beyond the sites of cryptographic activity. Although the British and Allied organisations for fighting the Battle of the Atlantic were necessarily on a much larger scale than those opposed to them, it is noteworthy that standards of cooperation seemed to be of a much higher standard. The Germans did appreciate the worth of Sigint, but appeared unable to exploit it to anything like the Allied model.[56] Here, the general tendency of Third Reich institutions to lead separate and competitive, rather than integrated and cooperative existences was reflected in the *xB-Dienst*–BdU relationship being considerably poorer than the GC&CS–OIC–CinCWA one.

The application of Sigint

As the last paragraph suggests, successful Sigint production is but the first step on the road to having a successful system which makes use of Sigint. Some aspects and considerations of this are to be found in the explanatory text of David Syrett's illuminating work on signals intelligence and the Battle of the Atlantic.[57] Aside from this it is necessary to take a number of general factors into account. The first of these is an enemy's dependence on signal-traffic in pursuit of his chosen strategy. Clearly, in those periods of the Battle of the Atlantic when pack-attacks were a dominant tactic, the signal-traffic was a highly salient factor. At other times, such as off the US east coast in early 1942 and in the latter part of the war when submarines were also operating independently, this was less helpful to the Allies. The next item of importance is the subject matter of the decrypted signals. This can vary greatly between say, for example, routine administrative material sent out on a submarine broadcast from shore or the reporting of meteorological information from submarines at sea to operational orders from shore and sighting reports from sea. Although there may be some indicators of the relative importance of these given away by certain parts of the whole signal which did not require full decryption or the form of the message itself, it might still be necessary for an entire reading of the signal to be made for its significance to be clear. At times when Ultra was at its very best, with keys revealed, then full decryption was a virtually instantaneous process, but when decryption was less certain and more lengthy, difficult decisions of priority would have to be made.

This leads on to understanding the significance of time in the process. It is dubious if there were any decrypts which were of no use at all to the British Sigint system. Even when blackouts were at their darkest, there were always occasional insights. Further, subsequent break-ins to the system would sometimes permit the decryption of material which had eluded solution for weeks or even months. It is fairly obvious that if the information thus revealed had a long currency in time, then it might still be of use. What is less directly evident is that much of the apparently dated material had utility, too. This might, for example, permit the reconstruction of an operation which had been concluded some time previously. By doing this, methods, procedures and doctrines might be revealed, many of which might still be in force and, perhaps more importantly, would continue to be in force for some time in the future, well beyond the actual date of the belated decryption. It is factors like this which make it more difficult to assess the true worth of Ultra. For the historical analyst, operations where Ultra was plentiful and timely are laborious and time-consuming to reconstruct: for this process of Bletchley and the OIC – separately and together – building the database, it is probably impossible now to reconstruct again the Bletchley/OIC reconstruction. At the other end of

143

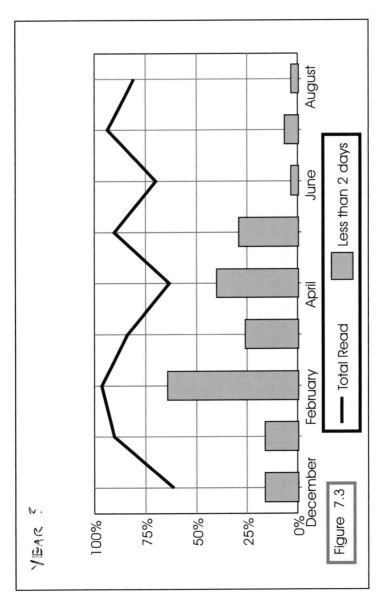

Figure 7.3 Decrypt reading times

this was the assessment of how current Ultra had to be for operational utility. For this, the best evidence is probably the statement of Patrick Beesly made at Annapolis when he considered 48 hours as the critical figure.[58] On first look, this would appear to be broadly correct. In very general terms, such a period might well allow the diversion or reinforcement of a convoy away from a reasonably remote patrol line of submarines. However once inside, say 350 miles, this critical time would rapidly become less.[59] A further comparison comes from looking at some global data on decryption times.[60]

What is interesting is the contrast between the two datasets. In the case of the number of days read, the situation would appear over a period – both lengthy and critical to the Battle – to be entirely satisfactory. The percentage of days read never drops below 60; and more often is at or above 80. However, the proportion of days with traffic read within less than 48 hours is much less reassuring; only once above 50 per cent and more often in the 15–40 per cent bracket with a quite abysmal coda.[61] It is only fair to point out that two further types of analyses could profitably be done. Firstly, greater detail of time, both chronologically and in terms of variance of decryption time might yield some useful insights. A second approach would be to compare either the present analysis or the more detailed one just suggested with some index of operational relevancy. Very roughly, it could be suggested that the poor performance in the summer did not matter very much because of Dönitz's *de facto* withdrawal from the main cross-Atlantic routes; on the other hand, this was also the period in which the CVE groups achieved a great deal of antisubmarine success. In any case, there is much fruitful work that could be done in this area.[62]

Ultra – Sigint – all intelligence

To complete this chapter, it is helpful to recall that important as Ultra was to the Battle of the Atlantic, it formed only part of the category normally described as Sigint. In turn Sigint was only one of several intelligence sources utilised during the battle. Others that were of importance were photo-reconnaissance and prisoner-of-war interrogations, and there were others.[63] It is probably correct to consider Sigint the most important of these but any such judgements are, by their nature, difficult to quantify. Lastly, and most importantly, anyone in danger of being carried away with the thrill of the romance of intelligence in general and Ultra in particular would do well to remember the judgement of David Kahn. Referring to the rapid Polish defeat in 1939, notwithstanding their mastery of Enigma, he wrote:

> The defeat demonstrated an elemental point about intelligence: unlike guns or morale, it is a secondary factor in war. All the Polish codebreaking, all the heartrending efforts and the heroic successes, had helped the Polish military not at all. Intelligence can only work through strength.[64]

8
Case-Study I – 1941

It was in 1941 that many of the most important characteristics of the Battle of the Atlantic first became truly evident and it also marked the ✓ first large-scale setbacks for the Germans, at least at the strategic and operational levels. There has been some recognition of the latter although this has also been coupled with some deductions about the causes which bear re-examination. This largely is what this chapter is about, although to do this thoroughly it is necessary to look at all aspects of the U-boat offensive against shipping in 1941 and the Allied response to it.

But perhaps it is necessary to start with some explanation of the word 'Allied' in the preceding paragraph. Surely, it can be argued, this is inac-✓✓ curate as Britain, or rather the British Empire, stood alone for almost all of this period, that is, until the declarations of war by Germany and Italy on the United States on 11 December 1941. This would be technic-ally correct, but it would overlook the progress of American involve-ment in the Second World War which was deliberate but gradual, rather than a sudden event on a single date in late 1941. It is an entire chron-icle on its own account and has been described extensively elsewhere.[1] It is enough to say that from mid-1940 onwards a process occurred which reflected an earnest desire on the part of the British leadership to involve the Americans and a growing awareness by political elites in the USA of the global implications of the European war. This was to lead to such measures as high-level communications, staff talks, defence scientific missions, the exchange of 50 old destroyers to the UK for western-hemisphere bases for the USA, Lend-Lease and eventually naval operations in support of the transatlantic traffic. In strategic and mili-tary strategic terms almost all of these were significant, as well as moving towards the Grand Alliance that was to dominate the latter part of the war; they fostered more generally a sense of trust that was to mature eventually into a much broader and deeper entity. They introduced the political, official and military leaderships of the two countries to each other, largely before the outbreak of formal war at the end of 1941, thus overcoming some but not all the difficulties inherent at the outset in any new and important relationship.[2]

But two of these items – the destroyers deal and American naval operations in support of convoys – were also important in operational terms. In the former case, this assertion is less easy to support as the ships were already over 20 years old, of obsolescent design and not always in the best material condition. They required a certain amount of work to fit them for practical service. Consequently although the agreement over their transfer was concluded on 3 September 1940, the first ships did not arrive in the UK until the end of that month and the others took several months to be transferred in a piecemeal fashion.[3] They also needed adapting for the escort role. They were hardly ideal for Atlantic escort work but several of them did play a part for a considerable period of the Battle of the Atlantic, including the periods of greatest difficulty. Even when not doing such work, they often managed to release newer or more suitable ships for such duty. In this way, their importance went beyond being just a symbolic act.

Of perhaps greater operational importance were the various American measures adopted progressively in the western and mid-Atlantic. By April 1941, the Americans declared a neutrality zone extending as far east as 26º West, that is, including Greenland.[4] At the same time, public admission was made of patrol orders for American warships in these waters. Less publicised were their instructions to report observations and contacts with German units to British authorities. In July 1941 these measures were extended to Icelandic waters. In the previous month, on the eve of Hitler's attack against Russia, a German submarine, *U-203* sighted the American battleship *Texas*. The submarine's captain had to resolve a dilemma. Although the battleship and her escorts were in the German-declared war zone, there was a prohibition on attacking American warships. He resolved this by deciding that *Texas* must have been transferred to the British, like the 50 destroyers: she had not. *U-203* attempted to torpedo the battleship but was unable over several hours to gain an attacking position. This was probably fortunate for both sides. Roosevelt and the Americans had no desire to provoke a full war at this point and neither had Hitler. The incident, however, led to an even stronger prohibition against German submarines attacking American ships.

1941

On 7 July, 4000 American marines landed in Iceland, effectively relieving a small British garrison. This was followed by the American escorting of convoys between the USA and Iceland. Although nominally for the ships of those two countries, ships of other nationalities were free to join such convoys. And so, escorted by either American or Canadian ships, these convoys were established by mid-1941. Although angered, Hitler held back from lifting his restrictions on attacking American ships. The autumn was to see further escalation in the overlapping German/American zones south of Iceland. In succession American destroyers *Greer*, *Kearny* and *Rueben James* were to be involved in ASW action, being torpedoed and the last sunk in action on 4 September, 17 October and 31 October respectively. Even this was to be insufficient to goad either side into a formal declaration of war. It did, however, confirm Roosevelt in the way in which his policies had led him and prepared the nation further for an eventual involvement in a war which they and at least some of their political leaders had striven so hard to avoid. At the military strategic and operational levels, this semi-war – the undeclared naval war – in the words of the subtitle of Bailey and Ryan's book, was of great significance.[5] For, especially in the latter half of the year, relatively few sinkings took place in the American zones. This German restraint effectively constrained their operating areas in the Western Atlantic quite considerably and was to have a significant influence on the nature of the operations they did carry out. Looking ahead in chronology and back in this book to Chapter 2, there is an interesting paradox in that, in a sense, the Americans contributed more to the immediate ASW war in the six months before they formally joined it than in the six months thereafter. This statement is not a criticism, as is often voiced, merely a reflection of the strategic realities of 1941–42.[6]

In another sense, too, it was an Allied war in 1941. As Bradley Smith has noted, there was a degree of intelligence-exchange in place well before the events of 11 December 1941 and this was of significance for the Battle of the Atlantic.[7]

The fundamental characteristics of 1941

There are several good accounts of the general trend of operations in 1941.[8] But in order to move to the questions of 'how' and 'why' it is necessary to look more broadly than these descriptions alone – apart from anything else, they tend to be heavily biased towards active events while the defence of shipping in particular and antisubmarine warfare in general is often a matter of 'the dog that did nothing in the night'.[9] And as Marc Milner has pointed out, it is the avoidance of encounters with submarines that is often important in historical terms.[10] So how does 1941 look as a whole?

The first point to note is the growing size of Dönitz's submarine fleet. Firstly, the total number of submarines available to Germany increased greatly over the period from the middle 1940 until the end of 1941. This was by any standards an impressive feat of shipbuilding, even in an era when these were relatively small and unsophisticated vessels compared to those of the late-twentieth century. The U-boat of 1941 probably represented the highest combination of technology compared to size other than in aircraft. But, of course, not all of these submarines were available for anti-shipping operations in the Atlantic. The first point to note is that every new submarine had to undergo extensive trials to establish its fitness for service. Then, each newly commissioned boat had to undergo an extensive period of shakedown and training. There was thus a significant lag between the emergence of a new boat from the building-yard and its transformation from a collection of gleaming metal components into an operationally ready *Frontboot*. In mid-1941, for example there were some 60 *Frontboote*, which was half of the total number. This reflected not only the lag just described but also the requirement for a number of submarines to be dedicated purely to the task of training; that is, in giving experience to and bringing submarine personnel up to a proper standard before they joined their first submarine. In mid-1941, this number was typically about 15 submarines. Often these were older boats, but they still diminished the number of front-line submarines.

There was a further diminution in the number of submarines that might be expected to be sinking Atlantic merchant shipping; this came

Table 8.1 U-boat fleet growth, mid-1940 to end 1941

Year/half	1940 H2 *July/December*	1941 H1 *January/June*	1941 H2 *July/December*
Total submarines Beginning/end	51/73	81/138	153/256
Growth (in period, %)	43	70	67
Growth (period on period, %)	–	89	86

from the various levels of the German higher command. Although the common English-language historical perception of the Battle of the Atlantic is that of an all-out onslaught on shipping, this perception would not have been shared by Dönitz in 1941. His views also serve as a corrective to his legendary position – at least in Anglo-Saxon circles – as the ultimate arbiter of submarine operations, certainly in this period of the war. Diversion of the 1941 submarine effort from the Atlantic war on shipping was noted for weather reporting, escorting of blockade runners, North Russian operations (some time before the Allied convoy system got into gear) and reconnaissance for surface-warship sorties (some of which did not occur).[11] But the greatest drain on Dönitz's Atlantic strength was undoubtedly the Mediterranean. Here, demands from the naval command led to a very considerable deployment of the available submarine strength. The first deployments there began in September 1941 and by 8 January 1942 there were 23 U-boats active in the Mediterranean.[12] Dönitz had two objections to the deployments: distraction from the main Atlantic task and the difficulties of Gibraltar transit, ensuring that boats once despatched to the Mediterranean could never return. In hindsight, it is difficult to avoid the view that he was right on both counts.

The upshot of all this was that, despite the very significantly greater number of submarines overall and even the considerable tally of *Frontboote*, the roster of submarines at sea for the war on shipping was to rise steadily from eight in January to stabilise, but only to reach the thirties in the latter half of the year, and dropping significantly below that again in December as the Mediterranean requirements ate into the Atlantic stock of submarines.[13]

These submarines enjoyed considerable success, at least in the first half of the year. This was to peak in May with the loss of well in excess of 300 000 tons of shipping to submarines but from then on was to decline, with only June, September and October showing figures significantly in excess of 100 000 tons.[14,15] This descent was to occur despite the greater numbers of submarines deployed in the latter part of the year and the contrast is striking. Indeed, the point of decline makes it very easy to conclude that there is a direct relationship between the decrease in sinkings and the advent of reliable and timely Ultra information. This, indeed, would appear to be a perfectly logical inference at first glance but it will be addressed more thoroughly later in this chapter.

But what is perhaps even more striking is the discrepancy until the middle of the year between tonnage sunk (monthly) and productivity expressed in tonnage sunk per day.[16] From June onwards tonnage and

151

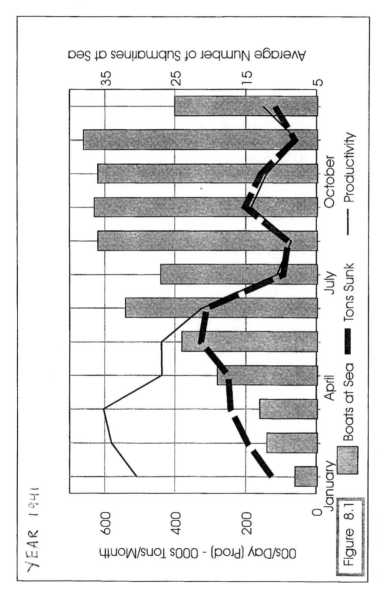

Figure 8.1   Tonnage warfare patterns

productivity curves are virtually coincident but their previous major divergence is very noticeable. What this means is that the German submarine force was very much more productive in the first half of 1941 than it was in the latter half, notwithstanding the greater numbers deployed at sea. Again the Ultra thesis appears an attractive explanation. However, if this is to be sustained, there is one very awkward fact that needs to be looked at in greater detail: the steady fall in productivity from March 1941 down to July–August, that is, starting well in advance of and showing a most marked descent well before the general availability of decryption intelligence.

Three types of anti-shipping operations

An aphorism of modern British submariners is that there are only two types of vessels at sea: submarines and targets. While this can be a useful invocation to the offensive spirit, it may be more helpful in the present case to consider instead that there were for the German submarine of 1941 the same classification but three types of anti-shipping operation: against independent ships, against convoys encountered relatively randomly and the specific mounting of pack operations against convoys. As an aside, it is worth noting that escorts were very rarely targets of choice during this period of the Battle of the Atlantic; they were relatively small, more likely to manoeuvre suddenly and, for these reasons, coupled with shallower draughts, were difficult targets. In any case, the stated priority was the sinking of merchant ships.

The concept of attacking an independent ship is relatively simple. This ought to be the easiest target for any submarine. It is likely to be the least well-equipped unit to deal with a submarine attack, be it by torpedo – from a submerged or surfaced submarine – or gunfire from one on the surface. By definition an independently routed ship is unlikely to have any form of military assistance – be it warship or aircraft close to hand. It may have some form of self-defence but in 1941, this was likely to amount to no more than a gun manned by a crew whose skill was probably less well developed than that of its adversary, and a merchant ship was a much larger target than a surfaced submarine. If a torpedo attack was used, even this means of defence was unlikely to be of any use. There was, perhaps, one asset that some independently routed merchant ships might be able to use, and this was speed. A surfaced Type VII U-boat was capable of a maximum surface speed of about 17 knots and, if the merchant ship could exceed this, then salvation might be possible if it appreciated its situation quickly

153

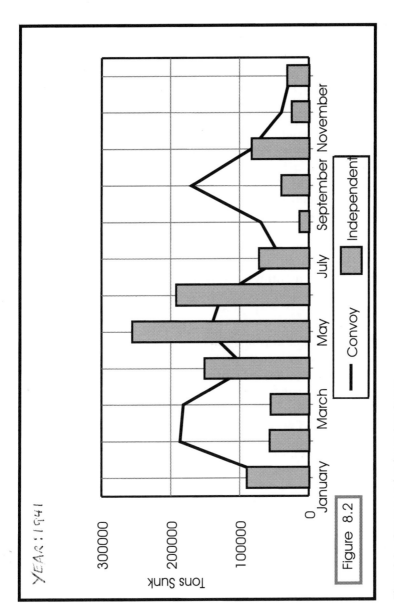

Figure 8.2   Convoy and independent losses

enough. However, not many merchant vessels operated at this speed. But even a lesser speed might suffice to render a submerged attack marginal or even impossible because a submarine could not reach a firing position in time. A merchant ship at say 14 knots might invalidate an otherwise good torpedo attack by means of an unknowingly well-timed zig-zag course alteration. But this could not be relied on. In the earlier part of 1941, independent ships whose speed was in the range 13–15 knots had been taken out of the convoy system on the grounds that the time lost in convoy because of their speed potential not being used would more than offset any occasional losses to such ships sailing independently. This proved to be a considerable miscalculation and losses were, in fact, significant. As a result these ships were again absorbed into the convoy system from 18 June onwards. This and other measures which extended the convoy system over more routes and to take in more ships were effective in reducing the independent losses considerably over the next few months and for the rest of the year; after July, they were only to rise above 50 000 tons once in any one month.

The contribution of this measure to improvement in the shipping situation was fully acknowledged by the British official history of intelligence:

> For the reduction in actual shipping losses the main cause was a change in the Admiralty's policy. From 18 June it raised the minimum speed limit for independently routed ships from 13 to 15 knots and there followed a dramatic decline in losses of 'independents', from 120 ships in the three months from April to 25 ships between the beginning of July and the end of September.[17]

It is clear from study of the German side that in 1941 there were two types of operations which resulted in sinkings against convoys. One involved a very deliberate allocation of resources and forces in an attempt to target specific routes or even convoys: the other a less structured approach, usually involving fewer forces. The second had no name: the first was known in German as the *Rudeltaktik*, normally translated into English as 'wolfpack'. Both played a significant part in 1941 and it is worth looking at both of them in attempting any analysis of the importance of specific factors in the outcome.

The *Rudeltaktik*, despite not being deployed until the autumn of 1940, has origins much further back. Certainly it was discussed and trialled in the 1930s and it has even been claimed that its origins lay with

Dönitz's own experiences in the First World War. In the early part of the Second World War, it was neither feasible, because of the small numbers of suitable submarines, nor necessary. This was because of the large numbers of independently routed ships which still fell outside the convoy system. Even when a convoy was encountered, it was likely to be, by the standards of the later years, weakly protected and even a single submarine had some chance of success. But as the events of 1941 unfolded, it became clear that such fortunate circumstances for the Germans were going to become less common. By the latter part of the year, the *Rudeltaktik* was to be the dominant form of operation. It is not intended here to describe this method fully, but it is important to note two salient characteristics of the system.[18] Over the years and in some of the literature, as well as the popular imagination, it has become commonplace to associate the term 'wolfpack' with the mass attack on convoys. This is certainly one of the aspects of the *Rudeltaktik*, but there is another which in the present discussion is at least as important: the use of submarine groups for reconnaissance. This has already received consideration earlier in this book,[19] but it is important to reiterate that this process was not merely an incidental detail of the *Rudeltaktik*, but was essential to it.

For the non-*Rudeltaktik* operations, some observations can be made at this point. They tended to produce results which reflected their relatively meagre allocation of assets. There are 47 identifiable cases where they carried out attacks on what might be called mainstream convoys.[20] Only about one in five could be considered as even a medium-level operation inasmuch as either three or more ships were sunk, the aggregate loss exceeded 20 000 tons, or three or more submarines were involved in the sinkings. The number of instances where two of these criteria were met was only six and in only three cases were all three conditions fulfilled.[21] The other point worth making was that these operations in aggregate were often relatively successful and at certain times, notably at the beginning of the year and briefly in the summer, they did better than the *Rudeltaktik* boats. Overall, however, it was these larger groups that did better during the year and they represented the greatest ASW problem.

It should be noted that some of *Rudeltaktik* operations, especially early in 1941, were of relatively modest size. The question thus arises of distinguishing between the two types of operations. The criteria adopted here are those used by *Fregattenkapitän* Gunther Hessler and his colleagues in producing after the war, under British Admiralty aegis, a history of the U-boat campaign from the German perspective.

156

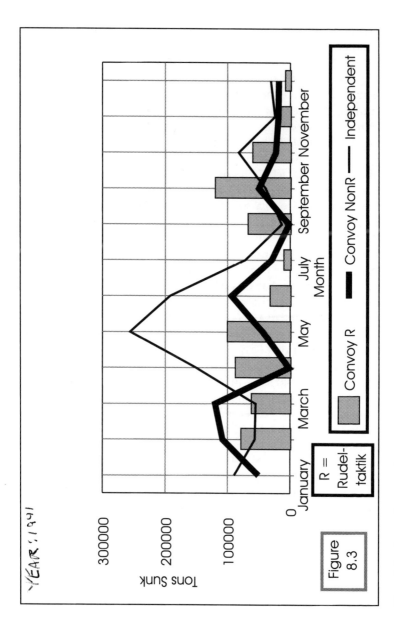

Figure 8.3   Losses by operation type

The diagrams in the first volume of that history provide a designation of anti-convoy operations specified as such together with much useful subsidiary information.[2]

Productivity – the key to the year

In order to understand what happened in 1941, it is necessary to look at productivity in greater detail. The results obtained by Dönitz in terms of tonnage were a conflation of two factors: the number of submarines that he had and their ability to sink as much tonnage as possible in the shortest possible time, that is, their productivity. As has been demonstrated earlier in this chapter, this latter quantity declined markedly in 1941. Before looking at this phenomenon more closely, it is necessary to reiterate the point that BdU were constantly interested in this figure and understood its importance. They did, however, have the problem that they were largely reliant on what they were told by their submarine captains with some assistance from Sigint. As a result, they were not always accurately informed of this important figure. In general, it was thought that they had sunk more than they actually had. Such overclaiming is usually the case in wartime. In the early part of the submarine war, when independent ships were often sunk in daylight, it was quite often possible to ascertain the victim's name and thus her tonnage without any difficulty. At night, submerged and convoy attack became more and more the staples of the Battle of the Atlantic and tonnage estimation became more difficult. It was also sometimes the case that ships were claimed as sunk either when they had only been damaged or even not hit at all. There were certain systematic elements of overclaiming too. On the Gibraltar route, many of the ships sunk were relatively small but often claimed as much larger. Certain submarine captains, too, had a propensity to overclaim.[23] To be fair, however, such propensities were not exclusive to the German submarine fleet and they certainly never reached the rococo heights of the Italian *Barbarigo* affair.[24] Having established the necessity for high productivity figures it is now useful to consider the components of productivity.

There are connections here with some ideas which have been established earlier, particularly the concept of ORCA.[25] However, despite the similarities of concept and language, that is essentially a tactical and procedural analysis whereas what follows is more to do with operational matters and the economics of warfare. Like ORCA, however, it has much to do with the use of time. The first divide in operational at-sea time is passage to (or from) the operational area and activities once arrived there. These are not infinitely extensible activities in either time or space and it is important to distinguish the proportions of each at any given time. There are some useful, if slightly extreme, examples out of the 1941 context. In 1939, German submarines had to make the long passage around the north of Scotland (or even further north) to reach the prime Atlantic traffic. This was not only hazardous; some of the submarines they used were neither designed nor suitable for oceanic operations. Similarly, but on a very different scale, the same factors obtained later in the war when deployments were made to southern Africa, the Indian Ocean and beyond. On the other hand, in the opening months of operations using the Biscay bases, submarines needed to do little more than make a short passage after leaving harbour to find themselves in an operational ara. Between these poles of difference and performance lies what happened in 1941.

Once in the operational area, there are three sequential areas of activity to be considered: finding targets, closing them and conducting an attack. Although these can be considered as serial events, it was not always necessary to start the process over afresh each time. If, for example, a submarine's target was in a convoy and there was little interruption from its escort because of either inadequate numbers or low skill-levels, then there was unlikely to be any need to find the convoy again from scratch before attempting a re-attack. But in considering these three phases of Reconnaissance (R), Closure (C) and Attack (A), to again use the ORCA terminology, some more detailed study is necessary.[26]

Of these, the first sequentially, and perhaps the most important in terms of the experience of 1941, was Reconnaissance. Here, a number of factors were involved. The first deals with the density of targets in the sea. This may be determined in part by geography. During the First World War, many German submarines operated in the areas such as the western English Channel and off Ireland. Here traffic was dense and ships sailed independently. As a result submarines did not have to work particularly hard to find targets. The organisation of oceanic shipping traffic into convoys from mid-1917 onwards made the submarine task of finding ships more difficult at a stroke, even in these relatively constricted areas. However, if sufficient submarines are deployed to cover every part of the ocean, this can be overcome. But this would be difficult enough to do even without any further interference from an enemy.[27] There are resonances too with the concept of carrying out cold-war ASW by nuclear barrage bombardment in which the proposal is put forward that it is not necessary to find submarines precisely, but to target their likely operational areas with a large number of nuclear weapons.[28]

But in the Second World War, such areas were contested only briefly and at the beginning.[29] By mid-1941, the arena was that of the mid-Atlantic, where it was unlikely that much could be achieved by chance encounter. The alternatives open to a submarine-force commander were either to persevere with the closer areas – probably accepting a high loss rate – or to head for open ocean and take what assistance he could from other quarters.

The first potential area for assistance was airborne reconnaissance for convoys and this was, in theory, an excellent direction in which to go. Aircraft had a much greater ability to search out vast areas of ocean looking for convoys or even individual ships than had unassisted submarines. Even if they only flew by daylight and suffered from some degree to the vagaries of North Atlantic weather, a relatively small number of aircraft regularly employed on such tasks should have provided the Germans with a highly significant adjunct to the striking power of the submarine. This happened to a limited extent, but there were difficulties. At an organisational level, the higher levels of the Luftwaffe wanted nothing to do with the Kriegsmarine. But neither were they very happy with the naval arm developing its own air force. As a result, air support for submarines was sporadic and not always of the highest quality. At the operational level, the liaison between the navy's BdU and the Luftwaffe's KG40, with its FW200 aircraft, was reasonable enough, not least because the latter's commander, Harlinghausen, had himself served in the navy; but above this level, matters were much less happy. The net result was that cooperation between submarine and aircraft, a skill that needs, above all, practice, never became developed to the extent that it might have done. Some of these problems belonged to the discipline generally and even the British who invested much more effort, both material and intellectual, in solving air-cooperation problems did not achieve success instantly.[30] In short, the Germans failed this test on material, doctrinal and administrative grounds.[31] In any case, many of the operations of 1941 (and indeed for the next few years) were to take place outside the range of German aircraft – or indeed those of all but a few Allied ones.

There was, of course, another possible way of targeting submarines on to convoys: intelligence. However, at this stage the cryptographic intelligence products of *xB-Dienst* were rarely available to assist Dönitz's submarines. In one instance, however, intelligence was of more use. The convoys that sailed from Gibraltar were susceptible to having their movements compromised by German agents across the bay in the nominally neutral Spanish port of Algeciras. The convoys on this route, too, were somewhat more prone to being reported, and indeed even being attacked, by aircraft, being closer to the Luftwaffe's French bases.

These measures were, on the whole, inadequate in themselves and seldom available as much as Dönitz would have liked. In the end, Reconnaissance ended up by being done from the bridges of the lines of submarines buffeted by the weather and only a few feet above the surface of the sea – hardly the ideal way in which to carry out this demanding task.[32]

Reconnaissance was undoubtedly the most difficult task facing German submarines in 1941.[33] However, Closure too could present difficulties although this was very much easier in 1941 than it was to be some two years later. But even in the relatively benign 1941 environment it was a process which required skill and, above all, time. This was especially so during *Rudeltaktik* operations when an initial sighting by one submarine had to be converted into a Closure involving several relatively widely spaced boats.

Attack, too, was a time-absorbing matter, especially when its synchronisation with Closure involved waiting until daylight had gone to allow the preferred tactic of surfaced attack. Experience suggests that it was not always possible for any submarine to go straight from one attack to another and post-attack manoeuvres might well lead to loss of contact with the convoy and the whole R-C-A sequence having to be started again. Thus, from a productivity point of view, the optimal sequence can be summed up as short passage to the operational area, followed by relatively short periods of time spent on Reconnaissance and Closure and the maximum number of attacks (preferably as lethal as possible with the minimum expenditure of weapons), and all carried out in the shortest possible period of time. Any failure to either achieve the sequence or indeed to spend too long on any or all parts of it resulted in a patrol less productive than was desirable.

The productivity flow diagram (Fig. 8.4) shows a somewhat idealised and time-compressed (inasmuch as there is virtually no dead-time between events) representation of a patrol. It covers all likely cases, such as the standard R-C-A (Attack 1), A-A (Attack 2), A-C-A (Attack 3) and A-R-C-A (Attack 4). However, the time spent on each activity and sequence will not always be the same; it will vary according to circumstances. The factors which affect this are partly to do with the basic dynamics of finding and closing targets and partly to do with Allied

161

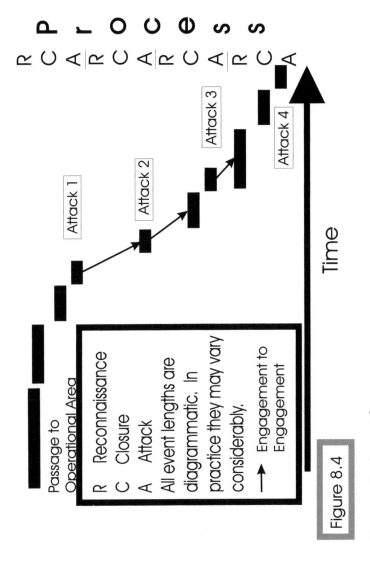

Figure 8.4   Productivity flow

intervention. As far as is known, no analysis identical to the one just described was ever gone through in any Allied headquarters or among the staff of an escort group commander. Nevertheless, these were the principles which informed Allied action and any attempt to either disrupt the movement between stages in the diagram or to prolong any or all of the events worked to Allied advantage. What happened in 1941 was, as at all times, a combination of the fundamental difficulties of the submarine operation, further frustrated by what their opponents' actions discounted in turn by the latter's ability to carry them out.

Before leaving productivity for a while it is necessary to add two further points, both affecting sinking; in one case, about merchant ships, and in the other, about submarines. The previous discussion has rather assumed that attack means successful attack. However, it has to be said that not all attacks were. Some missed, some experienced weapon-failures and some resulted in damage which was either relatively small-scale, involved significant salvage effort and subsequent considerable repair effort or sometimes resulted in total loss some time later – occasionally after a further submarine attack or even when the target – successfully salvaged and having reached port – was subsequently declared a constructive total loss (CTL) and then scrapped. However, 1941 was probably a period in which the proportion of fatal attacks by submarines on merchant ships was relatively high compared to later in the war. Clearly, too, a submarine's future productivity would drop to zero on its being sunk. This was not a particularly significant matter in 1941 as there were around 2000 sinkings by submarines and less than 40 submarines sunk.[34]

It cannot be stressed too strongly that following the progress of submarine productivity in 1941 is the best key to understanding the complex events of that year. This will be returned to later in this chapter.

Convoy routes and areas of operations

Attacks by submarines on convoys occurred in a variety of places in the Atlantic in 1941, ranging from well to the west in the north Atlantic to the west African coast as far south as 20° South, the latter areas being reached for the first time in that year. It was in 1941 too that the first ventures were made by individual boats south of the Equator,[35] though these did not achieve very much other than to generate alarm. They were not regarded as very successful by Dönitz. Three types of convoys received most attention: those on the main cross-Atlantic routes, the ones from the United Kingdom to Sierra Leone and lastly the Gibraltar route.

The main cross-Atlantic convoys were known by the designators HX, SC, OB and ON. The first two were both eastbound, starting, in this period, from Halifax and Sydney, Cape Breton Island, both in Nova Scotia. HX convoys were faster than SCs.[36] OB convoys went from Liverpool westbound to North America, at this stage Halifax. In the middle of the year this series of convoys was replaced by the ON series. In the case of the ON convoys a further designator sometimes denoted a slow convoy, thus ONS. These convoys had their routes determined by geography, weather and, latterly, attempts to evade submarine lines. These systems were the main conduits of imports to and exports from the United Kingdom.[37]

In the second category of convoys were those which were on their way to and from West Africa. There were two reasons for this route. Firstly, there was still a considerable UK–African trade and while a convoy system embracing all parts of the continent might have seemed worthwhile, this was not practicable with the assets available.[38] The other component of the African convoys was generated by the *de facto* closure of the Mediterranean in 1941, together with a continuing necessity to maintain sea communication with the Middle East, India and the Far East around the Cape of Good Hope. These convoys were known as SL which was inbound from Freetown, Sierra Leone and its outbound counterpart, OS, which did not start until the middle of the year. Although these two convoys were relatively unscathed by wolf-packs, they did receive some attention from single boats or the smaller groups of submarines.

Lastly, there were the convoys between the UK and Gibraltar, known as OG (to Gibraltar) and HG (back to UK). These had certain characteristics which rather set them apart from the other two systems. Although, for obvious reasons, they had to put themselves well to seaward of the peacetime transit of the Bay of Biscay, their general room for manoeuvre was nevertheless limited. As a result, they were considered quite an attractive proposition by the Germans. This was a compound of the range of German forces which could attack them with relative ease and their being less difficult to locate than the more oceanic convoys. In particular, the sailing of the HG convoys was easy to monitor from Gibraltar. But there were British advantages, too, as they were relatively easy to reinforce, being less expensive in assets – as they were tied up for less time than they might have been with cross-Atlantic convoys. Another factor working against the Germans was the generally much smaller size of ships in the Gibraltar convoys. Common sizes of ships in the other two systems were 6–8000 tons and upwards: many of the OG and HG ships were of only 1–2000 tons. From a tonnage warfare perspective, this was less useful to them.

The *Rudeltaktik* : the core of operations

Those operations which were carried out as deliberately organised examples of the *Rudeltaktik* form the core of the German effort in 1941. It is now apposite to look at these operations in greater detail, to note their commitment of effort and the outcomes. Further, although much of the previous literature has concentrated on those times when they were worse for the Allies and better for the Germans, it is intended here to also contemplate both the incidence of, and the reasons for, failure of the U-boats. Looked at broadly, 1941 might appear to consist of 10 not 12 months. This is because no such operations were attempted in January and only one in December. The former is probably attributable to the paucity of boats available for operations – caused by a combination of the operational cycle, a hard autumn of work in the Atlantic and winter weather – and the latter is explained by the preparation of submarines for the newly opened American waters and the diversion of submarines to the Mediterranean. The analysis that follows therefore looks at February to November.

In this period the number of *Rudeltaktik* operations initiated varied between two and five per month with an average of just over three, which was also the most common number of operations. This probably represented the upper limit of what could have been achieved unless a major redisposition of submarines had been effected. Even during the mid-1942–mid-1943 period, which is the best comparison with 1941, the number of operation per month did not always go into double figures, even when a much greater number of submarines was available.[39] The pattern of convoys attacked during the year changes to some extent. Early on, the targets of choice were often those outbound from the UK on the main cross-Atlantic routes. Thus in February and March convoys OB288, OB289, OB290, OB292 and OB293 all received the attention of from three to seven submarines for a number of days. In general these operations were supported by both air reconnaissance and German Sigint, and took place in the areas west and northwest of the UK and Ireland. Some success was achieved, too, the first operation being the best, with eight ships of 42 282 tons being sunk. But, despite these advances, not all went well. Before the first operation against

OB288, there had been an earlier one, which despite the relatively large number of five submarines, and the advantages of an air-sighting of a convoy as well as Sigint, had still failed. The March operation against OB292 sunk nothing at all and its successor sank only two ships.[40] Worse still, two submarines were lost in the process. These losses and lack of results resulted in a move to the west, out of the range of many of the shore-based aircraft and away from the perception that convoys were more strongly escorted there.[41] This move, which might be seen as only tactical manoeuvring, represented rather more than this: a move to more distant waters was, in fact, an operational defeat for reasons which will be explored later in this chapter.

So it was in the waters south of Iceland, then Greenland, that most of the efforts of April and May were centred. Operations against SC26, HX121, OB318 and HX126 all yielded scores in excess of 35 000 tons, twice in excess of 50 000. These were good results for the Germans, which also have to be seen in the context of large losses of independent ships during these months. However, three submarines were also lost, although such figures were acceptable against the sinkings of merchant vessels.

June was to produce only two such operations, one against HX133, at the time south of Greenland, where the efforts of 10 submarines, the first time such a number had been deployed against a single convoy, resulted in the loss of six ships of 38 000 tons. This was relatively meagre and was worsened by the loss of two submarines. Some escorts were transferred from the convoy OB336, as the two were about to cross in approximately the same area. A further relatively hastily arranged operation was also put together against the latter westbound convoy and this sank two ships as well as a straggler.[42] A further operation was mounted a few days later southwest of Ireland but, despite some air reconnaissance having sighted a convoy, no contact was made.[43]

July brought two further failed operations one in the middle of the month and one towards the end, the first west of the North Channel and the second southwest of Ireland. These problems, almost certainly brought about by Ultra, and the similarly poor results of the 'chance' encounters against convoys made July one of Dönitz's worst months in 1941. A slightly brighter event was the action west of Ireland against OG69 on its way to Gibraltar. Nine submarines were engaged for five days and seven ships were sunk. However, as was common with such convoys, a number of the ships were relatively small, totalling some 11 000 tons: hardly a large reward.

August saw a return to the areas west and southwest of Ireland, although the targets were not the ships on the main cross-Atlantic convoys but either those to and from west Africa – OS and SL – or the Gibraltar traffic. Four operations were mounted and there was a considerable commitment of effort, with around 35 boat-days being devoted to each one. As a result the two longer-range convoys attacked lost 23 000 and 31 000 tons of shipping respectively. The only complete failure occurred west of Gibraltar with convoy HG69 which, despite being cued by a German agent in Spain, suffered no losses whatever.

September repeated the same pattern as August inasmuch as there were two Gibraltar convoys attacked and two others. But this time the others were east and southeast of Greenland where two westbound convoys, SC42 and SC44 were set upon. The latter proved reasonably profitable from the German perspective, losing some 26 000 tons of ships but it was SC42 that was to present Dönitz with his best result of 1941 with 16 vessels of 68 000 tons being sunk. The relevant factors in this would appear to have been a large number of submarines (17) combined with a weak escort and a convoy close to the Greenland coast whose manoeuvres were confined by lack of sea-room. The Gibraltar convoys attacked were again profitable in number of hulls if not tonnage.

October saw the mix of cross-Atlantic and Gibraltar convoys repeated, although this time with much less success. Again the Gibraltar convoys repeated the pattern of a small tonnage for the number of hulls, with one operation against an outbound convoy failing totally. Another operation 600 miles west of the North Channel against the eastbound SC48 yielded nine hulls of 51 000 tons, a good result. But the month was to end with two failures, both about 500 miles west of Ireland and at the end of the month.

November, too, saw declining German fortunes. In early November SC52 was attacked off Newfoundland but, despite the efforts of 13 submarines over five days, a mere five ships of 20 000 tons were sunk. Two failures also occurred, ONS33 losing nothing in mid-Atlantic and a further operation at the end of the month north of the Azores also having no result for the Germans.

What trends can be picked out in all this to aid comprehension of the whole; to see the wood for the trees? Initially, perhaps it is best to start with a non-trend, the loss of submarines during *Rudeltaktik* operations. The only general observation that can be made here is that there are no discernible patterns at all, apart from losses being very slight indeed. On average, there were hardly any at all, and quite often long periods without a loss. The paucity of such occurrences almost suggests them to be random events. Nevertheless losses do occur most notably in March with the losses of the experienced captains, Kretschmer, Schepke and Prien. Similarly, although outside the period of main analyses, the five losses to the escorts of convoy HG76 in December are noteworthy. These specific actions certainly indicate that there was no fundamental lack of skill on the part of the British escorts; perhaps what they do suggest is that rarely were escort resources so generous as to permit the time required to make a kill more likely.

The number of submarines engaged rose slightly, although the figure drops back slightly towards the end of the period. What is more marked, however, is a tendency for the total number of boat-days devoted to operations to rise; from under 10 in February to figures in the twenties and thirties being the norm from June on for the rest of the year.

Results, too, show a number of trends. Once the early months of the period are over, there is a tendency for the number of ships sunk per operation to be in the upper half of the single-figure range, provided contact with a convoy is made. In one particular case, the action against SC42 in September, even this figure is exceeded by a handsome margin. However, this situation is not reflected in the tonnages sunk per operation which show a marked decline in the second half of the year, relieved only again by September's results. This suggests two things: the growing strength and competence of escort forces and the Gibraltar factor.[44] The former should be noted as important and denoting Allied progress; the latter needs further explanation. In the second half of the year, there was a trend away from the main cross-Atlantic convoys towards attacking those between the UK and Gibraltar. Some of the reasons for this have been described above.[45]

The central point remains, however, that whether individual victims were Gibraltar-bound short-sea traders of 1500 tons or ocean tramps of 6000 tons south of Iceland, convoy contact was all-important. Once contact was made, a number of sinkings were almost certain to ensue. Referring back to the productivity flow diagram (Fig. 8.4), the CA (Closure and Attack) stages were likely to be quite frequent and easily repeatable.[46] Perhaps more to the point, they were likely to absorb comparatively little time. A complement to this was that the R (Reconnaissance) stage became even more critical to the ultimate success or failure of the operation. To take a *leitmotiv* well out of its original context – 'only connect'.[47]

The 1941 analysis

What is clear is that 1941 fulfilled neither the promise implicit in a substantially larger fleet of submarines nor Dönitz's aspirations for them. However, attempting to unravel the reasons for this is far less easy. Perhaps the first thing to do is to dismiss immediately the idea that there is any simple monocausal explanation for this phenomenon of failure. The simple statement that the Germans did not win the Battle of the Atlantic in 1941 covers a number of complex systems at various levels of strategic politics, warfare and military economics. Nor did everything of significance occur at sea: the White House, 10 Downing Street, the Admiralty's OIC, the huts of Bletchley Park, the radar laboratories of navies and air forces, and the shipyards of several nations were all important locations, too. The other problem is that in all these places and concerning all relevant subjects little of significance stood still, even over the relatively limited period of a single year. As Paul Sutcliffe observed in 1993:

> it was rare for the complex Battle to change without other components changing separately, but concurrently. These changes might stem from the introduction of new Allied equipment, new Allied tactics, increased force levels, or new German equipment or tactics, perhaps in response to an Allied change. In practice, it is exceedingly difficult to disentangle the effects of the two or three changes all occurring at roughly the same time ... the situation was not static long enough for a useful data sample to be obtained.[48]

This encapsulates well one of the central problems in attempting to understand the Battle of the Atlantic in general. Rarely was this so evident as in 1941. However, it might be argued, Sutcliffe's remarks generally refer to the tactical and operational levels at sea – not to the other levels and aspects mentioned above. From an analytical point of view, this would appear a gloomy prospect – can nothing be done?

It should be obvious from some of the description and subsidiary analyses carried out earlier in this chapter that all is very far from being lost. Although it is unlikely that all factors can be totally teased out of the tangle, some progress can be made in sorting them out. At the very least it may be possible to draw a clearer perspective on some of the factors at the time and explanations proffered since then.

The How and Why of 1941

There are a number of mechanisms in operation in 1941, not all of them immediately obvious. It is also very difficult, if not impossible, to rank them in any order of importance. Perhaps this should not be attempted. The factors which accrue to German advantage are: The growing number of submarines and the development of the *Rudeltaktik*.

But significant as both of these were, they were greatly outnumbered by the points working in Allied favour:

- The largely covert assistance given to the British by the Americans
- The diplomatic constraints imposed on the Germans by a policy of not provoking the Americans
- The diversions both strategic and tactical of submarines from the main task
- The extension of the convoy system both geographically and taking in more ships
- The acquisition of near real-time decryption of German signals by the British
- Increasing numbers and skills of both escorts and aircraft.

There were some themes to the year, too, some exhibiting long-term trends, others cyclical. A knowledge of these allows a better understanding of what happened during the year. Some of the more important of these were:

- The trend away from the sinkings being dominated by those of independent ships to ships in convoys
- The attacks on convoys becoming predominantly those conducted using the *Rudeltaktik*
- The *Rudeltaktik* succeeding once it had gained contact but sometimes having difficulty in achieving contact
- The drop in submarine productivity being well established by the second quarter of the year
- Although there were many variations in the timely availability of Ultra, it was at its best in the second half of the year.

The most interesting phenomenon is the productivity drop starting in March. This can largely be attributed to the submarine move westwards, caused in part by a search for an area in which targets might be more readily found; in part because of a failure to connect with convoys in the areas of the northwest approaches to the United

Kingdom and also because of the pressure being brought on sub-marines in those areas by British aircraft and surface escorts.[49] This operational-level deployment was sufficient in itself to cause a significant drop in productivity but there were consequent factors which made the position even worse.

The first was inherent in the new areas chosen remote from any chance of air reconnaissance. In any case, even when this apparent asset had been present earlier in the year, it was far from being a guarantee of success. This had occurred as early as February and March when operations against an unidentified convoy and OB292 respectively had both failed. These are noteworthy for occurring relatively close to land and both having the advantage of air reconnaissance and some signals intelligence. Further, the British were not able to access German signals in a timely manner at this point. These two failed operations are significant because they indicate that *Rudeltaktik* operations were capable of failing despite the Germans holding several advantages and the British virtually none.

How much more difficult, therefore, from the point of view of finding targets, were those operations of the late spring conducted in much wider waters? Here, with less frequent signal intelligence, no air assistance and a greater area to sweep out, the successes were much harder-earned. The British, with growing assistance from the Americans, were, however, about to make Dönitz's task even more difficult in two different ways, both of which became effective at about the same time. A growing realisation dawned on the British that the policy of taking ships whose service speeds were in the range of 13–15 knots out of the convoy system was thoroughly mistaken. The rationale which had informed this decision was not totally unreasonable. It was certainly the case that confining these ships to convoys, the fastest of which could scarcely lurch up to a giddy 10 knots, meant that their overall capacity was severely constrained. The acceptance of the greater risk was felt to be offset by their ability to make more round-trip voyages over a given period of time. Experience, however, did not vindicate this policy and during the period April–June there were many independent ships sunk, of which a significant number operated at this speed.[50]

Despite the imperfections of the data now available, it is relatively easy to see that bringing such ships back into the convoy system was clearly advantageous, as has been acknowledged.[51] What is far less easy is attempting to produce a similar numerate analysis of the impact of Ultra on the Allied campaign in 1941. There are a number of reasons for this. Firstly, decryption must not only be carried out to be of assistance but it must also be done in a sufficiently timely fashion. Data exists to suggest the general time-lags for specific signal-decryptions but it is not possible to follow this all the way through the intelligence-operations chain. This could be quite variable and it is difficult to produce a single criterion of timeliness. Patrick Beesly suggested, some years after these skills were practised, that the figure was in the order of 48 hours.[52] This may have been a little generous to the British side and although it may have been adequate when lines were being formed up and convoys were still some hundreds of miles distant, the time-tolerance was probably far more critical as the process of search and passage developed. To truly gain an insight into this it would be necessary to examine the decision process, particularly within the OIC in some detail. This is unlikely ever to occur now as not only are most, if not all, of the participants no longer alive but many of the best evidential records have been destroyed. In any case, as has been stressed, by those there at the time, much business was done orally.[53]

In any case, there is some evidence to suggest that attempts – often successful – were made at evasive routeing before near real-time Ultra became available. This presents a paradox. Most of the credit has been claimed for the period of 'instant Ultra', that is, in the second half of the year, but it may well be that it was the patient application of the information gleaned from signals that were broken days, weeks or even months after their immediate operational significance had expired that was at least as important as the ability to know immediately what Dönitz's game plan was. It cannot be suggested that the effect of fast intelligence was even neutral, let alone negative, but the far less seductive accretion of old operations created the knowledge of the U-boat framework in terms of doctrine, method, performance and plans that enabled the products of near-immediate decryption to be used to best effect. It was this combination of ancient and modern and the structures to use them that made Ultra such a powerful weapon.

The million-ton myth

In the literature dealing with the Battle of the Atlantic, there has been an assertion made over several years which is fairly specific about the consequence of Ultra in the second half of 1941 and expresses this in terms of tonnage that would have been sunk had it not been for Ultra. This has taken the form of general statements about the effectiveness of Ultra in the second half of 1941 as well as the more precise claims.[54] Perhaps the broadest of these come from one of the loftiest authorities:

In 1941 Ultra had enabled the Navy almost to drive the U-boats back to their bases, such were their losses.[55]

This quotation is given to indicate the extent and pervasiveness of the ideas about Ultra which are now accepted. Without, however, considering the attribution of cause to effect, it is worth noting that not only were the U-boats never even close to being driven back to their bases, but it was only in one convoy battle, that against HG76, that they suffered significant losses.

Before moving on to the specific numerate claims, it is also worth noting another example of the persistence of the perception of Ultra as the sole cause of the 1941 turnround:

Ultra made its greatest contribution in the winning of the Battle of the Atlantic and at least in 1941 played a decisive role by itself in protecting British convoys. The results speak for themselves.[56]

The results certainly are evident but there is no explanation whatsoever of how they were reached. All, apparently, was Ultra.

More helpful, however, in terms of analysis, are the several statements suggesting that Ultra was responsible for the saving of some 1.5–2 million tons of shipping in the second half of 1941. This is stated in a number of places.[57] More helpful, still in attempting to understand this claim, is F. H. Hinsley's article which in part relates the average monthly sinking figures in the last six months and those of the four months which preceded them:

In this period [the second half of 1941] their sinkings were reduced to 120 000 tons a month. This has to be compared not with the monthly average of 280 000 tons they had sunk in the four months up to June, but with the sinkings they would have achieved with their greater numbers in the next six months had Ultra continued to be unavailable. It has been calculated that some 1.5 million tons of shipping was saved; and even if Britain's essential imports had not otherwise been reduced to a dangerously low level, the intermission was invaluable in enabling her to build up her reserves of merchant shipping and develop her anti-submarine defences.[58]

So now there was a numerate rationale for the claim. But does it stand up to close examination? The tonnages actually sunk in the two periods are certainly correct, but what about the numbers of German submarines? Perhaps it is best to start by working from the tonnage figures that are known and surmise what order of increase in submarine numbers is being sought. The difference quoted between the two periods is some 130 000 tons and the notionally saved increment is 250 000 tons (on a monthly average basis). This would therefore suggest that the increased number of submarines would have achieved a monthly average totalling 380 000 tons. This is a relatively modest increment suggesting an improvement of some 52 per cent over the first-period performance.

There are probably three ways of measuring submarine numbers: grand total, operational submarines (*Frontboote*) and those at sea. For the two periods, the average numbers are shown in Table 8.2. Both grand total and numbers at sea produce a good correspondence with the notional Ultra advantage and this would seem to vindicate the 1.5 million tons figure. However, this would ignore a number of factors which tend to vitiate this argument. These would include:

- The significant number of losses in the first period of independent ships, not repeated thereafter
- The general shift to the west of operations in the latter part of the first period and thereafter, leading to marked losses in productivity because of longer passage times

These are both important points and they have been taken into account to some extent already in the literature.[59] However, there are complications, especially with the second. By working in the wider Atlantic, in which there was not even a hope of air reconnaissance, the problem of finding convoys became much more difficult, even without the activities of Bletchley Park and the OIC. Ironically, the best illustration of this comes from the pre-Ultra period when a number of submarine operations in February and March failed to make contact despite being in much easier waters and having the advantage of both

Table 8.2   Growth in the numbers of submarine

	Total	Frontboote	At Sea
March–June	152	26	22
July–December	240	67	33
Ratios	57.8%	158%	50%

Note   All numbers averaged.

air reconnaissance and German Sigint. This suggests that there could well be a natural failure rate even without any specific British effort to induce it.[60] To suggest that this consideration no longer applied after Ultra became available is dubious; to attempt to quantify the respective and relative contributions of the basic problem and its complication by Ultra would be both complex and probably unsound on the evidence likely to be available now. But it is extremely dubious to attribute German failure to connect with convoys in the latter part of 1941 entirely to Ultra.

The extension of the convoy system more generally than the belated inclusion of the 13–15-knot ships, too, worked against the Germans. Now, independent shipping became even rarer than it had been before, reducing the non-convoy contribution to the tonnage figures. It is also useful to address another aspect of these statistics at this point: the claim that Ultra's true worth could be measured in the second half of 1941 by the enormous damage wrought on convoys on those occasions when Ultra had not been successful. The leading case for this must be convoy SC42 in September which suffered extremely heavy losses, but here as well as cryptographic delay, there were some other factors which led to the largest loss from any 1941 convoy. Weakness of the escort, the number of submarines deployed against this convoy and a lack of sea-room were all cogent factors. Apart from this case, the assertion that convoys contacted suffered higher losses than hitherto cannot be supported by the statistics.[61] In fact the opposite was true, with a reduction being seen. When the losses of merchant ships are considered against the deployment of submarines in terms of numbers and days involved in any given operation, then there is a marked drop in the number of ships sunk. When February–June and July–November are considered there is a drop to about two-thirds of the previous efficiency in the latter period. This might suggest greater difficulty – or at least a longer period being spent in the closure process – but equally it could also indicate a growth in the strength and competence of escorts. The statistics are even more persuasive where tonnage is considered, the drop here being from 2328 tons per boat-day in an engaged operation to 846 tons per boat-day for the latter period.[62] This is a marked divergence and is almost certainly caused by the 'Gibraltar phenomenon'.

Because these often had smaller ships sailing on them, rather than the ones on the cross-Atlantic and African routes, there was a tendency for their submarine victims to be of lower tonnage. This was by no means compensated for by sinking more of them: it took just as much effort to sink a 2000-ton ship as it did a 7000-ton one. Although from a strict comparison of ship-construction and explosive energy, they were probably easier to sink, the critical path was the submarine's problem of lining up an attack and carrying it out. Two further reasons suggested that this was probably, if anything, more difficult, than for a larger ship. Firstly, the smaller length and draught of the target made them a more exacting problem with reduced tolerances and thus more liable to failure, even were their true dimensions to be evaluated correctly. Secondly, such correct evaluation was rarely made. There was a tendency among submarine captains – and not just those who were chronic over-claimers – to consider their targets much larger than they actually were on this particular route.[63] So not only was there the tactical consequence of more difficult torpedo attacks, but there was also the operational point that Dönitz was under the impression that his submarines were doing much better in tonnage terms than they actually were. Whatever the detailed reasons, the overall result did not work to German advantage.

This does, of course, raise the subject of the German motivation for the switch to the Gibraltar traffic rather than either the cross-Atlantic or African routes. Could this have been indirectly caused by Ultra in the sense that continuing failure in other areas forced the decision to go for the less rewarding (in actual as opposed to perceived tonnage terms) and harder-fought Gibraltar route? A study of the literature on the German rationale that exists in English suggests that there was no indirect influence at work here.[64] Indeed, the tension in relations with Berlin, in either the indirect shape of the highest command or, more obviously, that of *OKM* on the subject of submarines deployed to the Mediterranean, provided a more cogent rationale for the selection of the Gibraltar convoys at the operational and, to some extent, the strategic level. By choosing these targets Dönitz was able to claim that he was addressing the main concern of *OKM* – British forces in the Mediterranean – whilst retaining his forces in the Atlantic for what he regarded as the more important matter in the longer term – tonnage warfare.[65] Nor indeed, do there appear to have been any claims made for this rationale post-Winterbotham.

1941: an Allied victory – but why?

In retrospect it is very clear that 1941 was not a good year for Dönitz and his U-boats: the result went very clearly in favour of what started the year as a *de facto* and incomplete partnership and ended as a *de jure* alliance. Perhaps even more important than the coming of a legal framework and the growth of habit, if not custom, was the deepening and broadening of that relationship during the year and the promise of that process being carried yet further in the future. These were not just fine words and sentiments, for some large schisms lay ahead, but they were of the type that were associated with a proper relationship and not just the casual and incomplete couplings that characterised the so-called Axis.[66] So 1941 saw the first true Allied effort – and the first success.

There can be little doubt about this judgement as far as the Battle of the Atlantic is concerned. Dönitz's forces increased throughout the year but became less effective. Even if nothing changed, common logic suggests that an improvement, not a deterioration, in performance should have followed. Certainly the analysis of other periods in the conflict suggests a general relationship between effort available and results achieved, but there were exceptions, although rarely sustained over long periods.[67] However, the discrepancy between the two halves of 1941 is very marked indeed and the place where the apparent break falls has led to a general acceptance of a monocausal explanation for this dramatic turnround in Allied fortunes.

If one very specific manifestation of this view – the saving of between 1.5 and 2 million tons of shipping – is examined, there are two comments that should be made. The first is that this is, of course, a hypothetical figure: it comes not from reality but from the speculative projection of reality. As such it is a perfectly legitimate construct to warn decision-makers at the time what the outcome of not taking certain actions might be: 'If we do not improve our overall ASW performance over the next six months, then an additional X.x million tons of shipping are likely to be lost.' In that context the specific figures derived from submarine numbers are quite feasible. However, as a post-event tool of analysis, this construct is not only somewhat crude but also wrong.

This lack of refinement is not just intellectually unsatisfying but positively dangerous, in a particular and very plausible scenario – one in which a number of salient causatory components change, not just one. It is hoped that this chapter has demonstrated that in this case there are several of these factors, that they sometimes interact in a complex fashion with others and it is difficult, if not impossible, to attribute quantitative contributions to individual causes.

As an example, it is useful to reconsider the German move westwards in the spring and summer of the year. This was 'caused' by the greater

concentration of surface and air forces by the British in the waters west
of the UK and Ireland and 'constrained' in its westward extension by
the increasingly robust diplomatic and military actions taken by the
Americans in the western Atlantic. Ocean reconnaissance became more
difficult 'because' of the open ocean spaces in which operations generally occurred and the lack of air reconnaissance. A further 'consequence' was a loss of submarine productivity, simply brought about by
the longer passage-times. At the same time, the convoy system was
extended in three ways: taking in more ships, more routes and protecting them more strongly – an important 'factor'. During part of the
period, cryptographic improvements occurred and as a 'result' not only
was the general understanding of the German submarine system
improved but it also become more likely that convoys could evade
concentration of submarines. This is only illustrative and there are
other instances.

What should be clear from this it is that is very difficult indeed to
attribute a single cause to what happened. It is suggested that it is far
more difficult still to adopt a single reason for what did not happen.
Thus the claim that 1.5–2 million tons was saved by Ultra in the
second half of 1941 cannot survive proper scrutiny.

But neither does this mean that Ultra had no utility at all. It did enable
– when available in a timely fashion – more reliable evasive routeing of
convoys. But this sometimes occurred even before Ultra, although less
successfully and, in any case, it was perfectly possible for the Germans to
fail to find convoys, even when no Ultra was helping the Allies and they
had the advantage of their own intelligence and even sighting by aircraft
to assist them. Ultra was a major factor in the events of 1941 but it was
not the only one and it is now all but certain that it was not responsible
for saving shipping in the order of 2 million tons.

9
Case Study II – Mid-1942 to Mid-1943

By the middle of 1943 – in fact by the end of May – an important point had been reached in the Battle of the Atlantic. This period saw the end of the large-scale convoy battles which had characterised much of the previous year and although Dönitz at the time saw his withdrawal from such tactics as a temporary state of affairs while he regrouped and re-equipped his battered submarine fleet, U-boats were never again to attain the same degree of actual as opposed to potential threat as they had during several prolonged periods in the last four years of war. But this was a judgement which could only be made with the benefit of hindsight enjoyed by historians and, to a lesser extent, operational analysts. The Allied path in the Atlantic from mid-1943 onwards for the remaining years of war was still to be a tough one and sometimes even hard-fought. 1943 thus has a Janus-like quality and two stories about it come together in the middle of the year. The first concerns the causation of the climax reached in May; the what, how and why of that remarkable outcome, and in this the role of Ultra forms a part of the account and analysis. The second deals with what happened next – not until the end of the war, but for the next few months, and in this too Ultra deserves evaluation and attention.

The hard road from July 1942 to May 1943

The phase of the Battle of the Atlantic that started in July 1942 was one of the hardest for both sides in the conflict. It is characterised by large concentrations of submarines, mid-Atlantic battles against convoys and increasing intensity of conflict. More coldly, certain long-term trends began to work in Allied favour and, despite the wildly fluctuating fortunes of the previous three months, the May 1943 outcome is perhaps better understood in terms of the longer picture rather than the shorter. The period that preceded this one saw U-boats running riot off the east coast of Canada and the United States largely because of the failure or inability of authorities there to institute an effective convoy system.[1] This combination of lack of escorts and dispersion of merchant vessels assured a plethora of targets for the submarines which had made the long passage from the Biscay bases. So much so, in fact, that submarines enjoyed one of their best periods in the whole war with both total sinkings and productivity at very high levels indeed. It thus led to the revival of their phrase *glückliche Zeit* to describe this period.[2] Although there were some at the time and more afterwards who criticised the Americans for being tardy in setting up a convoy system, a series of these were instituted and gradually extended. But as they spread in the western hemisphere, they were often anticipated at worst and reacted to at best by Dönitz moving his submarines further south and west. Thus the field of submarine operations moved slowly from the US east coast into the Gulf of Mexico and then the Caribbean. There weakly protected convoys or, more commonly, ships sailing independently, were easily picked off. It was only the ever-lengthening passage distances and times that limited the productivity of the U-boats. By the middle of the year it was obvious that Dönitz would either have to deploy his boats even further afield or else change his strategy entirely.

The latter was the course adopted and in July the first operation that year which employed more than 10 submarines was mounted against a convoy; ON113A was the object of attention and in the course of a four-day operation during 23–27 July it suffered the loss of two ships of some 12 000 tons, although one submarine was lost. July, too, was the last month for a year in which the sinking figures in the Atlantic were to be dominated by independents, not convoys. From then onwards the pace was to rise by spasms with more anti-convoy operations, more submarines tending to be allocated to each one and operations lasting for longer periods of time. Although some of these were to be undertaken against convoys in and going to or from the Caribbean, together with a few attacks against convoys to and particularly from West Africa, the bulk of the effort was to be deployed against the main cross-Atlantic traffic, that is, the convoys of the ON and ONS series westbound, and the HX and SC ones in the opposite direction. It is with this crucial traffic and these routes that the following narrative and analysis will be principally concerned.

At the operational level, this meant that Dönitz was forced to choose the most vital route, but also the one most likely to be defended well with sea and air bases which could contribute to the defence of convoys. For him, this was a policy of some risk but also the one that gave him, and thus German strategy more generally, the greatest chance of success. Should he not prevail, then the initiative for the Battle of the Atlantic would pass to the Allies almost completely.

The initial portents were good for the Germans as the year moved on. August was to see merchant-ship sinkings rising again over 500 000 tons, with the best result being at the beginning of the month against SC94 when losses were incurred of 12 ships of 53 000 tons sunk for a loss of two submarines. September saw a marked drop in number of convoy engagements attempted, from 11 to six, but a tendency for these to be on a larger scale. Typically here, packs were of 15 boats rather than the seven of the previous month and although one operation failed to make contact, that against SC99, no submarines were lost during any of these operations and results were obtained, albeit on the low side of Dönitz's expectations, averaging some 18 000 tons per operation. This, too, was one of the few months of the period in which losses of independents exceeded those of convoyed ships.

October saw the scale of the average anti-convoy operation moderating but with an increase in the number of operations attempted. Only one of these failed to make contact and the net result of these was an average loss per convoy of six hulls of 35 000 tons, nearly twice as bad as in the preceding month. All but one of these were against mainstream cross-Atlantic traffic, the exception being the Africa–UK SL125 which, despite a relatively small effort of 34 boat-days, nevertheless had the second-highest results of the month, with 12 ships of 80 000 tons being sunk over five days for no submarine loss. At the other end of the scale from both points of view was the attack on the westbound ON137, which occupied 25 boats for four days, the largest operation of this phase so far, but this was thwarted by poor coordination and bad weather, which denied continuous contact on the convoy.[3] As a result, only two convoy ships of 10 000 tons were lost as was one U-boat, a very poor return indeed for such a large expenditure of effort.

November presents a statistical paradox. On a strict calendar-month reckoning this is a better month for the Germans than October, resulting in the loss of over 530 000 tons compared with less than 430 000 tons and over 20 more ships. However, the two most significant operations in terms of loss were those against SL125 (mentioned in the previous paragraph) and that against SC107 both of which started in the

last days of October and continued into November. The latter started
on 30 October and did not complete until 6 November. Such apparent
statistical anomalies are bound to arise when analyses using two different time and function-basing systems are followed.[4] In order to understand the progress of the tonnage war, calendar-month statistics are
not only invaluable to the analyst but also have the happy property of
being one of the criteria used by Dönitz himself in assessing his
progress towards his own tonnage Valhalla. On the other hand, the
only sensible way of calculating both German and Allied success in
convoy operations is to look at the figures pertaining to individual
operations from both sides. Perhaps the greater problem in November
for the Germans, however, lay in a failure of strategic intelligence, and
thus of strategy. Only two days after the conclusion of the SC107
action, the Allies landed significant military forces in northwest Africa
– Operation Torch. These landings were carried out simultaneously on
both Mediterranean and Atlantic coasts. Mediterranean U-boats were
deployed in an attempt to intercept possible landings there but made
little or no impact on operations. Such submarines were in any case
irrelevant to the Atlantic struggle. They crossed that particular Rubicon
by the very act of entering the Mediterranean, a process which had
started as early as September 1941 against Dönitz's strenuous objections.[5] The Germans had also assessed that any Atlantic-coast landing
was unlikely and, in any case, the invasion convoys passed on their
business virtually unscathed. However, as soon as it was appreciated
that the operation had in fact been carried out, all available submarines were rushed to areas off the African coast. As a result the cross-
Atlantic convoys enjoyed relatively little attention for the rest of the
month. Only two operations were mounted, starting in November,
both against westbound convoys, and eastbound ones went untouched.
Nor did these two do well. ONS144 lost five ships of 25 000 tons and
the earlier ON143 had only one sinking; one submarine was sunk.

If November had contained components of failure for Dönitz, it at
least had the compensation that, taking the whole calendar month, the
sinking-figures were good. December was able to offer no such consolation. Operations were again carried out against convoys in each direction but a phenomenon not seen regularly since the failures of
mid-1941 returned to haunt German submarines: an inability to make
contact with convoys, and this was quite a strong theme during the
month with several failed operations. Even when contact was achieved,
success was scanty, despite significant commitment of submarine effort.
No convoy operation reached 15 000, far less 20 000 tons sunk and it

was a dismal month. One slight compensation was the relatively rare
sinking of an escort, HMS *Firedrake*, the Senior Officer Escort of
ON153.[6] The Atlantic tonnage count also came down to under 300 000
tons. The reason for these failures will be explored later in this chapter
but one feature of the month worth noting was very poor weather,
with heavy storms, to be repeated later in that winter.

January 1943 was no vintage month for the Germans either, with
very few operations attempted, partly reflecting a cyclical fall in submarines available. It is perhaps worth taking a rare excursion outside
the mid-Atlantic area to find the month's highlight when the Brazil-
bound *Delphin* group made a chance encounter with the all-tanker
convoy TM1 *en route* from Trinidad to the Mediterranean. A poor
escort in bad material repair was no match for the U-boat group and
the convoy suffered seven losses from nine, the highest proportional
loss of any in the whole war. This indicated the Allied difficulty of
trying to maintain significant strength on a worldwide basis. More generally, the month saw less than 200 000 tons of shipping despatched.

February, however, was a completely different story with a rise in
operational tempo, but more importantly, from the German point of
view, a considerable improvement in results. Not only was the overall
tonnage figure restored to nearly 300 000 tons, despite the month
being shorter than its predecessor, but there were some good individual convoy actions too. Particularly good results were obtained against
SC118 in the first third of the month but even better ones ensued from
the last-third onslaught on ON166 with losses of 60 000 and 88 000
tons respectively. It was also important to note that Dönitz was obtaining these results largely against convoys, not independents: no less
than 82 per cent of these losses by tonnage were from convoys.[7] Such
figures began to indicate that even the measure considered to be the
Allied best defence against submarines might be failing. Further, the
sheer numbers of submarines deployed in the Atlantic suggested that
the days were over when Ultra-informed evasion might by itself permit
effective avoidance of U-boat lines and thus the safe passage of all, or
at least most, convoys. The Battle was, according to much conventional historiography, about to reach its climax.

Whatever else March might be it was a month of superlatives: the
largest-ever pack-operation, with 42 boats involved and two others
using more than 20.[8] Casualties to merchant vessels were on a similar
scale, four actions producing over 20 000 tons of loss each and the
further case of the largest operation reaching the huge figure of 22 ships
of 141 000 tons. On such a basis, Dönitz would appear to have been

approaching all that he wanted; high tonnages sunk and minimal submarine losses. But all was not quite so rosy. Firstly, despite the undoubted successes, there were failures, too. Two operations, albeit with slight forces, failed to make any contact at all. Secondly, those operations which fell between failure and high success did not achieve very much at all. Principal among these must be HX230 which received the attention of up to 28 submarines over four days and lost only one ship – an Allied triumph not attained because of fate's compensation for what had gone before but as a reflection of hard work and some other factors discussed later in this chapter. The final judgement on this seesaw month must lie in the cold columns of the tonnage figures. A total of less than 510 000 tons – which includes independents – was good but not nearly good enough for the Germans. Since American entry into the war, barely 16 months earlier, this monthly figure had been exceeded on no less than four occasions; however, it was destined never to be reached again.

Despite these qualifications about German performance in March, it was still a good month. April was not. A similar number of operations was undertaken in April as in the preceding month but these were on a much smaller scale. The largest, against HX233, was only of 18 submarines and most were of less than 10. The HX233 operation was the most successful, netting six ships of 41 000 tons and losing two submarines, but no others reached 20 000 tons. Three of the nine operations failed completely; six submarines were lost on anti-convoy operations. The overall total sunk was under 270 000 tons and the proportion in convoy was only 60 per cent. Although not yet at the point of decision, the German offensive was failing and the Allied case improving.

This became even more marked in May. The Germans tried to carry out a similar number of operations as in the preceding months but returning to the large-scale as in March. Of the 10 operations attempted in the first 23 days of May, all but three involved a double-figure number of submarines; two exceeded 20 U-boats, two more were in the low 30s and one used 41. On this scale and with the relatively recent memory of March, Dönitz expected much: this was not to be. Firstly, half these operations failed to achieve anything at all. This did not appear to be a function of size of operation. Both 30-size packs fell into this category. Of the remainder, only three sank more than one ship and two reached sinkings in excess of 10 000 tons. Admittedly there was one 'success', the action against ONS5. That convoy, which had received relatively minor attention at the end of April, again was under pressure during 4–7 May. The 41 submarines pitted against it did succeed in sinking 12 ships of 56 000 tons. This, by itself, would not have been a bad outcome for Dönitz, but it was accompanied by the loss of six submarines, quite the worst outcome of any convoy battle of this period. This was disappointing to the German leadership but not sufficient to convince them to rethink fundamental methods. The subsequent operations – high on commitment of submarine-days and low on achievement – went from bad to worse with growing losses of submarines. The two last blows were the operations against SC130 which suffered no convoy losses but inflicted three on submarines during 17–19 May, and the similarly fruitless pursuit of HX239, involving 32 submarines which similarly gained nothing but lost two boats on 22–3 May. Dönitz had had enough. Submarines were ordered to the area southwest of the Azores to attack US–Gibraltar convoys, while those with insufficient fuel for this activity were left at sea in an attempt to deceive the Allies about the abandonment of the main routes. On 24 May Dönitz noted in his War Diary:

> The decision [to withdraw from the main routes] denotes a temporary abandonment of the fundamental principles which have so far governed the U-boat campaign. The change of policy is dictated by the need to avoid unnecessary losses in a period when our weapons are shown to be at a disadvantage. It must be realised, however, that as soon as our boats have been equipped with new weapons, the battle in the North Atlantic – the decisive area – will be resumed.[9]

Thus ended what was probably the most intense, hardest-fought and probably most evenly balanced prolonged period of the Battle of the Atlantic. The description of it above is very brief but much more can be said about the 'what' and the 'when' of the events of the Battle of the Atlantic. This can range from works dealing with the naval war as a whole, through the entire Battle of the Atlantic via this particular period to convoy monographs.[10] Accounting for these results is less easy to do, or at least to do so rigorously. There is no shortage of monocausal explanations, ranging from Ultra to the provision of a very few long-range aircraft, through the emphasis given to the antisubmarine war by the Allied high command to specific weapons and sensors. But perhaps, armed with the tools forged from the discussions of the previous chapters, it may be possible to go further along the road of explanation than hitherto.

In this context the key question is 'how', leading on to 'why'. This can best be attempted by looking again at the period for trends, if any, and then considering the causes for these phenomena, all the time bearing in mind the considerations already brought out earlier in the book.

Analysis of July 1942–May 1943

The Allied drivers at the grand strategic level in this period were the stemming then reversal of German advances in Russia – the first contemplated at the outset of this period but not happening until about half-way through it, and the second being set in motion some two months after the end of it; the continuing problems of war in other theatres; and the debate over when and where to re-invade Europe. But although these problems were somewhat abstract for the Allied redoubt in Europe – the United Kingdom – whose priority was survival, this did not mean that they were irrelevant to those islands. Whatever form the European re-entry took, with the possible exception of a most unlikely option making use of basing in the eastern Mediterranean, the British islands were necessary as a springboard, as a supply base and above all as a terminal point for all the facilities implied. Translated from grand strategic conception to military-strategic reality, all the vast material resources for the invasion of Europe had to make their way to Britain by one means or another. On top of this, Britain's basic requirements also generated a considerable requirement for cargo deliveries. This has been discussed in detail above.[11] Convoy was the agreed and accepted method of affording the greatest protection to these supplies and although most histories tend to accentuate those in which incidents occurred, it is worth remembering that even at its most intense, a large number of convoys saw no trace of a submarine.

The historiographical point is well summed up by Marc Milner's phrase 'Happy is the convoy that has no history', to which might be added the coda 'but it is also historically nearly invisible'. More specifically and numerately it is useful to look at an analysis conducted by W. A. B. Douglas and Jürgen Rohwer.[12] In this, among other things, they show, broken down by broad time-blocks, two pieces of data of great interest. The first is labelled 'percentage of convoys intercepted and reported by U-boats'. To use the classification adopted earlier in this book, this clearly takes the submarines beyond the Reconnaissance phase and into Closure.[13]

What is interesting are the three figures adopted by Douglas and Rohwer for the period looked at here – 34, 20 and 54 per cent with the

Table 9.1 Convoy losses by type (those with losses shown in **bold**)

Eastbound	HX	209 210 211 **212** 213 214 215 216 **217** **218** 219 220 221 222 **223** **224** 225 226 **227** **228** **229** **230** **231** **232** **233** **234** 235 236 **237** 238 **239**
	SC	**94** **95** 96 97 98 **99** **100** 101 102 103 **104** 105 106 **107** 108 109 110 111 112 113 114 115 116 117 **118** 119 120 **121** **122** 123 124 125 126 127 **128** **129** **130**
Westbound	ON	113 114 **115** 116 117 118 119 120 121 122 123 124 125 126 127 128 **129** 130 **131** 132 133 134 135 **136** **137** 138 **139** 140 141 142 **143** **144** 145 146 147 148 149 150 151 **152** **153** 154 155 156 157 158 159 160 161 162 163 164 **165** **166** **167** **168** 169 170 171 172 173 174 175 **176**
	ONS	New Series 1 2 3 4 **5** 6 **7**

lower middle figure applying to January 1943 only. But what this also means is that 66, 80 and 46 per cent of convoys for the same periods had no contact with German submarines.

Another way of expressing this is to look at the mainstream cross-Atlantic convoys during the period, that is the HX and SC convoys eastbound, and ON and ONS convoys in the opposite direction.[14] In Table 9.1 the first sequential mention of a convoy is initiated by one of that type being brought under attack and the last follows a similar criteria. Convoys attacked are shown in bold type.

Douglas and Rohwer make a similar point by showing percentages for convoys attacked by packs in the same periods as they used for their earlier analysis; that is August–December 1942, January 1943 and February–May 1943. Here the figures are 14, 4 and 24 per cent respectively. By now the analysis is concerning itself with Closure and Attack. Two points arise from this. Again using the complementary figures, this suggests that in Douglas and Rohwer's three subsections of the period 86, 96 and 76 per cent of convoys escaped pack attack altogether.[15] The further point is to look at the relationship between these two categories of data.

The general figure is derived by studying the same relationship for the other periods throughout the war. The relationship figure (as derived from Rohwer and Douglas's diagram) for the two longer periods shown is not very different from the general one in any statistically significant way. The January 1943 figure does stand out from the others. Two comments can be made on this. Firstly, by studying Douglas and Rohwer's entire diagram it is clear that the Relationship is at its most volatile when the Intercepted figure is also relatively low. The diagram shows two especially low figures in summer 1941 and the first half of 1942 when the derived relationships are 100 and 18 per cent respectively. Clearly the January 1943 figure may suffer from a similar problem. Further, when the actual number of operations attempted by the Germans in January 1943 is considered, this is very small indeed, suggesting considerable statistical unreliability.[16] What

Table 9.2   Douglas and Rohwer data – comparison

	Aug.– Dec. 42	Jan. 43	Feb.– May 43	General
A. % Convoys intercepted	34	20	54	
B. % Convoys attacked	14	4	24	
Relationship B:A %	41	20	44	c50

can be done, however, with rather more confidence, is to deduce a general relationship for the chances of converting an interception of a convoy into an attack: this would appear to run in the order of around, or more likely just under, 50 per cent both in this period (August 1942–May 1943) and more generally.

This is important in helping to determine the efficacy of various antisubmarine measures. When the 40–50 per cent figure is considered to be the norm and the Germans either do very much better or worse than this then it will probably be worth looking for an explanation. But perhaps this is a rather crude way of looking at the analytical problem, because although failure to attack is significant, so too is failure to achieve very much. Obviously in order to build up the tonnages desired by Dönitz, rather more than just carrying out one attack by one submarine is necessary: the more targets, and the bigger they are, the better. This suggests another approach which might be used in parallel – looking at each operation from the German perspective as input and output. This has the advantage of being readily amenable to numerate analysis although it is probably less easy to ascribe reasons, in other words to answer the 'why' question with quite such confidence. On the other hand it may make it easier to approach this latter stage of analysis if only by excluding some of the less likely explanations and hypotheses.

What then are the quantities that should be dealt with? In the first instance, commitment of submarines in terms of both numbers of boats and time spent on specific operations is perhaps the main thrust to the input side of the balance. If a holistic approach was to be taken to this then the whole field not just of submarine operations themselves but also operating cycles, turnround times, building rates, time for training and submarine losses would all have to be considered. These will not receive anything like a full treatment here not because they are unimportant but because these subjects and their interrelationships are so complex and extensive that they deserve study on their own account. As some indication of the breadth and depth of these topics, the work of Brian McCue is instructive.[17] In his book he attempts to look more closely into the relatively limited field of Bay of Biscay transits by U-boats in 1942 and 1943. This an important study, as it is his contention that submarines who returned to the Biscay bases spent ever-longer periods of time being turned round there and the avoidance of Bay transits – one in and one out – not only removed two potentially vulnerable operations from the submarine but also obviated the deleterious effect of long operational down-time between

them. The means of avoiding the return was replenishment at sea, possibly of weapons and certainly of fuel either by means of a surface ship
or, as the war moved on, more probably from another submarine,
sometimes specifically designed for that role. Clearly, there were limits,
both material and human, to how long a submarine could remain at
sea, even with this assistance. But even if 'double' patrols were all that
was to be attained on a regular basis, the effect on operational availability would be significant. The point of mentioning this is not to
look into that subject more fully but to realise that even this relatively
restricted investigation takes a whole book and within it certain facets
such as the repair and turnround times are taken as givens rather than
described in depth.[18] Here it is only intended to reiterate the point that
submarines available to attack convoys are a subset of boats at sea, in
turn themselves only a proportion of operationally available submarines (*Frontboote*), which are lastly part of the total of U-boats built.

These relationships are of course dynamic, and both size and proportion showed signs of change during the course of the war. It is rare to see
representation of the classification described above and to have an
explanation of their inter-relationships during the course of the war. Part
of the problem is methodological. Some parameters lend themselves
fairly readily to quantification, such as the total number of submarines,
but even here there can be difficulties. For example, from as early as
1941 there is a growing discrepancy between the total number of submarines as evidenced by BdU's war diary and base records. Initially this
is insignificant but by the end of the first quarter of 1943 it has risen to
20 and by the end of the war has reached 70.[19]

As the analysis approaches the combat area, the problem tends to
become one of definition. How frequently is the 'boats at sea' figure
compiled: quarterly, monthly, weekly, daily? Does it matter? What is
the definition of when a submarine is engaged in an operation against
a convoy? Does it matter which convoy it is? Does Dönitz know which
convoy (or convoys in the case of the HX229/SC122) his submarines
are up against? These all present difficulties and it is not always possible to write up every nuance of definition: this is, after all, a history
and not a laboratory report.

Nevertheless some trends and definitions emerge in this period.
These are:

- A sharp rise in the total number of submarines
- A less pronounced and more erratic rise in the number of operational submarines (*Frontboote*)

- A very similar rise curve for Atlantic *Frontboote*
- The proportion of *Frontboote* actually at sea on operations fluctuated a fair amount in this period but was typically of the order of 37 per cent
- The number of submarines at sea engaged in specific anti-convoy operations (as against general reconnaissance) at any one time was very variable indeed

For example on 18 March when the HX229/SC122 battle was in full swing statistics might be as in Table 9.3

It has to be pointed out that this was a fairly busy day by the standards of the Battle of the Atlantic but, even so, less than 70 per cent of Dönitz's North Atlantic boats are engaged in anti-convoy operations; put another way only 45 per cent of his total at sea; yet again, less than 20 per cent of *Frontboote* or just over 10 per cent of the total. To compile such data for every day of the period of interest would not only be laborious but would also be difficult to interpret. It was also the case that once Dönitz had his system working, there was a degree of stability to the system. This is best described as one in which submarines, once clear of Biscay, moved to a mid-North Atlantic grouping. These had no permanence in themselves, with new boats joining and others with fuel and other stores reaching the end of their endurance, departing. Nor did the groups maintain any long-term nominal identity. Sometimes two smaller ones would be joined into a larger one or a larger might be split. In March 1943 the following names were used: *Wildfang, Burggraf, Raubgraf, Stürmer, Dränger* and *Seewolf*. The ideal use of a group was to position it so that it could make successive attacks on convoys running in opposite directions. The area felt to be most productive was that which, at the start and for much of the period, lay outside reliable coverage of shore-based aircraft, known as the 'Air Gap'. There submarines might expect to have a few days of operations against any convoys it found, subject only to the attentions of the surface escort. The ideal was very rarely attained, with groups obtaining good

Table 9.3   Submarine deployment, 18 March 1943

Deployment	Number
Total	393
Frontboote	212
Operational at sea total – under BdU control	92
Operational at sea – BdU control – other than North Atlantic	32
Operational at sea – BdU control – North Atlantic	60
North Atlantic – specific convoy operations – HX229/SC122	41

results against a convoy moving in one direction before shifting their attentions to one bound in the opposite direction. The process in practice tended to be rather messier, for a number of reasons. Firstly, there was rarely precise and timely information on the location of convoys. Although Dönitz and his staff had built up a good idea of the general convoy system, there were too many variations of time and place to be able to intercept without further intelligence. But for the reasons described earlier in this book, even with such information there was rarely a precise forecast available. Nor did the intelligence system always reach even this imperfect standard. For example, the largest convoy battle of the war, that against HX229/SC122, was precipitated not by direct intelligence but by the chance sighting of one of the convoys.[20]

In analytical terms, this means that there tends to be a gap between two types of performance measurement: that of the overall tonnage sunk against the total of boats at sea (overall productivity and that derived from the specific anti-convoy operations of this period (tactical efficiency once engaged). Although having such a gap is philosophically unsatisfying, it can be argued that it matters little in significance. The former is the acid-test in determining the success or otherwise of the tonnage war as it actually happened. By using counterfactual hypotheses, it could be argued that a number of palliatives could have given the Germans better results than they experienced, but this is rarely done both rigorously and numerately.[21] Turning to the specific anti-convoy operations, these have the advantage of having reasonably discrete information that can be used for analysis. Further, they can look at inputs of submarine numbers and days of commitment. As outputs, tonnage sunk is also well known, as is the loss of submarines. It is not suggested that either Allied high commands worked on specific criteria of numbers as guides to their decision-making, but such information certainly assists in determining the underlying trends and thus in evaluating the various causal factors.

In looking at the specific anti-convoy operations, that is, those shown clearly in Hessler's diagrams as having been conducted, certain immediate trends become apparent:

- The tendency to have more submarines involved in each operation as time goes on, starting with an average of seven in July 1942, and never dropping below double figures after August
- At the same time having an even more pronounced trend for the maximum number in any one operation to rise. July's largest was 10 but by October an operation using more than 20 boats had taken

place. In 1943, this rose even more with twenties becoming relatively commonplace and ones involving more than 40 submarines occurring twice

- There is very little variation in the length of each operation, very few months showing averages different from 3–4 days
- Average results by month for 1942 are not especially good, with only one month, October, rising above the barrier of three ships or 20 000 tons sunk per convoy attacked
- In 1943 the first three months all pass this barrier: April and May do not
- On the Allied side, submarine sinkings, averaged monthly, only exceed one per anti-convoy operation in the last month of the period
- Sinking two or more boats per operation only becomes relatively common in some months in 1943.

Such characteristics help in understanding the situation a little more clearly because they indicate some of the characteristics of convoy warfare in this period but presented individually they rarely convey very much and even collectively they may seem unremarkable. But this in itself is important to convey the thesis that what happened in 1943 (up until late in May) was not the playing out of an intense see-saw struggle which started in March of that year but rather that the much longer period which started in July 1942 has marked, if progressive, homogeneity. In this context white knights, be they Ultra in December 1942 or B-24 Liberators in the following spring, remain important but only because they form part of a whole, like the poor bloody infantry (the convoy system, perhaps) and primitive artillery (surface escorts) as well as a number of other factors. It is also important to consider not just the list of characteristics adduced immediately above but also their relationship to each other in a number of bilateral comparisons, because these too have an important story to tell. Those considered are:

- The tonnage of merchant shipping sunk per boat-day on anti-convoy operations
- The number of merchant ships sunk per submarine sunk (known generally as the exchange rate).

In examining these it is sometimes useful to look at direct comparison before proceeding to look at relationships where two parameters are combined in an arithmetical way. Thus it is with boat-days engaged on operations and tonnages sunk (see Fig. 9.1). What this indicates is that

YEARS 1942-1943

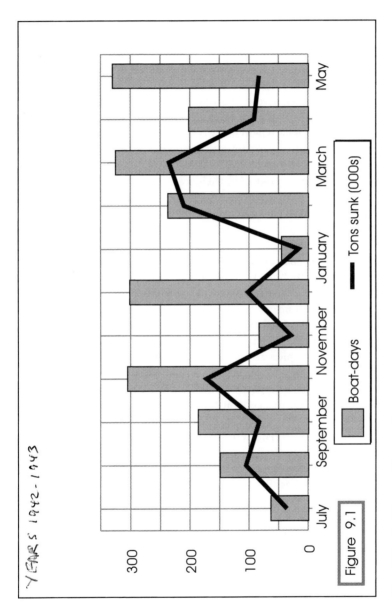

Figure 9.1   Boat-days and tons sunk

there is a general relationship between the commitment of effort and the attainment of results. This is to be expected, but there are also two sorts of anomalies. Firstly, there are two instances of adjacent month pairs – August–September 1942 and April–May 1943 – when there is a ratio of greater effort leading to lesser results. The latter is hardly surprising as it corresponds to the ultimate German failure and collapse. The former is less easily understood as there is no obvious cause for the phenomena of both increased effort and reduced result, which is not only counter-intuitive but also does not accord with the data-trends for the other months. There are perhaps two clues to this German reversal, one obtained from numerical data and the other from Dönitz's writings. Looking at the operations for the months of August and September, there is one very important change in their scale. No operation in 1942 up to August had used more than 10 submarines. In August, there had been some employment of packs amounting to double figures but the average number per operation was still only seven. In September this leapt up to 15 and single figures as a monthly average were never to occur again in this period. The change was not gradual; in September the average doubled to 15. It might be postulated that both at the level of individual submarines and of BdU that there was a learning process in dealing with these larger formations. Dönitz noted as early as the second half of 1942 that the Allies had gained tactical dominance.[22] This is obviously a fairly non-specific remark, especially as to time but it is a clear acknowledgement of prowess, which at this point would have had little connection with either Ultra or VLR aircraft. In short, Allied surface escorts, their sensors, weapons and support systems were of a good standard.

Secondly, despite the general trends coinciding, there are marked scalar differences. With the data in Fig. 9.1 being shown in boat-days and (thousands of) tons, there is a ratio between the two parameters which is sometimes close to unity (July 1942 and January, February 1943) and sometimes as far apart as a factor of three (December 1942 and, less markedly, April 1943). There are other times, too, when there is a noticeable divergence, especially in October 1942. Not all of these would correspond with some of the known and suggested advances, such as success with Ultra and the rise in numbers of VLR aircraft, so it must be assumed either that the data is random or else that causation is either unknown or compound. The random data supposition cannot be supported because of the obvious correlation of the parameters in general.

The other way to look at this data is to examine the relationship already discussed with greater clarity by looking purely at the

195

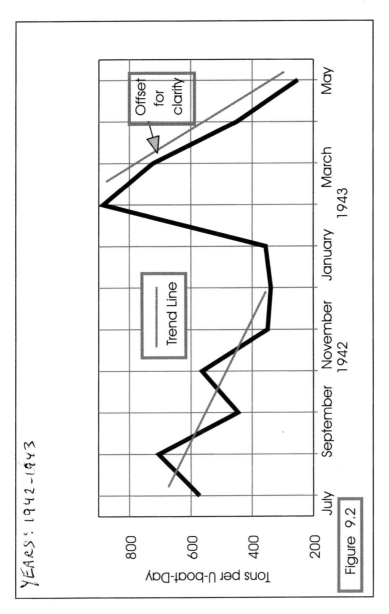

Figure 9.2   Tons sunk per U-boat day

parameter of tons sunk per boat-day. Here what in effect is being looked at is the specific productivity of anti-convoy operations. Although this is dangerous in the sense of considering the overall productivity of the submarine force for the whole time that it is at sea, it can be justified here on the grounds that what is being examined is the relative efficiency of anti-convoy operations over the period of interest, that these formed the backbone of Dönitz's efforts at the time and it was on the failure of these that his attempt at stopping the Allies foundered.

What is evident from this is that there is considerable coherence in the pattern of operation productivity over the period, or rather that there are two separate coherences. One extends without any difficulty from July to at least November and, without too much trouble, on to January. The second trend line which can be ventured is that from February to May, which is all but a straight line. But the difference between January and February is very striking indeed and represents a considerable Allied setback, not only reversing the previous steady progress but also putting German performance on to a peak not enjoyed for over half a year. Nor is it clear why this should be so. As far as is known there was no general and critical Allied weakness which might account for this result. Certainly, the air gap still existed but the same was true of earlier and later months, too. On the cryptographic front, February was a reliable month for the Allies. Certainly *xB-Dienst* regained its mastery of the No. 3 Cipher in February but this is hardly persuasive by itself as it had enjoyed several months of good results earlier in the period, often when the Allies had not had the advantage of Ultra.

The only obvious factor changing to German advantage was the weather after an especially foul January. But this too by itself can hardly account for the improvement in German performance. It was, however, to be Dönitz's swansong.

There are several conclusions which can be drawn from Fig. 9.2:

- There was a significant long-term decline in the operational productivity of German submarines from July 1942 to January 1943
- After an anomalous rise in this parameter in February there was a very rapid decline indeed in German fortunes after February
- The steepness of this decline in itself should have been a cause for German concern by May 1943 although the point that it had reached by then was not significantly lower than had been the case in the past.

Another point worth considering is the exchange rate, that is, the number of merchant ships sunk per submarine sunk. This might be considered as another investment criterion. Whereas the ratio of tonnage sunk per commitment of a number of submarines for a given number of days can be related to a result (tonnage sunk) and might be seen as evaluating the efficiency of a given commitment, the latter is related to the maintenance of a capital asset. Here, too, it can be argued that the boats committed at sea to attacking mid-Atlantic convoys represent the tip of this asset and they are in turn reinforced successively by the whole number of Atlantic-allocated boats, the corpus of *Frontboote* and, beyond that, the total of all submarines. Nor is this merely theoretical. Assuming that Dönitz knew instantly that he had lost a submarine (and he rarely did) and wished to replace it at its task as soon as possible, then further assuming that a submarine lay poised at the exit of La Rochelle or Brest, it would still take some days at best to reach the required station. Further, it would need replacing in its originally allocated task or else that would be weakened by the loss of a unit, or the task abandoned. Much of this process was unlikely to be quite as reactive as suggested but looking at the numbers previously adduced in Table 9.3 the following numbers can be derived:

- 1 U-boat lost at sea on mid-Atlantic operations
- = $1\frac{1}{2}$ in the North Atlantic generally
- = $2\frac{1}{4}$ of submarines under Dönitz's control at sea
- = 5 *Frontboote*
- = 10 of total number of U-boats.

Such figures are, of course, largely theoretical but they do give some clue as to the significance of loss. Turning to the actual exchange rates in evidence in the mid-Atlantic arena during the period, it is evident that these fluctuate quite rapidly (see Fig. 9.3).

There are no obvious trends here except at the very end of the period when the exchange rapidly becomes unfavourable for the Germans. What may be more helpful and cogent is to look at the absolute submarine losses during the period (see Fig. 9.4). Figure 9.4 indicates a very close relationship between overall Atlantic sinkings of submarines and those associated with the mid-Atlantic convoy operations. The latter rarely dominate the total but they do show signs of correspondence. More importantly it was both the trend and number of losses that led to the German decision to effect a withdrawal from the North Atlantic – intended as a temporary measure.

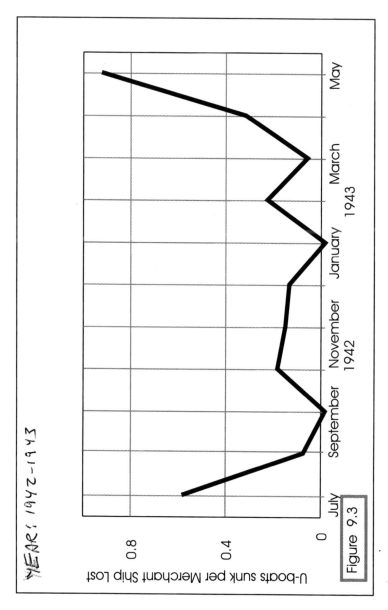

Figure 9.3 Merchant-submarine exchange rate

199

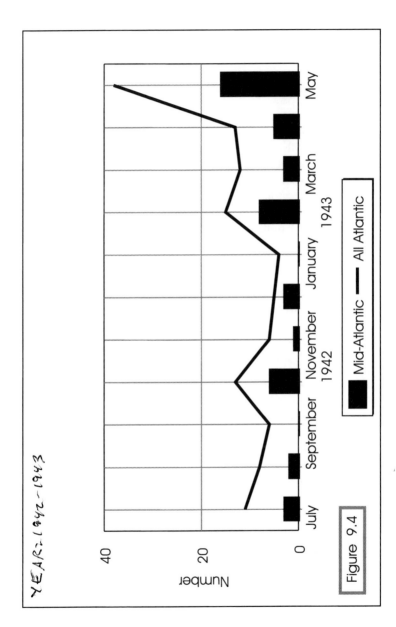

Figure 9.4 Submarine losses

So what were the factors behind this decision and what causation can be attributed to them? The most cogent would appear to be:

- A long-term decline overall in submarine productivity
- A particular – if interrupted – specific decline in mid-Atlantic convoy operations productivity
- The acute burden of large losses of submarines in May 1943.

To what specific cause or causes can these three phenomena be attributed? It is plain that no single influence is constant over the period and is equally applicable and significant in all circumstances. For example, Ultra was not generally available at the beginning of the period or for some months thereafter. There is also the difficult point that qualitative factors are also relevant when they are to hand. Even if a universally agreed methodology were available for assessing this difficult area, there would still be a vast amount of work necessary to establish significance. The fact that only one known historian has attempted to do such analysis, on an individual convoy basis, is as good an indication as any of the problem.[23]

When looking at the general decline in U-boat productivity the keys to understanding this are strategic and economic. At the strategic level Dönitz had suffered from the progressive if relatively gradual closing-off of the sources of easy targets and high-tonnage sinkings. This process had actually started in the autumn of 1939 with the establishment of a partial convoy system. There had nevertheless been an adequate supply of targets for the first two years of the war, although this was latterly constrained by political considerations of maintaining American neutrality on the one hand and the growing extent and competence of the convoy system on the other. Coming nearer the period discussed in this chapter, there was initially a new source of easy targets along the east coast of the USA and, latterly, further south. But as these areas became better resourced and organised for antisubmarine warfare, these too were effectively closed to Dönitz, effectively leaving him with two choices:

- Going even further afield which was costly in submarine time and not always practicable[24]
- Attacking the better defended mid-Atlantic convoys.

In either case, the economics of the attack on shipping were now starting to work against Dönitz and his submarines. The general decline, too, exhibited some of the features relating to the more particular decrease in effectiveness experienced in the mid-Atlantic described below.

Looking into this area, it is clear that Ultra is one of several factors involved. As has been established earlier in this book, it is clear that Ultra's main merits in this period lay at the operational and not the tactical level or, put from the German perspective, was most likely to benefit the Allies during the Reconnaissance phase (R) and the first part of the Closure phase (C).[25] Under the circumstances pertaining in 1942–43, with large, wide-ranging packs of submarines, it would be unreasonable to expect that Ultra would have been able to do very much in the way of allowing evasive routeing of convoys. Indeed that was not the only factor working against such a technique being successful. As well as the perennial problems of uncertain navigation (compared to the modern era) and wide oceans, there were also the important, but not always omnipresent, difficulties caused by the parallel German efforts of the *xB-Dienst* and that of chance sightings of convoys. But as the statistics of convoy-action indicate, before reliable Ultra was again available in mid-December 1942, the key to engagements was the difficulty encountered by the U-boats in sinking ships. Here a comparison with the events of 1941 is instructive. In that year a good general rule was that if contact was made by a group of submarines then a number of sinkings would ensue. This compares very favourably with the 1942–43 period, when in only one month, October, does the average number of ships sunk per operation exceed five. In 1941, when fewer submarines were used, the situation was that nearly seven ships were sunk for every successful operation.

Here can be seen at least a dual causation at work, operating on more than one level. In one instance the latter part of the Closure process (C) was rendered more difficult by a greater Allied ability to put surfaced submarines down and a submerged submarine could not, in general, close a convoy. This came about through a greater quantity of escort resources on the surface and in the air, and qualitative improvements, too. Putting any submarine down which was attempting to attain torpedo-firing range was useful; if that submarine was also the contact-keeper, the improvement in the tactical situation was even greater. The potential to carry out such tactics had three sources:

- *Quantity.* An adequacy of escort forces allowed one or more units to be detached from the immediate vicinity of the convoy without the concomitant fear of exposing it recklessly to attack from another direction. A further benefit was to allow this process of prosecution to be carried out for some time – not just one quick thrust, then back to the convoy.

- *Aircraft.* These allowed much greater reach than hitherto beyond the area just a few miles from the convoy. They were also much quicker in reaction.
- *HF DF.* Ship-fitted direction-finding provided a sensor of greater range than anything else that an escort-force commander had previously enjoyed. By this period it was fairly widely available, allowing best use of the previous two items. It did, of course, depend critically on a submarine transmitting on radio but with the submarine tactics employed this was not a problem.

Similar advantages worked, but coming from slightly different sources, when submarines started on the process of Attack (A). Here radar and sonar made the above- and underwater environments more difficult for the attacker. These sensors were never enough by themselves to destroy submarines but in the early months there was little enough of this in any case. More importantly, they played a part in limiting, disrupting and in some cases breaking up attacks altogether. Further, submarines not only had to move into firing positions, they had to leave them afterwards. This too provided an opportunity for similar Allied activities. None of these activities owed anything directly to Ultra.

But, at the same time, it would be wrong to say that intelligence in general and Ultra in particular contributed nothing at all. Even when the long black-out ensured no near real-time Ultra product; even when the delays were so long as to render their information useless tactically and to some extent at the operational level, there was still utility. This came in the shape of providing background information about the submarine force in general: its size, state of training and operating methods. Nor was this of purely historical significance. Dönitz, despite occasional forays on to the wilder shores of fantastical assessment, was a pragmatic operator. If a tactic worked it was persisted with until, and even sometimes beyond, the point of usefulness. The insight into such methods, extracted retrospectively by Ultra, became a large and growing Allied asset.[26] If Ultra was more timely, but perhaps not sufficiently so to permit evasion, it might nevertheless allow reinforcement of a threatened convoy.

It would be easy to attribute the spectacular Allied successes of May 1943 entirely to Ultra or the arrival of very long-range aircraft, or the combination of these two factors but this would deny the reality of the situation.

After May – the Allies become aggressive

The period that succeeded Dönitz's virtual withdrawal from the mid-Atlantic might seem to be quieter, and certainly as far as Allied convoys were concerned it was. It was not until September that any serious attempts against convoys were made and in the event these did not do very well. Worse still, U-boat losses, which might have been expected to decline steeply with the switch in operating pattern, did no such thing. In May some 40 submarines had been lost to all causes, June saw 17, July 37 and August 25 losses, all against both much reduced activity and very little by way of achievements. This was not just a defeat; it was a rout. As has just been suggested, this period saw not just some form of statistical quirk but a fundamental change in the nature of operations. Two points are worth noting especially: the actions in the Bay of Biscay and the operations, largely in the Central Atlantic, carried out by United States escort carrier (CVE) groups.

Before looking at these two types of operation in greater detail, it is worth considering Dönitz's aims for the period. Acutely conscious of his defeat in the mid-Atlantic, his mind turned in a number of different directions:

- Turning south to the central Atlantic in an attempt to tackle the convoys from the United States to the Mediterranean
- A renewed series of campaigns against the distant theatres ranging from the US east coast and Caribbean to the West African coast, Brazil and even into the Indian ocean
- A materially based strategy which involved improving submarines, most especially in their ability to deal with aircraft.

Not one of these worked out as planned, for a number of different reasons. The complete design for the latter did not occur during the period now being discussed, that is, until the end of August. Further, a proper assessment of its results lies outside the period of this chapter, but it would be true to say that even when fully implemented, these were only partially successful. Thus, for example, the adoption of the schnorkel, while it did a great deal to render the submarine invisible again to aircraft did little or nothing to improve the submarine's operational effectiveness, other than perhaps to prolong its life somewhat. The other two aspects of Dönitz's strategy merit closer examination.

The intention of shifting his attention to other lucrative traffic was understandable, but probably misconceived. Little prior effort had been turned towards the USA–Mediterranean convoys and, as a result, little real understanding of their method of operation had been built up. Their existence, approximate periodicity, and start and end points might be known but, most importantly, precise routes were not. Thus, there was much more of a speculative element to these operations than there had been in the case of the mid-Atlantic operations that had dominated the previous ten months. It was rather as if the clock had been turned back to the middle months of 1941 when Dönitz had first tackled true oceanic warfare and experienced difficulty in finding convoys in the vast space of the Atlantic – but now there was one very important difference.[27] In 1941 when a pack succeeded in finding a convoy, there was at least the consolation that sinkings in some numbers almost invariably followed; this was not the case in 1943 when adequate numbers of escorts, equipped with good sensors and effective weapons, and buttressed by doctrine based on hard experience, backed up by rigorous training and, perhaps most importantly, well supported by aircraft, saw to it that a submarine in the vicinity of a convoy would not have enjoyed a pleasant and productive life.

This was very much borne out by the German experience in June and July of Group *Trutz*, 16 submarines which attempted to make contact with various UGS and GUS convoys, operating initially several hundred miles southwest of the Azores. Despite the absence of timely Ultra information to the Allies to allow effective evasion, no results were achieved by *Trutz* at all.[28] This can almost certainly be attributed to two factors: the amount of sea that needed to be searched by submarines unsupported by any form of other reconnaissance, and the effect of carrier-borne aircraft. It should also be pointed out that at this stage the German cryptographic asset was declining as the Allied realisation that the No. 3 Cipher had been compromised was growing. The absence of near real-time Ultra should not lead to the conclusion that it was of no use at all. Although it was incapable of tracking *Trutz* on a regular basis it still enabled much to be known about its general pattern of operation. The very knowledge that the Germans had carried out this switch at all was of considerable value to the Allies. However, even that had been arrived at with some difficulty. Ralph Erskine gives a good account of the problems of good decryption, but owing to ambiguities in interpretation, on this occasion the Americans, junior in experience, assessed the position correctly.[29] However, the credit for carrying out the tactical and, to some extent, the operational confounding of the German group undoubtedly belongs to the aircraft of the escort carrier *Bogue*. Their presence resulted in general harassment of the submarine group and, more importantly, occasional breaking-up of the German reconnaissance line when it might have led to convoy-sighting. Only one ship of a threatened convoy was sunk in this period and that was caused by a chance sighting by a single submarine on its way to the Caribbean; *Trutz* was not involved. Further, although the activities of *Bogue*'s busy air group did not account for every one, five of the 16 *Trutz* boats were lost. From an Allied point of view, the most important aspect of this undoubted further victory was that Dönitz attempted no further anti-convoy operation until September. This, by itself, was a worthwhile outcome.

His subsequent plan to return to the more distant theatres was largely forced on him by the mid-Atlantic failure. It was not a strategy of truly free choice. Certainly, such distant areas had yielded results in the past and there was no reason why they should not continue to do so in the future as viewed from Berlin in the mid-summer of 1943. However, it is difficult not to feel that Dönitz must have realised that this was, at the very best, a second-best choice. The reasons for this are not hard to find. Although Allied strength by this point was very considerable it was still insufficient to be as strong in all places and at all times as it was in the mid-Atlantic. Nevertheless, if submarines could be deployed to any particular location covertly, it would take some time for the Allies to effect the necessary relocation of assets to that area. By this time, considerable damage might be done. Further assuming the continued capability to relocate to another remote area without Allied foreknowledge, the process might be repeated more than once with the same degree of success. It was true that this could never be regarded as true tonnage war, not only because its absolute results were relatively poor when compared to the glory days of 1941 or 1942–43, but also because of the very low productivity caused by extremely long passage-times.

Nor was this the only problem; there were two particular ones which were interlinked and proved to be the practical undoing of such schemes. Firstly, the whole plan was likely to become unravelled if its general lines were known to the Allies. They did not need to know the mile-by-mile progress of every submarine over every hour of its transit: just the general trend of where it was heading for and when it might reach that area. This would allow the allocation of effort and the putting into effect of certain measures. For example, it was the common practice in the Indian Ocean only to institute convoy when perception of a threat was acute. This does not vitiate the case for convoy but it has to be recognised that convoy has its costs and, although these are more than compensated for in an area such as the North Atlantic or the eastern seaboard of the USA where threat levels were high, the case is not nearly so good when the problem is a sporadic one. Secondly, the Germans could not just decide to go to, say, the Indian Ocean or even somewhere closer, such as the Caribbean, at whim. Such an operation needed a good deal of planning, preparation and, most of all, support. Even the longer-range Type IX submarines had range and endurance limitations and the need for refuelling was almost inevitable. Once past Biscay and the Iberian area, this meant taking on diesel oil at sea either from a surface ship or another submarine. By mid-1943, the former option was very rarely possible, because of the Allied dominance at sea. The latter was, technically at least, the more feasible option. Even for the lesser distances, refuelling could still be very important. As Brian McCue has pointed out, had Dönitz been able not only to maintain but actually increase his U-tanker fleet then the U-boat arm could have been very much more effective.[30] But this dependency was also an Allied opportunity, the key to which was Ultra.

This use of submarine tankers was not new to this period; they had been utilised for some time. Thus, in the year ending in May 1943, as many as 170 refuellings for distant operations had occurred and no less than 220 for those engaged in mid-Atlantic operations.[31] Not one but two specialist designs of submarine – the Types X and XIV – had been built, although it was perfectly feasible for standard submarines to transfer surplus fuel to others.[32] Sinkings of U-tankers had occurred prior to May 1943, but these were incidental rather than deliberate and it is arguable that a deliberate policy of seeking out these submarines could only have been carried out at the expense of convoy protection. In any case, any hypothetical earlier loss of these submarines would probably have been a marginal inconvenience to Dönitz and may have also involved taking a further risk with Ultra security. In any case, for much of the July 1942–May 1943 period Ultra was probably of insufficient timeliness to have permitted the deliberate targeting of U-tankers.

After the end of May 1943, circumstances altered radically. German strategy demanded greater reliance on refuelling; the withdrawal from anti-convoy warfare for a while, and from the main mid-Atlantic routes in particular, permitted the allocation of forces to look specifically for targets such as U-tankers, and Ultra was generally available to guide Allied forces to these desirable victims.

This is indeed what ensued over the summer months. As the Germans observed between May and September, the number of U-tankers declined from 12 to four and 'little could be achieved with such a small number'.[33] As Ralph Erskine has demonstrated Ultra played a considerable part in this significant Allied victory.[34] However, despite cooperation between both the British OIC and its American equivalent, F-211, there was also a degree of tension. This was caused by the combination of the American intention to make the best possible use of the intelligence information, usually by means of carrier-group operations and British fears that too positive and direct conduct of operations would clearly signal to the Germans that their communications were insecure. In any case, not only was the tanker-strength much depleted, but so too was the general stock of seagoing submarines, sometimes by the sinking of boats in the vicinity of refuelling rendezvous, and in this, the efforts of the American CVEs were prominent, with particular credit going to *Bogue*, *Core* and *Santee*.

Nor were all of Dönitz's problems in the operational areas themselves. His new perceptions of how to deal with the aircraft problem in the Bay of Biscay transit area more or less played into Allied hands for a significant period of time. Quite correctly perceiving the aircraft as his greatest problem, his further analyses and the solutions deriving from them did not work to his advantage. Specific misjudgements were made of radar capabilities and the performance of the submarines' own radar warning devices. These led to the effective deprivation of warning by both day and night.[35] A further miscalculation was the decision to keep submarines on the surface as the best way of dealing with aircraft. Although this appeared successful for a while, especially once submarines had started to carry a more substantial anti-aircraft armament and had been instructed to stay in groups, this was ultimately a developmental blind alley. The additional armament adversely affected boats' stability, and also generated a need for extra crew members, whose presence did nothing to aid the already poor living conditions on board. Further, the additional equipment was only likely to be of use for a relatively limited part of a U-boat's operational sea-time. A further problem was that the Allies reacted quickly and well to each shift in German plans. Thus a concentration of aircraft on Bay operations often meant that an aircraft which encountered a submarine did not have to attempt a penetration of its daunting flak alone; it was often possible to call for assistance which might arrive in relatively short order, complicating the flak gunners' task and tending to increase aircraft lethality against submarines. Nor

was this all. As the Germans appreciated this tactic and gave some airborne support to submarines on passage, the Allies reacted by deploy-
ing their own aircraft which might tackle the German ones, as well as
planes such as Beaufighters and Mosquitos, which could not only
perform this task but also, being cannon-armed, attack submarines
directly. Further German difficulty came from the employment of
surface groups into the Bay such as the sloops of the 2nd Escort Group
under the famous Captain F. J. Walker. This put the submarines into
an awkward quandary; stay on the surface to be outgunned by the
surface ships or submerge, making a slower and slightly less certain
outcome occur by way of sonar and underwater weapons. The whole
Bay campaign took on the appearance of a miniature war on its own,
culminating in the deployment by the Germans of Hs293 glider bombs
which successfully accounted for the sloop *Egret* at the end of August.

The other distinguishing feature of this campaign was the employment of Ultra in a number of different ways. Firstly, indications of Bay
departures and arrivals might come from Ultra and not always from
the highest-level cyphers such as Shark, but rather from the more
mundane, but sometimes just as revelatory, indicators, concerning
everyday matters such as port-movements and preparatory operations.
Secondly, the various shifts in perception and policy practised by BdU
were readily monitored by Ultra. Contrary to some views, the activities
carried out in the Bay of Biscay had not started in mid-1943; they had
been carried out for some years before.[36] But their success rate up to
mid-1943 had not been very high. What changed things in 1943 were
two connected factors: the German reading of their defeat in the mid-
Atlantic in May and the measures taken to remedy one perceived
aspect of this; and the Allied ability to devote fresh forces to the Bay.
One of these factors, the first, was completely outside Allied control
but the second stemmed from their quick appreciation of what the
Germans perceived and were doing. As far as intelligence in general
and Ultra in particular is concerned there are analogies with the
convoy battles. At low tactical levels Ultra was of little use, rarely being
timely and accurate enough to influence matters much.[37] However,
matters were different at the operational level where much, if not all,
of the information on which tactics and the allocation of forces was
based came from Ultra.

Looking at the hinge in the Battle of the Atlantic which is represented by late May 1943, the influence of Ultra can be clearly discerned on both sides of that division. Before then, it provided a great
deal of background data and, in retrospect, often made it possible to

forecast medium-term movements of German submarine groups. It was important in this context of hard convoy battles but it could hardly be claimed as decisive, even by its most ardent proponents. This is not a pejorative judgement, merely a reflection of the realities of a series of situations, the causations of any one of which are hard to unravel. To take this further, analysis of the whole period is no easier but what can be done suggests that Ultra's importance changed from time to time within this period and tended to be greater at the higher levels of warfare. From June 1943 onwards, perhaps Ultra gained more import-ance at the operational and tactical levels but this reflected not only the technical success of codebreaking and growing expertise in exploitation, now taking place in more than one centre, but also the differing nature of the operations to which the intelligence product could be applied.

The hinge itself is Dönitz's mid-Atlantic withdrawal of 24 May 1943. As early as 1 June an appreciation that this had occurred was sent from COMINCH to all task forces in the Atlantic as well as the commanders of sea frontiers, and this is a very fast reactive notification to operational level commanders.[38] The importance of this appreciation and of ones like it was that it enabled a number of shifts at the operational level; the realisation that mid-Atlantic convoys were unlikely to be threatened allowed the reinforcement of the direct USA–Mediterranean convoys; more aircraft and ships could be released for operations such as the re-inforcement of the Biscay operations. Thus the Allies moved from pro-tecting convoys, albeit with an ever-growing strength and competence, to an era where submarines became hunted rather than being hunters. Such a series of operational-level changes, it is argued, cumulatively constitute, in automotive terms, a strategic gear-shift. There can be little doubt that the main enabling factor of that shift was Ultra and that this single facet is at least as important as Ultra's contributions to some of the processes at tactical and operational levels.

10
Conclusion: Evaluating Plays and Actors

Ultra did not exist; Ultra was the most important and critical factor of the Second World War; Ultra was nowhere near as significant as it was claimed to be. All of these statements are true and all are false depending on the state of knowledge and attitude of the person making them. They are also to a large extent time-related to the decades from the 1940s to the present day. As perceptions, their truth is unquestionable: as judgements, they deserve critical examination. As this work draws to a close, it is necessary to synthesise the points made in the preceding chapters and draw concluding assessments but it is helpful to understand first that previous evaluations of the subject have not always been illuminating or correct, for a number of reasons. Perhaps the most useful initial approach is to note the chronology of Ultra's historiography and also draw a theatrical analogy.

Ultra as theatre – of demon kings, critics and ephemera

Some years ago, a comparison was made of Ultra's dramatic appearance on the historical scene and its consequent effects on historians and published history in the years following the announcement.[1] The specific analogy then used was of the melodramatic appearance of the demon king, normally achieved by means of a trapdoor lift and accompanied by noise, smoke and other pyrotechnics. In theatres this tends to be shocking and holds the attention for some time but hardly for the rest of the performance. But there was no doubt that Winterbotham with the publication of *The Ultra Secret* achieved a major *coup de théâtre*.[2]

This is not the only useful theatrical analogy that can be deployed. The historian can also be seen as a form of critic, and criticism is the form of literature probably most liable to fashion. Any reasonably frequent attender of the London theatre will have encountered the phenomenon of attending a performance of a work which plays to an audience which either enjoys or is challenged by the work watched and leaves contented or stimulated, or even both. Within a matter of days or weeks, however, the production's run will have come to a premature end killed by critical denunciation. The connection between real worth and that transmitted by critics is not always a well-established one.

The other similarity that might be deployed is that of the ephemeral nature of theatrical work. A play, unlike a film or book or piece such as a painting leaves no direct trace behind – it lives only in the minds of its audience.[3] It might be argued that such a problem is a general one in history. However, where intelligence matters are concerned this effect is normally accentuated, as much material useful to the historian tends to be disposed of prematurely in the interests of security. It is also the case that much contemporary internal communication was of an ephemeral kind either because of security or the limitations of technology, or both. These observations both apply to Ultra.

When these various comparisons of the history of Ultra with theatrical performance are taken together, it is hardly surprising that the myth of Ultra's pervasiveness and significance arose from the mid-1970s onwards. Indeed it might have been more unusual had such a distortion not occurred. However, as a quarter of a century has elapsed since the demon king's first appearance, the time is more than ripe to lay the mythical aspects to rest. That, however, as the first chapter of this work has suggested, is easier to propose than to do.

Evaluating Ultra

Even in a work of this length it is not possible to explore completely one question: what was the significance of one factor in the conduct of one aspect only of the Second World War. Even if it were possible to do so, it would still have to place considerable reliance on the work done by others – or at least make it clear why it should not be used. Here lies one of the basic problems of such an analysis: what can be used and what should be rejected – and why? This is a fundamental question which suggests two yawning traps on either side: repeating work already done or uncritically accepting dubious work. This applies to all types and levels of analysis.

Here a number of different approaches have been taken in attempting to put Ultra in its proper place. These can be classified in four ways:

- Top down
- Bottom up
- Temporal
- Specific themes.

Sometimes these overlap or are combined. This is not sloppy thinking, but rather a reflection of the way in which these different vistas of the problem are mutually connected.

Top down: contexts

This approach emphasises not just that Ultra existed in a single context but that it operated in a series of multiple and simultaneous contexts. Perhaps the simplest to comprehend is that of signals intelligence.[4] Even in this it is evident that, important as Ultra was, it was not the only contributor to the Allied Sigint effort. Indeed, and bringing in an overlap with other analyses at an early point, it was not always available (temporal) nor of utility (thematic). The connection between intelligence and the other contexts – such as the economic – is often less easy to see and, even making the most generous interpretation possible, is almost certainly because it was more tenuous rather than less observable. The problem of producing a balanced assessment of Ultra is made worse by the concentration of five decades of literature on certain aspects of the history at the expense of others. Thus the relative neglect of the economic content of the Battle has led to both a diminished understanding of that dimension and also to a tendency to undervalue its importance.

One of the more obvious contexts is that of the conduct of the Battle at sea, broadly at the operational and strategic levels. Here some would see Ultra's greatest contribution having occurred. But even here some important caveats have to be entered.[5] Ultra's strengths, when operating at its best, might be seen in three different fields – sometimes mutually connecting, sometimes not. Firstly, it might provide a considerable degree of background knowledge of submarine total order of battle, operating methods and specific techniques. Secondly, information might be available which was good enough to suggest to a commander at sea the scale of deployment of German submarines that were likely to be encountered during a convoy's passage. Lastly, and most specifically, the information might be sufficiently accurate and timely enough to permit either evasion of submarine concentrations or else reinforcement of a threatened convoy. In even these three instances of an operationally relevant context it is not at all certain whether either a sound method can be devised to evaluate Ultra beyond question, or whether sufficient data has survived to support such a hypothetical method. The most reliable statement that can be made is that the great image of all convoys during the war effortlessly gliding round huge submarine concentrations guided by the unseen hand of Ultra is false.

Bottom up: detailed analyses

Going back to basics in looking at the Battle of the Atlantic tends properly to concentrate on events at the tactical level at sea. Here the important questions tend to be of the sort: what efforts did the enemy put into a given convoy battle, for how long, what was achieved and what did this cost Dönitz and his submarines?[6] Certainly this makes clearer the nature of the battles and their salient characteristics, as well as gaining a lucid insight as to how such struggles changed, not only between the periods of the two case-studies but also within them. In particular this makes it rather more evident why a climactic point was reached towards the end of May 1943 than has often been apparent in the past. In the two case-studies here it is evident that Ultra played a part, both in the three aspects of the operational nature mentioned in the last section and in reaching the particular outcomes that occurred. Thus, although it would be wrong to consider Ultra as the sole factor of importance in either case, it would be equally erroneous to write it out altogether.

Indeed in the second instance, concerning the events which followed the German May 1943 collapse, Ultra's significance was probably greater than it had been beforehand and now it was arguably operating at the strategic rather than just the operational and tactical levels.[7] Analyses of these types also tend to indicate such points as the relative difficulty of submarines finding, closing and attacking convoys under different circumstances and what causes these difficulties. Here again, it may be possible to say where Ultra may be of most use and when perhaps its utility was of a lesser order.

Time and themes

Yet another way of looking analytically at Ultra is by means of time periods. This may pervade the two previous forms of assessment. The point has already been made that there were times when Ultra was either unavailable or of little utility. When the whole battle of the Atlantic is examined it is probable that on a strict month-by-month basis, that is, without allocating any differential value of importance to different periods, it is probable that the 'not available or not as useful' periods may exceed their opposites. The problem with this approach is twofold: the question (where utility is involved) of judgement and different significance at different levels. Availability is relatively easy to determine but utility is open to differing interpretations. It might be argued that in the first six months of 1942 (when, incidentally, Ultra was not generally available) Ultra would have been of little use in any case, because submarines in general were engaged in independent operations, not pack ones. Somewhat more contentious is the much longer period from June 1943 until the end of the war when concerted actions against convoys were rare. On analysing utility using different levels it is fairly clear that Ultra was often produced with such delays that its main use was in building a general picture of the U-boat fleet, its size and methods. When this happened, it was of little value for operational and tactical direction. Taking all these factors into consideration, it is difficult to avoid the conclusion measured against the whole timespan of the war, that the combined product of Ultra's availability and use was patchy rather than consistent. This is not a criticism of those devising and using this intelligence product, rather a reflection of the realities of war.

A further approach would be to consider assessment in terms of specific themes. This is distinct from the consideration above of broader contexts above. Perhaps the greatest drawback here is that one of the potentially most interesting themes is all but inaccessible: that of Ultra's influence on decision-makers. The negatives are easy to amass; it is known that none of the seagoing commanders in this period had such knowledge. It is also a commonplace that no permanent record exists recording decisions in juxtaposition with the direct Ultra information, or indeed any information obviously derived from it. In any case, unless a smoking gun exists in which the decision-maker said 'Because of this piece of Ultra, I did A rather than B' it is dubious to attribute too much credit to such a source, no matter how ingenious or dramatic. On the other hand, the decision to switch the emphasis of strategy and the allocation of resources in the summer of 1943 from convoy defence to more aggressive antisubmarine operations may have been arrived at in any case, but Ultra and other intelligence probably provided decision-makers with a degree of confidence in their choices that would otherwise have been absent.

Combining the approaches

The best way out of this analytical maze almost certainly lies in syn-
thesising all the analytical approaches and extracting the useful
common and recurring themes. The first of these has to be the inter-
mittency of both Ultra availability and the circumstances in which it
was likely to be of greatest use. There is a qualitative aspect to the
first of these concerning timeliness. From the viewpoint of both cryptographic accretion and providing a background picture of German
strength and operational methods, there was virtually no practical
limit to how long it took to break German signals. But this did not
apply to information which was likely to be of tactical use – here,
timeliness was all.

The question of when even timely Ultra might be of use is probably
easier to answer. There are very considerable periods when a notional
timely reading of German signals would have been of very little tactical
value – at least in the central and critical context of convoy warfare.
These include:

- The period from the outbreak of war up to the beginning of 1941,
  when group attacks on convoys were relatively rare (15 months)
- The first half of 1942, when most attacks were made against independent shipping on the US east coast (6 months)
- The period after May 1943 when convoy warfare was rare
  (24 months)

When added together, these represent a period of about two-thirds
of the war in which available Ultra would have been of almost no
tactical significance for convoy defence. In order to propose Ultra as
the critical factor for the remaining periods – all of 1941 and the
year from mid-1942 to mid-1943 – it would have to be argued
further that these periods were not only critical but also more – and
very much more – critical than the others. This point might be
argued for the former period but is less easy to support for the latter
when the other Allied advantages were growing, and virtually all
underlying trends were going in their favour. Using the somewhat
difficult concept of criticality, it is certainly easier to support the
premise that 1941 was more critical. This was because the British,
then largely on their own, were very heavily stretched and the eventual salvation achieved largely in American shipyards was certain in
neither Alliance nor industrial terms. This might have represented
the Germans' – and in particular Dönitz' – best chance to ensure an

approach to victory. However, this was thwarted by a combination of factors, presented chronologically:

- In the spring, the German reaction to British pressure of moving submarine operations westward
- Their consequent difficulty in locating convoys in ocean waters with minimal outside support
- A further compounding of their problems caused by deliberate evasive convoy-routeing, made possible in part by Ultra
- The redeployment of considerable submarine forces to theatres other than the Atlantic in the last part of the year.[8]

For part of the case-study periods, too, Ultra was also not available or sometimes so only with delays rendering it tactically useless. There were undoubtedly times during the war when convoy warfare was either more difficult or more critical than at other times, but it would be difficult to suggest that both of the case-study periods were of such high criticality, thereby accentuating the value of any of the operative factors of the time and, especially, Ultra.

Perhaps the difficult matter of assessing comparative criticality at the tactical and operational levels does not always provide the best guide to the value of Ultra, in any case. A good example of this would be not so much the German submarine defeat of May 1943 but the nature of the operations in the succeeding months. Here a distinct change in emphasis was made, moving more resources to the attack on submarines away from the direct vicinity of shipping rather than the direct defence of convoys. Although no smoking-gun evidence can be found associating intelligence in general and Ultra in particular with this change in strategic gear it is very difficult to see how it could have been done without the assurance that large-scale attacks on convoys were improbable in the near-term.[9]

Moving even further away from the struggle round convoys was the neutralisation of the potential threat from the new-technology submarines late in the war. This was clearly not a tactical-level problem and the solution was implemented largely by aircraft which hardly ever saw the sea. Alerted by signals intelligence from a less obvious source – the communications between the Japanese embassy in Berlin and Tokyo – it became possible to delay both production and deployment of these dangerous boats.

In the totality of antisubmarine warfare, there is a clear progression here – from fighting submarines where they pose the greatest problem, to tackling them elsewhere at sea, to disposing of their threat before operational deployment. This is good war-fighting practice and it is clear that Ultra played an important part in all these struggles and as an enabling factor of this benevolent progression.

One test that might be applied in assessing the significance of Ultra is the counterfactual one of looking at the situation had Ultra not been available at all. A broad assessment would have been that the Battle of the Atlantic would have been harder and costlier. Conjecturally, the new-technology submarines might have been deployed, although not necessarily in the numbers desired by the Germans. It is also possible that the war would have lasted longer. However, it is difficult to suggest that the Allied economic preponderance would not have led to eventual victory. As Sir Harry Hinsley once suggested, one consequence might have been the first deployment of atomic weapons against Germany rather than Japan.[10] But such projections are very difficult to sustain, as changing one factor might very quickly lead to a chain of events quite different from that which occurred. It also has to be remembered that the Battle of the Atlantic was but one, albeit a very important, part of the world war.

Final assessment

One facet of analysing war which is apparent from the preceding chapters is the futility of attempting to discover 'the most important factor'. It is similarly specious to produce rankings of many steps as three points argue against producing such neat and superficially plausible classifications:

- The complexity of the Battle of the Atlantic as a whole
- The difficulty of producing a unified method of ranking such disparate fields as tactical antisubmarine warfare, intelligence and economics
- Even were the ranking method to be feasible, the inadequacy of the surviving data.

It is probable that no more can be done than to produce such a vague and probably unsatisfying classification such as 'less important' or 'more important'. Against such a test it would certainly be reasonable to put Ultra (especially when combined with other intelligence sources and products) into the latter category.

Advancing from importance to criticality, in which a stricter if still imprecisely defined test should be used, it is difficult for the reasons given in this book as a whole and outlined above in this chapter to sustain the argument that Ultra was critical at a sufficient number of levels and times to say that it was a factor of great, far less ubiquitous, criticality. This in no way denies either utility or importance. What it does, however, is suggest most strongly that many of the claims made for the significance of Ultra over the last quarter of a century are over-drawn at best and specious at worst.

Despite this somewhat downbeat conclusion, it is suggested that there is still much useful work that might be done in uncovering the employment of Ultra in the Battle of the Atlantic and how it was applied specifically at the levels of grand strategy and military strategy, as well as at the operational and tactical levels. Such studies ought to be works of substance rather than dramatic conclusion, displaying solid work situating the subject in the proper contexts. This chapter started with an extended metaphor from the field of drama. To draw both chapter and book to a close, let us return to the theatrical comparison. It is clear that Ultra was no mere member of a chorus but neither was it a star shining above all others. Indeed such a concept in the context of the Battle of the Atlantic is probably thoroughly unhelpful: there were spear-carriers and character actors, but probably no stars. Perhaps an even more helpful analogy in this context might be that of a first-rate repertory company performing a season of Shakespeare works, a mixed bag of comedies and tragedies. Further, the best parts (Hamlet and King Lear, Lady Macbeth and Cleopatra) are not always taken by the same leading players but are shared out among the more adept actors. What is clear is that the previous representation of Ultra as a demon king – either *diabolus* or *deus ex machina* – is a gross misrepresentation which, after 25 years, deserves to be put thoroughly and finally to rest.

Notes

1 The World War and the Atlantic Campaign

1. There were also a number of Italian submarines which played a subsidiary part until 1943.
2. See p. 5 below.
3. It is an interesting reflection of the time that a common mock definition of strategy was 'tactics talked through a brass hat', in other words setting the definition by personal status rather than functionally. However, by 1957 when the first of a number of similarly titled volumes appeared, the term 'grand strategy' at least was reasonably well known.
4. Directorate of Naval Staff Duties, *The Fundamentals of British Maritime Doctrine* (London, HMSO, 1995), 42–3, 47.
5. See p. 2 above on human scales.
6. Here were also some Japanese submarines which reached the Atlantic, but only to transport relatively small quantities of scarce raw materials.
7. See Alberto Santoni, 'The Italian Submarine Campaign', in Howarth and Law (eds), *The Battle of the Atlantic 1939–1945: The 50th Anniversary International Naval Conference* (London, Greenhill Books, 1994), Chapter 18.
8. Paul Sutcliffe has suggested privately that when employed in the less demanding areas, they were no less competent than the Germans carrying out similar tasks.
9. A relatively rare example of such a perspective in English is that of N. M. Naumov, 'The Soviet View', in Howarth and Law, 554–66, although this is largely a review of the Soviet-era historiography of the Battle.
10. Because of the combined problems of weather, long daylight hours in summer (which favoured German aircraft particularly) and enemy activity, most Arctic convoys took place in the winter.
11. Attention might also be drawn to the relative quantities of material reaching the USSR by other routes such as the Soviet Far East and through the Persian Gulf route.
12. It is approximately 600 miles from Cape Sable to Cape Race, a considerable proportion of the cross-Atlantic distance.
13. See William Glover 'Manning and Training the Allied Navies', in Howarth and Law, Chapter 10 and David Zimmerman, *The Great Naval Battle of Ottawa* (Toronto, University of Toronto Press, 1989). The wartime/peacetime expansion ratio of the RCN was in the order of 50:1, well above any of the other significant maritime nations. Sir Peter Gretton, in his foreword to Marc Milner, *North Atlantic Run: the Royal Canadian Navy and the Battle for the Convoys* (Toronto, University of Toronto Press, 1985).
14. The battleship *Tirpitz* only entered service after the outbreak of war but her existence was known about from the outset.
15. PRO ADM 234/322 BR1736(3/50), Battle summary No. 5, Chase and Sinking of German Battleship Bismarck, 23–27 May 1941.

16. S. W. Roskill, *The War at Sea* (London, HMSO, 1961), Volume III, Part 2, Appendix ZZ Table I.

17. See E. N. Poland, *The Torpedomen* (1993, no place or publisher given), especially Chapters 7, 8 and 10.

18. Less than 3 million tons to the submarines' 14 million.

19. PRO ADM 234/579, Defeat of the Enemy Attack on Shipping (hereafter Barley and Waters), Volume 1B, Plan 43 gives figures by quarter for numbers of ships sunk in British home waters and the North Atlantic (without distinguishing the two areas).

20. Some accounts of the German advances on the Eastern Front make an oceanic analogy about progress on the featureless steppe.

21. *Shorter Oxford English Dictionary* (Oxford, Oxford University Press, 1975), 1174. However, it does include the sea meaning, perhaps making the point that it was the advent of steam propulsion which allowed the setting of non-weather-determined courses and thus introducing the concept to shipping of the shortest route also being the fastest.

22. *The Fundamentals of British Maritime Doctrine*, 235.

23. See above, p. 27.

24. Convoy battles, especially latterly, tended to involve both sea and air forces on one, or sometimes even both, sides.

25. See Chapter 3 for a fuller treatment.

26. Preceding by a short head the actions in the Pacific War – many of which took place in any case fairly close to land. A further post-Cold War reflection might be that oceanic warfare was not so much an advance as a high-water mark, with the stress from the 1990s onwards being on expeditionary warfare in littoral areas – for those nations whose strategic vision is that far advanced.

27. Howarth and Law, 596–601.

28. A different viewpoint based on the chronology of the secondary literature is given in W. J. R. Gardner, 'An Allied Perspective', in Howarth and Law, 528–32.

29. Jürgen Rohwer, *The Critical Convoy Battles of March 1943: the Battle for HX229/SC122* (Shepperton, Ian Allan, 1977); Martin Middlebrook, *Convoy: the Battle for Convoys SC122 and HX229* (London, Allen Lane, 1976); David Syrett, 'Prelude to Victory: the Battle for Convoy HX231, 4–7 April 1943', in *Historical Research*, Vol. 70, No. 1 (February 1997), 99–109.

30. No examples are known to this author.

31. Michael Gannon, *Operation Drumbeat: the Dramatic True Story of Germany's First U-boat Attacks along the American Coast in World War II* (New York, Harper Perennial, 1991) and the same author's *Black May: the Epic Story of the Allies' Defeat of the German U-boats in May 1943* (New York, HarperCollins, 1998).

32. Robert Stern, *Type VII U-Boats* (London, Arms and Armour, 1991); Willem Hackman, *Seek and Strike: Sonar, Anti-submarine Warfare and the Royal Navy 1914–1954*, (London, HMSO, 1984); Richard Baker, *The Terror of Tobermory: Vice-Admiral Sir Gilbert Stephenson KBE, CBE, CMG* (London, W. H. Allen, 1972).

33. S. W. Roskill, *The War at Sea* (London, HMSO, 1954–61); S. E. Morison, *History of United States Naval Operations in World War II* (Boston, Little,

Brown, 1947–62); John Terraine, *Business in Great Waters: the U-Boat Wars 1916–1945* (London, Leo Cooper, 1989); and Dan Van der Vat, *The Atlantic Campaign* (London, Hodder and Stoughton, 1988) are all examples. General surveys may also be approached through aggregation of specialised studies, for example, Howarth and Law.

34. A man wandering in a street at night with his eyes fixed firmly on the ground is asked what he is doing. 'I have lost my wallet,' he replies. He is further asked if this place, under the lamppost, is where the wallet was lost. 'No' he responds, 'but this is where the light is.'

35. C. B. A. Behrens, *Merchant Shipping and the Demands of War* (London, HMSO, 1955) and Kevin Smith, *Conflict over Convoys: Anglo-American Logistics Diplomacy in the Second World War* (Cambridge, Cambridge University Press, 1996) are separated by some 40 years with very little of substance in between.

36. Marc Milner, 'The Battle of the Atlantic' in *The Journal of Strategic Studies* (March 1990), 45–66.

37. Not just because of Ultra but for many other reasons, as this work will bring out.

38. Donald McLachlan, *Room 39: Naval Intelligence in Action 1939–1945* (London, Weidenfeld and Nicolson, 1968). This was not the only instance but it was by far the most blatant.

39. Roskill, *The War at Sea*, Vol. II, 208. Roskill's wartime knowledge was indisputable as he had served as Deputy Director of Naval Intelligence.

40. F. W. Winterbotham, *The Ultra Secret* (London, Weidenfeld and Nicolson, 1974). Winterbotham was not an assiduous researcher and had little to do with the Battle of the Atlantic but the work's importance lies in opening the gates to the historical study of Ultra.

41. For examples, see Chapter 8, pp. 171–5: 'The million ton myth'.

42. F. H. Hinsley *et al*, *British Intelligence in the Second World War* (London, HMSO, 1979–88), 3 volumes in 4. There were further volumes but these are not germane to the subject under study.

43. Alluded to in Gannon, *Black May,* 55 and W. J. R. Gardner, 'The Battle of the Atlantic, 1941 – the First Turning Point?' in Geoffrey Till (ed), *Seapower: Theory and Practice* (Ilford, Frank Cass, 1994), 121.

44. It is invidious to select, but the work of Jürgen Rohwer, Ralph Erskine and David Syrett deserves especially to be noted.

2   Chronology, Time and Measurement

1. 'Chronology n. (pl. -ies) 1 science of determining dates. 2 a arrangement of events etc. in order of occurrence. b table or document displaying this. (Greek khronos time, *-logy).' Definition in the *Pocket Oxford Dictionary* 1994.

2. S. W. Roskill, *The War at Sea* (London, HMSO, 1954–61), 3 volumes in 4, and S. E. Morison, *History of United States Naval Operations in World War II* (Boston, Little, Brown, 1947–1962) (especially, vols I and X).

3. J. Rohwer and G. Hummlechen, *Chronology of the War at Sea: The Naval History of World War Two,* (London, Greenhill Books, 1992).

4. PRO ADM 234/578 and /579 Defeat of the Enemy attack on Shipping (hereafter Barley and Waters) (now published in an edited single volume edition,

1998, the Navy Records Society). Professor Rohwer's similar classification has appeared in a number of places, including *Les Marines de Guerre du Dreadnought au Nucléaire* (Chateau de Vincennes, Service historique de la Marine, 1988), 297–330. Barley and Waters identify specific dates whereas Rohwer uses months; the latter approach is adopted here.

5. The notion that there was no intention to have a convoy system (as occurred during much of the First World War) cannot be supported, but resources were very scarce.

6. There was a bias towards independents at the beginning of the period and convoy shipping towards the end.

7. However, in reality, the British accession of tonnage from the occupied countries more than cancelled losses to the actual submarine fleet. See Chapter 3.

8. Dealt with more fully in Chapter 8.

9. See also Chapter 8, note 16.

10. The term 'Allied' might be questioned at this point in the war. See Chapter 8, pp. 146–7 for a justification of its use.

11. There is division among historians about the underlying reasons for this. Much of what is written centres on the office and personality of the American Chief of Naval Operations, Admiral Ernest King. In general terms, British historians excoriate King while most Americans support him. See Michael Gannon, *Operation Drumbeat: the Dramatic True Story of Germany's First U-boat Attacks along the American Coast in World War II* (New York, Harper Perennial, 1991) and Robert W. Love, Jr, 'The US Navy and Operation Roll of Drums, 1942', in Timothy J. Runyan and Jan M. Copes (eds), *To Die Gallantly: the Battle of the Atlantic* (Boulder, Colorado, Westview Press, 1994), 95–120.

12. Described and analysed fully in Chapter 9.

13. The last victim of the Battle of the Atlantic, the *Avondale Park*, was sunk on 7 May by a new-generation submarine, one of only three attributed to the coastal Type XXIII. The larger Type XXI, intended for oceanic warfare, was not credited with a single success.

14. See Chapter 3.

15. Some aspects of operational research and the Battle of the Atlantic are described in Chapter 6.

16. Described and analysed in greater detail in Chapter 8.

17. This is a slightly dubious example for two reasons. Firstly, because it is not very clear when the Germans first took the possibility of American entry seriously and their subsequent actions were largely intended to keep her out of the war. Secondly, even when America had become a full combatant, her industrial capacity was underestimated for a long time by the Germans.

18. Strictly speaking the replacement rate, which encompasses accession other than building and losses other than sinking by enemy action. In practical terms, however, for much of the war, building and sinking were directly opposed. See Chapter 3.

19. Surface escorts tended to have weapons systems whose ranges were much less than their sensors. The aircraft's much greater speed was an excellent solution to this problem. See also Chapter 5.

20. There is an underlying philosophical and metaphysical point as to what a fact is, but this is taken no account of here. However, the reliability of apparently factual information is a different matter and receives some attention.
21. Andrew Gordon, *The Rules of the Game: Jutland and British Naval Command*, (London, John Murray, 1996), 603–19.
22. In this instance 'operational' refers to operations of war rather than, as elsewhere in this book, as a level of war and distinguishes it from such fields of naval history as policy and administration.
23. The leading examples of these must be the convoy monographs of Professor Syrett. See Bibliography for details of some of these.
24. G. R. Elton, *The Practice of History* (London, Fontana, 1967), 152–3.
25. See Chapter 5, p. 80–2, 'Navigation in the 1940s' for more detail on the reasons for this. For aircraft, it was likely to be worse. See, for example, C. H. Waddington, *OR in World War 2: Operational Research against the U-boat* (London, Elek Science, 1973), Chapter 4.

3   The Economic Context

1. Philip Pugh, *The Cost of Seapower: the Influence of Money on Naval Affairs from 1815 to the Present Day* (London, Conway Maritime Press, 1986), 3.
2. For the latter, see Norman Rich, *Hitler's War Aims: the Establishment of the New Order* (New York, Norton, 1974).
3. Pugh, 9–19. This work is largely related to the procurement of ships and their weapon systems but his exposition of factors is still relevant.
4. Certain aspects of this reduction actually had adverse effects on efficiency. Kevin Smith, *Conflict over Convoys: Anglo-American Logistics Diplomacy in the Second World War* (Cambridge, Cambridge University Press, 1996), 35.
5. This was, of course, a gradual rather than an instant process. Further, it was not self-regulating, needing continual adjustment.
6. Geoffrey Till in Stephen Howarth and Derek Law (eds), *The Battle of the Atlantic 1939–1945: the 50th Anniversary International Naval Conference* (London, Greenhill Books, 1994), 586.
7. A good overview of all main participants is given by Richard Overy in *Why the Allies Won* (London, Jonathan Cape, 1995), Chapter 6.
8. While it is true that many other industrial plants, especially in the USA, were physically larger, this was usually because of economic desirability rather than manufacturing necessity. It is not generally possible to produce what is still mankind's largest mobile artefact in a backstreet toolshop.
9. There is no specific consideration of manpower in this chapter but this, too, is a likely constraint and likely to be the greater the more thoroughly the population is mobilised, in one form or another, for war.
10. Frederic C. Lane, *Ships for Victory: a History of Shipbuilding under the US Maritime Commission in World War II* (Baltimore, Maryland, Johns Hopkins University Press, 1951), 7.
11. Martin Doughty, *Merchant Shipping and War: a Study in Defence Planning* (London, Royal Historical Society, 1982), 176.
12. Although most general cargo ships had limited ballast tankage, allowing the use of sea water, these were generally for trimming purposes only. Thus

some form of solid ballast had to be embarked, occupying time. Ships might also have to be held awaiting the next outbound convoy.

13. It has sometimes been asserted that, despite known British inefficiencies, more effective shipping was lost because of this by the Americans. Marc Milner, 'The Battle of the Atlantic', *The Journal of Strategic Studies* (March 1990), 52.

14. Thomas Wilson, *Churchill and the Prof* (London, Cassell, 1995), 118.

15. C. B. A. Behrens, *Merchant Shipping and the Demands of War* (London, HMSO, 1955), 11. This work is recommended in any case for a fuller understanding of the problems of shipping. It has been claimed, notably by Kevin Smith, that some revision of Behrens' work is overdue. Certainly it is worth noting that his book *Conflict over Convoys* is one of the very few, if not the only one, to revisit this important subject in over 40 years. On the point made here, see Smith 48, 59.

16. C. I. Savage, *Inland Transport* (London, HMSO, 1957) and Doughty, 166, 7.

17. It can be argued that it bore most heavily on the Japanese.

18. Kevin Smith's *Conflict over Convoys* is a rare example of attention being turned to this topic.

19. A good illustrative example lies in the problems confronting chiefs of staff of two countries over Indian Ocean or Pacific strategies in the east. H. P. Willmott, *Grave of a Dozen Schemes: British Naval Planning and the War against Japan, 1943–1945* (Annapolis, MD; Naval Institute Press, 1996).

20. Pugh in Howarth and Law, 33.

21. See Behrens, Chapter V, especially 102.

22. There were also drawbacks. The resultant routes tended to be longer, thus absorbing more shipping, and some commodities had to be brought from further afield. In particular, the Mediterranean was all but closed to shipping. See Smith, 29–30.

23. Derived from the various tables in S. W. Roskill, *The War at Sea* (London, HMSO, 1954–61), 3 vols in 4.

24. For example in tonnage, there are two systems in general use: deadweight tons (weight that the ship can carry), and gross and net register tons which are actually a volumetric measurement.

25. Amalgamating data from Adams in Howarth and Law, 160, Table 3 and Behrens, Appendix VIII.

26. Behrens, Appendix VIII.

27. Lane, 7.

28. ADM 234/579, Defeat of the Enemy Attack on Shipping (hereafter Barley and Waters), Volume 1B Plan 15.

29. Doughty, 191.

30. As an example, after the Allies began using Antwerp in late 1944, it came under considerable bombardment from V-1 and V-2 rockets. Their intended target was the docks through which much Allied supply flowed. But despite delivering 150 V-1s and 152 V-2s to the port area, only two large cargo ships were sunk and there was little overall effect on the port. L. F. Ellis and A. E. Warhurst, *Victory in the West: the Defeat of Germany* (London, HMSO, 1968), 235.

31. Philip Pugh in Howarth and Law, 31 argues that if the 1940–41 exchange rate (number of merchant ships sunk per U-boats lost) had been maintained

until June 1943, the proportionate loss with the growth of the submarine fleet would have wiped out the Allied merchant fleet. However, the exchange rate tends to be – for warfare purposes – an artificial construct, as is discussed further in Chapter 9.

32. This important traffic is referred to throughout the literature as the 'French Coal Trade', a nomenclature which obscures its strategic significance.

33. PRO ADM137/1392, War History Case HS1392; Paul Halpern, *A Naval History of World War I* (Annapolis, Maryland, Naval Institute Press, 1994), 352.

34. John Ellis, *Brute Force: Allied Strategy and Tactics in the Second World War* (London, André Deutsch, 1990), 160 and Clive Ponting, *Armageddon: the Second World War* (London, Sinclair-Stevenson, 1995), 121.

35. Brooke, who was the British Chief of the Imperial General Staff, said this at the Casablanca conference in January 1943. Quoted, among other places, in Behrens, 328, where it is used as a chapter heading.

36. A good example of this was the logistic operations associated with the land campaigns in France then the Low Countries from the summer of 1944 onwards. Ingenious and prodigious as were the efforts to make Mulberry harbours and other improvised port facilities work, their performance could not approach the efficiency of a large-scale deep-water port. This problem became an even greater logistical nightmare as the Allies made progress on the ground, taking themselves ever further from the entry ports for their supplies.

37. Milner, 'Battle of the Atlantic', 52.

38. It is certainly the case that knowledge and inference as to the enemy's intentions did much to allow the sense of confidence at high levels that formed a background to gambles involving shipping such as Operation Torch – the invasion of northwest Africa – a point made by Kevin Smith. Private communication, 6 July 1998.

39. At either end of the supply curve, there were two traps into which Britain might fall. Doing badly, because of Dönitz, at one end and doing too well and thus suffering the withdrawal of large-scale American support, at the other, a position which was enthusiastically espoused by such as General B. B. Somervell, the American head of the Army Service Force, who was keen to utilise as much shipping as possible. Again, this point is well made by Kevin Smith.

40. C. I. Savage, *Inland Transport* (London, HMSO, 1957); D. J. Payton Smith, *Oil* (London, HMSO, 1971); and M. M. Postan, D. Hay and J. D. Scott, *Design and Development of Weapons* (London, HMSO, 1964).

41. PRO CAB86/1.

42. For an account of this committee, see Gardner, 'An Allied Perspective', in Howarth and Law, 522–4.

43. Ellis, *Brute Force*, 160 fn.

44. This is a theme which runs throughout Clay Blair, *Hitler's U-Boat War: the Hunters, 1939–1942* (New York, Random House, 1996).

45. PRO ADM 234/67 The U-boat War in the Atlantic (hereafter Hessler) II, 2 quoting PG32615, page 39.

46. There were three months (March, June and November 1942) when the figure from all causes – not just submarines – was exceeded worldwide but

the first two of these reflect initial Japanese successes in the eastern theatre and all three took place after American entry into the war. Figures are from tabular data in Roskill's *War at Sea*.

47. This is very much a counterfactual point. Such was the global reach and considerable size of the American shipping commitments that such a large-scale reallocation of output solely to the Atlantic would seem unlikely in policy terms. On the other hand, it is similarly difficult to see the European theatre, both actual and potential, at any one time being cast totally adrift, especially in the light of the considerable investment of American resources into that area, even before June 1944.

48. As just one example of this, profligate use of the amounts of additional shipping might have degraded the Allied effort, either through gross inefficiency of use or through loss to the enemy. The particular way in which this limit might have been reached could have been through a consequent shortage of competent merchant seamen.

49. Pugh, 120.

50. W. J. R. Gardner; *Anti-submarine Warfare* (London, Brassey's, 1996), Chapter 4, 'The Spectrum of ASW'.

51. It is notable that Pugh's work, which is probably the most thorough study of the subject, makes no attempt to consider warfare areas either in chapter headings or index. Perhaps a more surprising omission is opportunity cost.

52. Both the precise form of words and even the speaker are not clear, alternatives being given as either Göring or Goebbels.

53. The complement of divisions varied with type and period of the war.

54. Roskill, *The War at Sea* (London, HMSO, 1956), II, 351.

55. See 62–4 (German perspective on tying down).

56. Being defined, somewhat tongue in cheek, as deciding what to do, then producing a numerate study to prove that it is the right thing to do.

57. PRO ADM 234/68 The German U-boat War in the Atlantic (hereafter Hessler), III, 62–3 quoting BdU KTB of 15 June 1944. An earlier and fuller account of the problems with the numerate rationale is given by W. J. R. Gardner (cited as John R. Gardner) in *Les Marines de Guerre du Dreadnought au Nucléaire* (Chateau de Vincennes, Service historique de la Marine, 1988), 341–2.

58. S. G. Gorshkov, *The Sea Power of the State* (Annapolis, Maryland, Naval Institute Press, 1979), 120.

4 A German Perspective

1. A good example of over-assessment is the German perception of sinking more tonnage than it had – on Gibraltar convoys especially; see Chapter 8, pp. 157, 175. A rare example of the latter is the British failure to perceive that they had attained an advantage over the U-boat force in the spring of 1941. W. J. R. Gardner, 'The Battle of the Atlantic, 1941 – the First Turning Point?' in Geoffrey Till (ed.), *Seapower: Theory and Practice*, (Ilford, Frank Cass, 1994), 109–13.

2. See Chapter 1, p. 14.

3. Quality and qualities are used in the sense of both judging the worth of characteristics and the characteristics themselves.

4. Alan Bullock's duo-biography *Hitler and Stalin: Parallel Lives* (London, BCA, 1991), lists several pages of books in different languages, only one of which is explicitly naval, that of Jost Düllfer. In the week when this passage was drafted a book was reviewed claiming that the childhood meeting of Hitler and Wittgenstein bore a large responsibility for the former's subsequent anti-Semitism and a leading newspaper claimed that Hitler had had an affair with a member of the Wagner family. These stories are both unimportant to this account but indicate the continuing interest in the man. George Steiner has also noted not only the continuing interest in Hitler but, possibly even its growth. *Observer*, 12 July 1998, Review Section, 17.

5. In practical terms he thought himself superior as most of the generals, being members of the general staff, he thought unacquainted with the front-line practicalities of warfare.

6. Anon, *Fuehrer Conferences on Naval Affairs 1939–1945* (London, Greenhill Books, 1990).

7. For a concise discussion of this, see Louis L. Snyder, *Encyclopedia of the Third Reich* (London, Blandford, 1989), 106. A brief contemporary prewar American impression of it is in John Gunther, *Inside Europe* (London, Hamish Hamilton, 1936) 25–6.

8. According to Keith W. Bird in his essay on Raeder in Stephen Howarth (ed.), *Men of War: Great Naval Leaders of World War II* (London, Weidenfeld and Nicolson, 1992, 51, 10 battleships, four aircraft carriers, 15 *Panzerschiffe* (normally called pocket battleships in English), five heavy cruisers, 68 destroyers and 249 U-boats were planned for 1948.

9. See Chapter 8, p. 150. The first submarine arrived in the Mediterranean in September 1941. By the end of the year some 21 U-boats were there and they had sunk one aircraft-carrier, one battleship and a cruiser among others. Their subsequent achievements were to tail off somewhat. PRO ADM 234/578, Defeat of the Enemy Attack on Shipping (hereafter Barley and Waters), Volume 1A, Appendix 8 and Jürgen Rohwer, *Axis Submarine Successes 1939–1945* (Cambridge, Patrick Stephens, 1983, 227–9.

10. This is very much the view of Keith Bird in Howarth, 72. Perhaps he is right, but other things stood between Raeder and his sufficient, balanced and technologically advanced fleet, particularly material resources, the bureaucratic inefficiency of the Third Reich and a strategic culture centred on land-based forces.

11. Initially his duties were confined purely to the operational, but as his reputation and influence grew he was able to deal with other matters too. The submarines which operated later in North Norway and the Mediterranean came under separate operational command.

12. Effective control was practised by his previous chief of staff, Eberhardt Godt.

13. Dönitz produced memoirs, available in English as *Ten Years and Twenty Days* (London, Greenhill Books, 1990) and there is also a biography in English: Peter Padfield; *Dönitz, the last Führer: Portrait of a Nazi War Leader* (London, Victor Gollancz, 1984). The former is both selective and self-serving, whilst the latter is more balanced.

14. For Dönitz's effect on them, see Eric C. Rust; *Naval Officers under Hitler: the Story of Crew 34* (New York, Praeger, 1991), Chapter 4.

15. J. D. Brown suggests that although it is difficult to prove, the additional responsibilities and the shifting of the headquarters can hardly have helped efficiency and morale. Timothy J. Runyan and Jan M. Copes (eds), *To Die Gallantly: the Battle of the Atlantic* (Boulder, Colorado, Westview Press, 1994), 155.
16. *The Economist*, 23 May 1998, 29.
17. Originally known as FdU – *Führer der Unterseeboote* (Leader of Submarines).
18. Jürgen Rohwer, 'Manuskript für Vortrag', London 21 Oktober 1997 (unpublished), sent to author 24 October 1997.
19. Graham Rhys-Jones, 'The German System: a Staff Perspective', in Stephen Howarth and Derek Law (eds), *The Battle of the Atlantic 1939–1945: the 50th Anniversary International Naval Conference* (London, Greenhill Books, 1994).
20. See also the discussion of productivity in Chapter 8.
21. For the loss of tactical choice, see Chapter 5, pp. 90: 'Convoy Warfare'.
22. See Chapter 9, pp. 203–8.
23. See p. 52 above.
24. For a fuller description of the centre of gravity, see Directorate of Naval Staff Duties, *The Fundamentals of British Maritime Doctrine* (London, HMSO, 1995), 110–11. The role of shipping is discussed above p. 12.
25. There is also the question of whether the specific aim, that is, number of tons sunk per month is correctly assessed. This is, to some extent, looked at above pp. 48–9).
26. *Fuehrer Conferences on Naval Affairs*, 334–5.
27. Economic aspects are discussed above (pp. 52–3).
28. This ranges from relatively early memoirs such as Herbert Werner, *Iron Coffins* (New York, Holt Rinehart, 1969), through fictionalised accounts by Lothar-Günther Bucheim, *U-boat (Das Boot)*, (London, Collins, 1974) to biographies of both individual commanding officers, such as Jordan Vause, *U-boat Ace: the Story of Wolfgang Lüth* (Annapolis, Maryland, Naval Institute Press, 1990) and a considerable late flowering of works on both the careers of individual submarines and submariners: David Stevens, *U-boat Far from Home: the Epic Voyage of U 862 to Australia and New Zealand* (St Leonards, New South Wales, Allen and Unwin, 1997) and Theodore P. Savas (ed.), *Silent Hunters: German U-Boat Commanders of World War II*, (Campbell, California, Savas, 1997). Some of these works have been criticised on the grounds of either factual accuracy or false *Zeitgeist* or both, but coverage of the subject is undeniable.
29. The BdU KTB, for 1941, for example, is almost entirely factual in nature. There is a very little operational-level interpretation and even less by way of perception and forward thinking. It is not suggested that this did not occur, only that it was not necessarily recorded in this important document at the time. The document can be accessed at NARA RG 242, PG 30280-30301/b, T1022, 4063.
30. PRO ADM 186/802, 234/67 and 234/68, The U-boat War in the Atlantic (hereafter Hessler). These have since been published by HMSO, London in 1989. The chronology of issue of the three original volumes is of interest, being in 1950, 1952 and 1977 respectively. The last carried an introduction making it clear that, although this (internal) publication came after the revelation of Ultra, the findings of its author had not been altered to take

these into account. This is quite proper as it would have almost certainly changed the German view.

31. A fuller description of the events of 1941 is given in Chapter 8. See also Gardner, *The Battle of the Atlantic, 1941 – the First Turning Point.*
32. Hessler I, Chapter III, especially p. 73. An analysis stressing the positive reasons for the move is given in a paper by Graham Rhys-Jones 'The Riddle of the Convoys: Admiral Dönitz and the U-Boat Campaign of 1941' (unpublished, Newport RI, United States Naval War College, 1992).
33. For aircraft, see Hessler II 43, 85 and 109; for radar, 86 and 99.
34. Hessler III, 6, 7, 97 and 98.
35. See Chapter 6, p. 97 on Metox.
36. Hessler III, 51–3.
37. An observation reinforced indirectly by a contemporary well-placed observer on Dönitz's staff – Victor Oehrn. Jordan Vause, 'Victor Otto Oehrn: The Ace with No Name' in Savas, 132 quoting from Oehrn's *Dönitz Nähe Gesehen* (unpublished memoirs).

5   Convoy Warfare

1. Ministry of Defence: Directorate of Naval Staff Duties, *The Fundamentals of British Maritime Doctrine: BR1806* (London, HMSO, 1995) lists offensive action as one of 10 principles of war. There is no corresponding entry for defensive action. Sometimes, in the general literature, this preference is expressed in such terms as the fashionable 'pro-active' or in aphorisms such as 'getting your retaliation in first'.
2. Earlier reinforcement (and associated protection) had been required for the invasion of northwest Africa in November 1942 and Sicily in July 1943.
3. PRO ADM 234/578, Defeat of the Enemy Attack on Shipping (afterwards Barley and Waters), 1A.
4. Barley and Waters 1A, 228–31.
5. Barley and Waters 1A, 2. This does beg the question of whether an exclusively air-mounted escort would qualify. The view of this writer (and one suspects, the spirit of the quoted text) is that it would.
6. Until the introduction of end-to-end convoys on the main cross-Atlantic route, a process begun in mid-1941, this situation almost certainly obtained for the first day or so after convoy dispersal, when merchant ships would be unescorted but to some extent grouped.
7. Latterly, the Germans made some use of hydrophones to detect convoys acoustically and some limited tactical Sigint was also carried out
8. There is a highly theoretical case where convoy ships are stationed so far apart that the advantage disappears. Such would not only be tactically imprudent but also impossible to manage.
9. See Chapter 8.
10. As is argued later, the German problem in this phase was not so much finding convoys as obtaining results against an increasingly competent opposition see Chapter 9.
11. This situation changed in the last year of the war when a combination of the difficulty of carrying out open ocean warfare and the positive development of

the schnorkel made inshore operations less hazardous, but still far from risk-free.

12. Karl Dönitz, *Memoirs: Ten Years and Twenty Days* (London, Greenhill Books, 1990), 220.

13. See explanation of ORCA, below, pp. 83–5.

14. For example, see Julian S. Corbett, *Drake and the Tudor Navy: with a History of the Rise of England as a Maritime Power* (Aldershot, Temple Smith, Gower, 1988) on the Spanish *Flotas*; Jaap R. Bruijn, *The Dutch Navy of the Seventeenth and Eighteenth Centuries* (Columbia, South Carolina, University of South Carolina Press, 1993) on the Netherlands.

15. A number of conjectures might be made, such as a greater estrangement of the naval and mercantile seagoing professions than previously, the fallacy of progress changing everything and the lack of maritime warfare at the higher levels. There is also a methodological problem. Dealing with the loss of knowledge, evidence is by its nature difficult to find – it is what might be called a smokeless-powder gun problem.

16. There are a number of good accounts of the problems, principally Henry Newbolt; *Naval Operations*, Volume V (London; Longmans, Green, 1931), Chapter 1; but none satisfactorily relating how it was resolved. One important factor was the successful demonstration of convoy on other routes than across the Atlantic.

17. The main cross-Atlantic routes tended typically to involve the USA, UK and Canada but might also involve warships of French, Belgian, Polish, Dutch, Greek and Norwegian manning.

18. See Chapters 8 and 9 pp. 162–4 and pp. 204.

19. The aggregate activities of these vessels resulted in about 10 per cent of the losses caused by submarines for the whole war. Data extracted from S. W. Roskill, *The War at Sea*, 3 vols in 4 (London, HMSO, 1954–61). As far as the Atlantic was concerned, their activities were constrained relatively early.

20. See next paragraph.

21. These were a rare example of independent shipping being given direct, evasive routeing directions from the OIC in the Admiralty. Patrick Beesly, *Very Special Intelligence: the Story of the Admiralty's Operational Intelligence Centre, 1939–1945* (London, Hamish Hamilton, 1977), 147–8.

22. The temporary exclusion of 13–15-knot ships from the convoy system is dealt with in Chapter 8 p. 154.

23. These were considered at high level by the Anti U-boat Warfare Committee in 1943. See Stephen Howarth and Derek Law (eds), *The Battle of the Atlantic 1939–1945: The 50th Anniversary International Naval Conference* (London, Greenhill Books, 1994), 527; PRO CAB86/3 AU(43) 92 22 Mar 43 and CAB86/4 AU(43) 131 3 May 43.

24. PRO CAB86/2 AU(43) 9th 3 March 43, Item 10.

25. In practice this was exceeded considerably; sometimes more than 100 ships were in convoy.

26. PRO CAB86/2 AU(43) 9th 3 March 43 Item 10; Howarth and Law, 526; P. M. S. Blackett's own 'Recollection of Problems Studied' in *Brassey's Annual* (London, Brassey's, 1953) 229–33. For a fuller mathematical treatment of the subject, see D. W. Waters, 'The Mathematics of Convoy', *Navy International* (May 1978), 25–26, 78.

27. The American method of having a separate escort force commander was tried briefly by the British but was not popular.

28. An account of this is given by H. P. Wilmott in Howarth and Law, Chapter 9. He is right to note that the exact reconstruction of the decision trail is now probably almost impossible.

29. D. A. Rayner, *Escort: the Battle of the Atlantic* (London, William Kimber, 1955), 40 recounts that only a seagoing spell by the then CinCWA, Sir Percy Noble, in February 1941 had revealed a degree of nugatory shore control and he had promptly changed the system.

30. Peter Gretton, *Convoy Escort Commander* (London, Cassell, 1964), 188 explains the useful point of ordering this not on a specific course which might require constant adjustment as the wind direction changed but, rather, keeping the wind on one bow, making the further point that he would use low-power radio because of the impracticality of flags in such conditions.

31. See p. 76.

32. Barley and Waters 1A, 39 suggests 0.66 per cent per sailing for an independent ship and 0.33 per cent for one that was convoyed. This is probably a convoy worst-comparison calculation.

33. Arnold Hague, personal communication, 30 April 1998.

34. In this era, changing oceanographic conditions had little real impact, other than a marginal one on the performance of sonar. In any case, the participant's understanding of this factor was very limited by modern standards.

35. It was normal to restrict shipborne star-sights to these times as not only had the stars to be visible but so too had the horizon. Aircraft obviated the problem (largely of the horizon varying because of altitude) by using bubble sextants to generate an artificial horizon. These were not available at sea.

36. For a study of these, see Ralph Erskine, 'U-Boats, Homing Signals and HF DF', *Intelligence and National Security* 2 (April 1987), 324–330.

37. A Survey of the DNOR papers in PRO ADM 219 and other places indicates no specific study of convoy navigation.

38. C. H. Waddington, *OR in World War 2* (London, Elek Science, 1973), 90–91. This data was for the second half of 1941 before considerable steps were taken to improve the situation, which met with some success. In the latter case, there were almost certainly three components: convoy navigational error, aircraft error and convoy manoeuvres since last report.

39. See discussion of precision and accuracy in Chapter 2.

40. Blackett, 232.

41. Although latterly some detections on convoys were made by dived submarines listening on their hydrophones, the eye was the principal convoy-detection sensor for most of the war.

42. See note 36.

43. See Rayner's judgement on Commander C. D. Howard-Johnstone and his philosophy of the task of an escort group. Rayner, 87.

44. See Richard Baker, *The Terror of Tobermory: Vice-Admiral Sir Gilbert Stephenson KBE, CBE, CMG* (London, W. H. Allen, 1972); on Tobermory, Mark Williams, *Captain Gilbert Roberts RN and the Anti-U-Boat School* (London, Cassell, 1979); on the anti-U-Boat school, see especially Goldrick, in Howarth and Law, Chapter 12.

45. See Rayner, 163.
46. This is, of course, not a process which was pursued in these terms at the time, or at least not explicitly.

6 Technology on Both Sides

1. Richard Harding, *Atlantic Seapower and Naval Warfare, 1650–1830* (London, University of London Press, 1999), pp. 59–60.
2. PRO ADM 186/802, The U-Boat War in the Atlantic (hereafter Hessler), I, 2, figures for 31 August.
3. Eberhard Rössler, *The U-boat: the Evolution and Technical History of German Submarines* (London, Arms and Armour, 1981), and Robert Stern, *Type VII U-Boats* (London, Arms and Armour, 1991) provide thoroughly researched work on the whole development of German submarines and on one of the two workhorses respectively.
4. See p. 98.
5. All performance figures come from Hessler I, Appendix II. The data is for the basic Type VII.
6. For more detail on this process, see Chapter 5.
7. Rössler, Chapter 6.
8. The technology was considered to be sufficiently promising to be tried, at least experimentally, by several nations postwar. However, it never succeeded, begging the question as to how good the Germans were at assessing technological risk. In any case by the mid-1950s there was little point in continuing down this path with the advent of nuclear propulsion.
9. Exact chronology is a little difficult to tie down, but it is thought that it should start in late 1942 with the suggestion of these types of submarine being made, and approval for their production coming from Hitler in July 1943. PRO ADM 234/68, The U-boat War in the Atlantic (hereafter Hessler), III, 6; see also Rössler, 208–10.
10. A very succinct summary of the features of the Type XXI is given by Axel Niestlé in Stephen Howarth and Derek Law (eds), *The Battle of the Atlantic 1939–1945: the 50th Anniversary International Naval Conference* (London, Greenhill Books, 1994), 434–6.
11. For one of the few descriptions of this period, see Marc Milner, 'The Dawn of Modern ASW: Allied responses to the U-Boat, 1943–1945, *Journal of the RUSI*, Vol. 134 No. 1 (Spring 1989), 61–8.
12. Clay Blair, *Hitler's U-Boat War: the Hunters, 1939–1942* (New York, Random House, 1996), x, xi.
13. These submarines used prefabricated construction rather than traditional building techniques.
14. The Baltic mining campaign is one of the most productive yet under-reported events of the Second World War. It was efficient in assets and low in British casualties. It was very successful, purely as a mining campaign partly because of its exploitation of the German routeing system gleaned through Ultra. Immensely disruptive generally it hit submarine activities especially hard. It was even used at times to provoke German signal traffic to aid the solution of particularly difficult Enigma keys. Some aspects of the campaign are described in ADM 234/560.

15. F. H. Hinsley *et al.*, *British Intelligence in the Second World War: Its Influence on Strategy and Operations* (London, HMSO, 1979–88), 3 vols in 4, III part 2, 474–84.

16. ADM223/358, 15 Jan. 45, 2. Assault Unit 30 was a specialist formation attempting to obtain technical intelligence material for naval use. It was originated and for some time controlled by Ian Fleming, later better known for his works of spy fiction.

17. Rössler, 198.

18. ADM223/172 OIC SI1036 of 11 August 44 – Notes on U-boats fitted with Snort. Although put out under OIC cover, the nature of the text and sub-scribed typed initials indicate that this was the work of Leon Solomon and, less commonly, E. J. Williams of the Directorate of Naval Operational Research and the Operational Research Staff, Coastal Command respectively.

19. Peter Padfield, *War beneath the Sea: Submarine Conflict 1939–1945* (London, Pimlico, 1997), 337. It is right to point out that the Americans were operating against less adept ASW opponents, which were not themselves fitted with either radar or radar detectors. Although speculative, in the event of the Germans developing in a similar direction, it is probable that Allied intelligence would not only have gained knowledge of this but would also have taken rapid countermeasures, probably in the form of a device for radar-detection and direction-finding.

20. See also Chapter 6.

21. Useful works are Alfred Price, *Aircraft versus Submarine: the Evolution of the Anti-Submarine Aircraft, 1912 to 1980* (London, Jane's Publishing, 1980); Stern and PRO AIR 10/5555, Radio in Maritime Warfare, as well as PRO ADM 234/67 and 234/68 (afterwards Hessler), II and III.

22. Other cargoes could be surprisingly hazardous too, such as grain or coal, if dust explosions were initiated.

23. Details of torpedoes can be found in John Campbell; *Naval Weapons of World War Two* (London, Conway Maritime Press, 1985), 260–8. Stern; Part Three is also good on this subject, in particular dealing with the weapons in service, their handling and firing.

24. Hessler I, 69. None of this should be too surprising. Torpedoes were probably the most sophisticated terminal munitions at the outset of the Second World War. They are also very difficult to test realistically under wartime conditions. Germany was far from being the only country to have torpedo problems; the Americans too were badly affected in 1941–42. Padfield has more index entries for torpedo-faults for the USA than he does for Germany.

25. *Federapparat* (literally spring-device) and *Lage unabhängiger Torpedo* (position independent torpedo). Described fully in Campbell, 261–2.

26. Also known as the *Zaunkönig* or GNAT (in Allied terminology).

27. Hinsley 2, 685 notes the significance of POW interrogations on this subject although the first indication of German acoustic torpedo work would appear to have come from an unsolicited human source in the form of the 'Oslo letter'. See also Hinsley 1 Appendix 5 Para 10 and R. V. Jones, *Reflections on Intelligence* (London, Heinemann, 1989), 266–7.

28. It was possibly even more useful for the Allies. On the verge of protesting to the Spanish government about the Spanish stations, it was realised that it would benefit the Allies at least as much as the Germans and possibly more.

It was therefore used by Allied forces for the rest of the war and, for civil use, for several decades thereafter.

29. Hessler II, 49.
30. Hinsley 3 part 1, 218.
31. Stern, 131–5 gives good descriptions of all of these.
32. Hinsley 3 part 2, 852.
33. ADM223/261 SI1254 19 March 1945. This is again an example of DNOR work being issued through the OIC.
34. On illuminants, see Gerald Pawle, *The Secret War, 1939–1945* (London, Harrap, 1956), 158–63.
35. Ships were equipped with searchlights but their relatively limited range meant that they were of little tactical use most of the time.
36. The Leigh Light, its origins and use are described very thoroughly in Price, principally 61–3.
37. See C. H. Waddington, *OR in World War 2: Operational Research against the U-Boat* (London, Elek Science, 1973), 164–5.
38. After the war, the former usage became universal. There is a famous and often repeated canard about the origin of 'Asdic' attributing it to a non-existent committee during the First World War. Willem Hackmann, *Seek and Strike: Sonar, Anti-Submarine Warfare and the Royal Navy 1914–1954*, (London, HMSO, 1984), xxv.
39. This tended to increase during the war as developments were made and experienced gained. An insight into the spread of ranges can still be obtained; PRO ADM 219/334.
40. The development of British sonar is well covered in Hackmann, *Seek and Strike*.
41. A partial exception to this might be made for operations conducted in the Strait of Gibraltar, but the relatively narrow waters helped MAD somewhat.
42. Price, 108–9. These were crude by modern standards, capable of producing non-directional information only against a submarine making a fair amount of noise.
43. See p. 109 below for the Mk24 Mine.
44. For the development of radar in the Royal Navy, see Derek Howse (ed.), *Radar at Sea: the Royal Navy in World War 2* (London, Macmillan, 1993) and F. A. Kingsley, *The Development of Radar Equipments for the Royal Navy, 1935–1945* (London, Macmillan, 1995), 2 vols. The description of radar in convoy warfare in Howse 276–281 is especially useful.
45. David Zimmerman, *The Great Naval Battle of Ottawa* (Toronto, Canada, University of Toronto Press, 1989), especially Chapters 6 and 9. The author notes a tendency for national self-sufficiency as a significant impediment to progress.
46. For radar generally, on board naval aircraft, see J. D. Brown's essay in Howse, 307–313.
47. Price's *Aircraft versus Submarine* is a very useful guide to both general development and application. For more detail of the technology, see PRO AIR 10/5555, *Radio in Maritime Warfare*.
48. See Chapter 7.
49. Peter Kemp, *Decision at Sea: the Convoy Escorts* (New York, Elsevier-Dutton, 1978), 90 among others.

50. ADM 223/7 ULTRA/ZIP/ZWTG/77 OF21 June 44 VIII(ii). Rohwer discusses the German intelligence failure at some length in his *The Critical Convoy Battles of March 1943: the Battle for HX229/SC122* (Shepperton, Ian Allan, 1977), 198–200 and some further aspects are considered in Ralph Erskine, 'U-Boats, Homing Signals and HF DF', *Intelligence and National Security* 2 (April 1987), 326–8.
51. A very full and balanced account of American shipborne HF DF is given by Kathleen Broome Williams, *Secret Weapon: US High-Frequency Direction Finding in the Battle of the Atlantic* (Annapolis, Maryland, Naval Institute Press, 1996). The best account of the British development is given by Redgment in Kingsley.
52. Although never put to the test, it is doubtful if this technology would have been adequate to deal with *Kurier* (see p. 102) signals. Fortunately, this never came to pass.
53. For the tactical application of HF DF, see Chapter 5.
54. Even at the time it was not especially prominent. See Gardner, in Howarth and Law, 525–6 on the lack of HF DF salience at the Anti U-boat Warfare Committee's meetings.
55. There were also a very few cases in which submerged Allied submarines engaged with torpedoes surfaced German submarines.
56. PRO ADM 234/578 Defeat of the Enemy Attack on Shipping (afterwards Barley and Waters), Volume 1A, Appendix 2(iii), as corrected by the research of R. M. Coppock of the Naval Historical Branch, Ministry of Defence.
57. ADM 234/560, Chapter 11.
58. For details of British mines, see Campbell, 94–7.
59. ADM 234/560, Chapter 11.
60. This activity known as 'gardening' has some claims for being one of the first examples of a 'smart' campaign, even if the individual weapons deployed were relatively unintelligent. The Baltic mining activity deserves much greater attention than it has received, especially as it was a major factor in the German inability to deploy its new technology submarines operationally.
61. For details of Allied depth-charges, Campbell, 88–90, 94, 163–6.
62. For some of the consequences of this feature see p. 117.
63. Price, 98–9. Waddington, Chapter 7 gives a more extended account of the theory and practice of air-weapon delivery.
64. Campbell, 91 and 164–5 provides further information.
65. Campbell, 91.
66. Campbell, 93.
67. Campbell, 162. It was also known as the Mark 24 mine or Fido. See also Price, 109–10.
68. Much of the specialist material is, in itself, of high quality, such as the World Ship Society monographs, e. g. Arnold Hague, *Sloops 1926–1946* (Kendal, World Ship Society, 1993). However, those which consider ships as the places where systems are located, are themselves systems, and in turn form part of larger systems, such as in the writings of Norman Friedman, are comparatively scarce.
69. For details of the long-range conversions to the destroyers transferred from America, see Arnold Hague, *The Towns: a History of the Fifty Destroyers*

Transferred from the United States to Great Britain in 1940 (Kendal, World Ship Society, 1988), 15.

70. The twin-engined Mosquito, armed with cannon, was used during the Bay of Biscay offensive, largely against surfaced U-boats attempting to act as flak-traps. Similarly, the single-engined Swordfish aircraft (capable of carrier operations) were deployed successfully from Gibraltar. The other honourable exception, and possibly what can be argued as the only specialist ASW aircraft, was the twin-engined PBY or Catalina.

71. Kenneth Poolman, *Allied Escort Carriers of World War Two* (London, Blandford Press, 1988) and David Hobbs, *Aircraft Carriers of the Royal and Commonwealth Navies: the Complete Illustrated Encyclopedia from World War I to the Present* (London, Greenhill Books, 1996) are useful works on the escort carriers.

72. J. Gordon Vaeth, *Blimps and U-Boats: US Navy Airships in the Battle of the Atlantic*, (Annapolis, Maryland, Naval Institute Press, 1992).

73. See above, p. 99.

74. Barley and Waters, 1A, 118.

75. Because of this last characteristic it tended to have a deleterious effect on sonar. Thus, some officers, notably Captain F. J. Walker, neither liked nor used it. The Canadians claim to have produced a better and more durable device. Marc Milner; *The U-Boat Hunters: the Royal Canadian Navy and the Offensive against Germany's Submarines* (Annapolis, Maryland, Naval Institute Press, 1994), 72–4.

76. Corelli Barnett, *Engage the Enemy More Closely: the Royal Navy in the Second World War* (London, Hodder and Stoughton, 1991); David Zimmerman, *The Great Naval Battle of Ottawa* (Toronto, Canada, University of Toronto Press, 1989).

77. John Ellis, *Brute Force: a Study in Defence Planning* (London, André Deutsch, 1990), inside front cover. Ellis does have a chapter on the Battle of the Atlantic and his thesis is somewhat more moderate than suggested by the blurb.

78. There are resonances with some of the economic arguments employed earlier in this book. See Chapter 3.

79. Paul Sutcliffe in Howarth and Law, 419 makes the point that Dönitz used this as a barometer of effectiveness, even although he had no formal OR staff.

80. For example, both Solly Zuckerman and C. H. Waddington fell into this category.

81. Both extracts from NARA RG 38 10th Fleet Box ASM-42, folder 'United States Naval Forces in Europe'. The former item also indicates the spread of Ultra information (referred to here as 'Z') in the British community, including the information that two Admiralty OR scientists and two in Coastal Command were privy to such knowledge.

82. The basic argument is described by Sutcliffe in Howarth and Law, 425–6, and in greater detail in J. G. Crowther and R. Whiddington, *Science at War* (London, HMSO, 1947), 101–2. See also P. M. S. Blackett's own 'Recollection of problems studied' in *Brassey's Annual* (London, Brassey's, 1953) 229–33.

83. PRO CAB 86/2 AU(43) 9th meeting 3 March 1943. See also Gardner in Howarth and Law, 526–7.

84. Useful accounts are in Waddington, and Keith R. Tidman, *The Operations Analysis Group: a History of Naval Operations Analysis*, (Annapolis, Maryland, Naval Institute Press, 1984).

85. Waddington, 172–205.

86. Sutcliffe in Howarth and Law, Chapter 23 gives a good general survey . In particular, he draws attention to the Pratt survey of naval OR work.

87. Waddington, 35.

88. ADM 223/172 SI1036.

89. Waddington, 88–110. See also Chapter 5.

90. Waddington, 110–121 and Chapter 3.

91. Sutcliffe, in Howarth and Law, 426–8 makes some attempt at assessing the overall impact of OR on the Battle of the Atlantic but properly notes the difficulties and limits of such an exercise.

92. ADM 223/261 OIC SI1254 covering minute dated 19 March 1945. The report itself also carries the autograph signature of Leon Solomon, a DNOR researcher.

93. Hinsley, 3 part 1, 286 asterisked footnote referring to Appendix 16 (actually 15).

94. One way in which this might have occurred is by disguising the true source of information. This was a technique quite common at the time. Thus, for example, some positional data obtained by Ultra was passed off as a product of HF DF: Professor David Syrett; staff seminar; National Maritime Museum, Greenwich, London, 10 January 1996. By its nature, proof that this occurred between intelligence and non–Ultra cleared OR staffs is unlikely to be available.

95. Keith R. Tidman, *The Operations Analysis Group: a History of Naval Operations Analysis*, (Annapolis, Maryland, Naval Institute Press, 1984), 59 suggests that some access was given after American researchers had grown suspicious of the unexpected accuracy of other data. However, this account is not dated or supported by documentary evidence.

7 Signals Intelligence and the Battle of the Atlantic

1. The former is well described in R. V. Jones, *Most Secret War: British Scientific Intelligence 1939–1945* (*The Wizard War* in the USA) (London, Coronet, 1978), Chapter 11. The latter was the subject of an informed decision by the Allies not to disrupt it but rather to make use of it. It had the advantage of needing no special radio equipment, only specially prepared charts and was used for several decades after the Second World War.

2. For some of the twists and turns of this debate see Ralph Erskine, 'Ultra and Some US Navy Carrier Operations', in *Cryptologia*, XIX, No. 1 (January 1995), 81 fn1.

3. F. W. Winterbotham, *The Ultra Secret* (London, Weidenfeld and Nicolson, 1974). It should be noted that there are works in other languages prior to this, as well as some literature which contained clues only conveying their full meaning to the initiated as well as some indiscreet works. In English see S. W. Roskill, *The War at Sea*, Vol. II (London, HMSO, 1956), 208; in the former category, Ronald Seth, *The Fiercest Battle: the Story of North Atlantic Convoy ONS5, 22 April–7 May 1943* (London, Hutchinson, 1961) and

Donald McLachlan, *Room 39: Naval Intelligence in Action 1939–1945* (London, Weidenfeld and Nicolson, 1968).

4. For a discussion of some of the confusion surrounding the definitions of terms, see F. H. Hinsley *et al.*, *British Intelligence in the Second World War: its Influence on Strategy and Operations* (London, HMSO, 1979–88), 3 vols in 4, Vol. 1, 21 asterisked footnote.

5. An earlier method of alluding to frequency was by wavelength, that is the distance between peaks or troughs of a cycle. The two are intimately related by the speed of light, which is also the speed of radio waves.

6. Strictly speaking, this form of communication is limited to line of sight, so the ranges can be much greater if one or more of the stations is in the air or space.

7. However it proved of great use for tactical ASW communications, not so much because of its basic characteristics, but because it permitted direct distortion-free voice communications between captains of ships. It is best summed up by its American name TBS – Talk Between Ships.

8. See Chapter 6.

9. U862, as probably the most extreme example, was not within several thousand miles of any other U-boat for several months. See David Stevens, *U-Boat Far from Home: the Epic Voyage of U-862 to Australia and New Zealand* (St Leonards, New South Wales, Allen and Unwin, 1997).

10. See Karl Dönitz, *Memoirs: Ten Years and Twenty Days* (London, Greenhill Books, 1990), Chapters 1 and 3, and Peter Padfield, *Dönitz, the Last Führer: Portrait of a Nazi War Leader* (London, Victor Gollancz, 1984), Chapters 2 and 4.

11. PRO ADM199/575, ADM199/576, ADM199/580, ADM199/1489, ADM199/1491 and Jürgen Rohwer, *The Critical Convoy Battles of March 1943* (Shepperton, Surrey, 1977), David Syrett, 'The Battle for Convoy TM1' in *The American Neptune* (Winter 1990), 42–50, Marc Milner, *North Atlantic Run: the Royal Canadian Navy and the Battle for the Convoys* (Toronto, Canada, University of Toronto Press, 1985), especially Chapter 3. Perhaps the most unusual item in the literature is E. J. Pratt's *Behind the Log,* a narrative poem on SC42 (cited in Derek G. Law, *The Royal Navy in World War Two: an Annotated Bibliography* (London, Greenhill Books, 1988), 260, item 1827).

12. John Prados, *Combined Fleet Decoded: the Secret History of American Intelligence and the Japanese Navy in World War II* (New York, Random House, 1995), 171–4.

13. Submariners, especially, might take issue with being described as semi-autonomous, their function and tradition stressing near-complete independence. This might be so with some nations and times but the *Rudeltaktik* was a clear espousal of not only coordinated working but also a deliberate surrender of autonomy to BdU.

14. See Chapter 6, p. 105.

15. Ultimately to comprise 51 stations. NARA RG457 SRH-277, Lecture on communications intelligence by RADM, E. E. Stone, DIRAFSA, 5 June 51, 21.

16. NARA RG 457 (edited edition of SRH 008, 009, 024 and 025 by Jeffrey K. Bray (Laguna Hills, California, Aegean Park Press, 1994), Vol. VI, Appendix 14, Table D. It is not clear whether the figure being discussed is in miles or square miles, although the former would seem more likely.

17. Although the American study referred to in the previous note is useful, there are no known similar works which look at the application of HF DF and its accuracy to specific operations – especially those in which contact was avoided. It is not even known whether sufficient data has been preserved to permit such work.
18. See pp. 140–1 below.
19. Perhaps the best example of this comes from sea and the better-integrated and -led escort groups where formal orders (which would be good as evidence for posterity) were not always necessary 'because we all knew what to do'.
20. Hinsley refers to these as low- or medium-grade. No distinction between these two categories is drawn here and normally they will be referred to as low-grade.
21. For example, Shark was broken for 88 out of 99 days from 12 December 1942 to 10 March 1943 entirely from cribs of weather signals, a point made by Ralph Erskine.
22. Robert Stern, *Type VII U-Boats* (London, Arms and Armour, 1991), 113–14 notes that this main (200-watt) set was backed up by a lower-power emergency set, but this would not have been used from choice.
23. Hinsley 2, 232.
24. TINA was a codename not an acronym.
25. There are chronic problems of definition and these have altered in different times and places. For example Hinsley 1, 21 first footnote, draws attention to this difficulty, noting in particular that for at least a part of the war the definition of traffic analysis included both low-grade codes and DF. These would not normally be considered part of TA now. What is evident, however, both for the points made by Hinsley here and for the whole of his work, is the importance of these subjects being considered as part of a whole and not merely on their own.
26. Hinsley 2, 551.
27. Kahn, x.
28. As Ralph Erskine has pointed out, this judgement does depend on both the specific characteristics of the machine system and it's being used properly.
29. For a fuller description, see F. H. Hinsley and Alan Stripp (eds), *Code Breakers: the Inside Story of Bletchley Park* (Oxford, Oxford University Press, 1993), 83–8. For those who would like to take matters a little further, a working Enigma simulator can be downloaded from the Internet, currently [May 1999] at *www.blueangel.demon.co.uk/crypto/* then follow the links to Enigma.
30. In the former case, some idea of working conditions is given in Len Deighton; *Blitzkrieg: from the Rise of Hitler to the Fall of Dunkirk* (London, Pimlico, 1996), facing page 234. Another version of a similar photograph published two decades earlier does not show the machine: Kenneth Mackesy, *Guderian: Panzer General*; (London, Purnell Book Services, 1975), facing page 116 and outside back cover, although any cropping may have been done for compositional purposes rather than any other.
31. The compromise problem was dealt with by an additive modification system known as *Stichwort*. See Ralph Erskine, 'Ultra and Some US Navy Carrier Operations'.
32. This judgement takes no account of timeliness, addressed below: see pp. 142–4.

33. Ralph Erskine, 'The German Naval Grid in World War II', *Cryptologia* (Jan. 1992), 39–51.
34. Ralph Erskine, 'Ultra and Some US Navy Carrier Operations', 82–4.
35. Most notably in Hinsley, Rohwer and Kahn. Mention also should be made of the many articles by Ralph Erskine, some of which are mentioned in the Bibliography.
36. See Chapters 8 and 9 below.
37. The capture of U-110 is probably the best described, in a sense, being the subject of a full-length book, S. W. Roskill, *The Secret Capture* (London, Collins, 1959). This pulls off the interesting feat of describing the incident fully but without mentioning the main result (of which Roskill had knowledge).
38. It is clear that the limited success that was obtained after the blackout in 1942 was attributable to unusual occurrences rather than reliable ones. Also very evident was the fact that three-wheel bombes were not entirely useless for dealing with the four-wheel Enigma; for example all Shark traffic read before 1 June 1943 was broken with these bombes. But their employment on this task could be uneconomic. Perhaps more importantly, their relative slowness meant that the product might not be available in such a timescale as to be tactically useful. Hinsley II, 749–51.
39. Most of the information on *xB-Dienst* comes from notes supplied by Professor Dr Jürgen Rohwer. German readers can also derive much from Heinz Bonatz, *Seekrieg im Äther: Die Leistungen der Marine-Funkaufklärung 1939–1945* (Herford, Germany, Mittler, 1981).
40. Hinsley 2, 636.
41. To refer back to the apparently long lag between the first realisation that No 3 Cipher had been compromised and the implementation of a new system, it has to be realised that one of the worst possible reactions to such a problem is to initiate a partial introduction of a new system, as this risks having a false sense of new security while giving an enemy cryptographic opportunities to understand the new system by means of comparing old ciphertext (Cypher No 3) to plaintext (obtained through decryption) to new ciphertext (Cypher No 5). It was by using just such methods that Bletchley was able to obtain some of its insights into the four-rotor Enigma.
42. For awareness of this, see NARA RG457 SRMN-054 (Part 1) Section 13 and SRH-009, chapter VI (Bray edition) and Bray Volume VI, Appendix 13.
43. Kahn, 91.
44. PRO ADM 186/802, The U-Boat War in the Atlantic I (hereafter Hessler), especially Sections 124–9 and 163.
45. Norman Dixon, *On the Psychology of Military Incompetence* (London, Jonathan Cape, 1976), 164–6.
46. Such as the use of the British submarine *Clyde* against German submarines in the Cape Verde Islands in September 1941. Hessler I, 96.
47. This introduces one of the more intriguing sidelights of the Battle of the Atlantic. The Germans had suspected for some time that the Metox radiations were a problem. This suspicion became (in their minds) certainty when confirmed for them by a British aircrew prisoner of war. This is described in Alfred Price, *Aircraft versus Submarine: the Evolution of the*

Anti-Submarine Aircraft, 1912 to 1980 (London, Jane's Publishing, 1980), 169–170. Subsequent discussions with both Dr Price and Professor David Syrett suggest that this story has certain inconsistencies. It would be very difficult to infiltrate a suitably briefed crew-member of a maritime aircraft into the German POW system, so either the POW story is a cover (on one or both sides) or the admission was a purely fortuitous piece of invention which just happened to play on current German suspicions. It is unlikely that the truth of this will ever be known.

48. Hessler III, Section 410.
49. Expanded on below – see p. 141.
50. See also the section on operational research in Chapter 6.
51. There were, of course, many more, principally the Americans and Canadians, with the British as well as other countries, and even Germany received some assistance from her Italian ally as well as (probably more usefully) some covert assistance in the way of facilities from the Spanish, at least in the earlier years.
52. And similarly, there were more organisations, principally the American Op-20G with many valuable assets such as a generous supply of four-rotor bombes.
53. There are good reasons to limit it thus. Op-20G was not engaged operationally for much of the time and a proper three-way (or one-and-two-halves) analysis would introduce considerable complication without necessarily clarifying any conclusions.
54. See the various Syrett examples of convoy monographs in the Bibliography.
55. NARA RG457 SRH368 Annex 2.1 Table II.
56. For German appreciation of Sigint, see Hessler II, section 303.
57. David Syrett (ed.), *Signals Intelligence and the Battle of the Atlantic* (London, Navy Records Society, 1998).
58. Patrick Beesly, 'Special Intelligence and the Battle of the Atlantic: the British View', in Robert W. Love Jr, *Changing Interpretations and New Sources in Naval History: Papers from the Third United States Naval Academy History Symposium* (New York, Garland Publishing, 1980), 416.
59. Based on the movement in one direction generated by the speed of a slow (7 knot) convoy and making no allowance for the likely movement of a submarine line towards it. This factor is covered in greater detail in Chapter 2.
60. NARA RG457 SRH009 25. The data has been extracted from a table on this page.
61. The reasons for this are probably twofold: changes in the Enigma system in use and the general withdrawal from the Atlantic, lessening the radio traffic and thus the amount of material for the cryptographers to work on.
62. It is probable that there is enough potential work here to occupy a book by itself.
63. McLachlan lists no less than 17 sources without (apparently) even mentioning Ultra.
64. Kahn, 91. Slight issue might be taken with the last sentence – intelligence is, surely, no substitute for strength. Nevertheless, Kahn's insight is all the more significant for having been made by one noted as being a cryptographic historian.

8   Case-Study I: 1941

1. Most notably by Patrick Abazzia, *Mr Roosevelt's Navy: the Private War of the US Atlantic Fleet* (Annapolis, Maryland, Naval Institute Press, 1975), S. E. Morison, *History of United States Naval Operations in World War II: the Battle of the Atlantic, September 1939–May 1943* (Boston, Little, Brown, 1947), Warren F. Kimball, *Forged in War: Churchill, Roosevelt and the Second World War*, especially Chapters 3 and 4.

2. For a clear and concise account, see David Dimbleby and David Reynolds, *An Ocean Apart: the Relationship between Britain and America in the Twentieth Century* (London, Hodder and Stoughton, 1988) Chapter 7.

3. The last – a long way behind the others – did not turn up until November 1941. Arnold Hague, *The Towns: a History of the Fifty Destroyers Transferred from the United States to Great Britain in 1940* (Kendal, UK, World Ship Society, 1990), 17.

4. Technically, Greenland was a Danish possession and therefore under German control. However, the practicalities of strategic location made this difficult to implement.

5. Thomas A. Bailey and Paul B. Ryan, *Hitler vs. Roosevelt: the Undeclared Naval War* (New York, The Free Press, 1979).

6. See Chapters 2 and 9 for more detail on this point.

7. Bradley Smith, *The Ultra-Magic Deals and the Most Secret Special Relationship, 1940–1946*, (Novato, California, Presidio Press, 1993) and PRO ADM 223/15. See also David Syrett, *Signals Intelligence and the Battle of the Atlantic* (London, Navy Records Society, 1998).

8. See S. W. Roskill, *The War at Sea* (London, HMSO, 1954–61), 3 vols in 4, F. H. Hinsley *et al.*, *British Intelligence in the Second World War: Its Influence on Strategy and Operations* (hereafter *British Intelligence*) 3 vols in 4 (London, HMSO, 1979–88), and ADM 234/578 and /579, The Defeat of the Enemy Attack on Shipping (hereafter Barley and Waters). A perceptive but overlooked version is given by Arthur Hezlet, *The Submarine and Sea Power* (London, Peter Davies, 1975). More recently, both Corelli Barnett, *Engage the Enemy More Closely* (London, Hodder and Stoughton, 1991) and John Terraine, *Business in Great Waters: The U-Boat Wars 1916–1945* (London, Leo Cooper, 1989) have also produced workmanlike accounts.

9. Arthur Conan Doyle, *Memoirs of Sherlock Holmes* (1894), 'Silver Blaze'. Often misquoted as the dog that did *not* bark in the night.

10. This is very much the *leitmotif* of Marc Milner's 'The Battle of the Atlantic' in *The Journal of Strategic Studies* (March 1990), 45–66.

11. PRO ADM 186/802, The U-Boat War in the Atlantic (hereafter Hessler), I, 87–89. No numbers are given to illustrate this point because there is some uncertainty about the level of detail in BdU's KTB.

12. Barley and Waters, 1A, 317–19. It should be noted that not all boats sent there succeeded in transiting the Strait of Gibraltar, some being damaged, so the effective Atlantic loss was that much greater.

13. Hessler I, Diagram 7.

14. Hessler I, Diagram 7. There are discrepancies between these figures and those derived from aggregating the individual figures shown in Jürgen Rohwer, *Axis Submarine Successes* (Cambridge, Patrick Stephens, 1983). But

as the latter source cannot be used for submarine deployment statistics, the former is preferred for the sake of consistency of source. In any case the patterns would appear to be the same.

15. The September peak is largely attributable to one single very successful convoy action, that against SC42.

16. The method adopted here is to divide the monthly sinkings by the average number of submarines at sea for the month and then reduce this to a daily figure by dividing by the appropriate number of days in the month. This has two benefits: the production of an order of numbers for productivity that readily fits (making a times-10 allowance) on to the same graph-scale as tonnages sunk and also taking account of different month lengths. An incidental benefit is that the productivity index is the same as that employed by Dönitz – not analytically necessary but historically pleasing.

17. Hinsley, *British Intelligence* 2, 169.

18. See Chapters 4 and 5.

19. See Chapter 5.

20. See below, p. 163, for analysis by routes and convoys. One ship was also sunk in a WS convoy.

21. The Gibraltar convoys were a special case as many of the ships in them were of smaller size than on the cross-Atlantic convoys. See also note 20.

22. Hessler I, Diagrams 9–14. This is preferable to using the BdU War Diary which at this point in the war is insufficiently structured and rigorous to draw useful conclusions.

23. A point brought out well in Clay Blair, *Hitler's U-Boat War: the Hunters, 1939–1942*, (New York, Random House, 1996).

24. Alberto Santoni 'The Italian Submarine Campaign', in Stephen Howarth and Derek Law (eds), *The Battle of the Atlantic, 1939–1945: The 50th Anniversary International Naval Conference* (London, Greenhill Books, 1994) 329–32.

25. See Chapter 5.

26. The capitalisation of Reconnaissance, Closure and Attack indicates the use of the definitions adopted in Chapter 5.

27. The relatively limited aim covering the 100 or so miles from Ushant at the northwest corner of France to the Lizard in southwest England would require 10 submarines permanently on station at 10-mile intervals – a reasonable compromise to allow for night and poor visibility conditions. Even here, with the limited ASW resources available to the British in 1940, submarine life would probably have been nasty, brutish and short.

28. See Tom Stefanick, *Strategic Antisubmarine Warfare and Naval Strategy* (Lexington, Massachusetts, Institute for Defense and Disarmament Studies/Lexington Books, 1987), 37–8. As well as the undoubted ethical objections to such a strategy it would also depend on good intelligence and might well be strategically ineffective.

29. And latterly by single submarines – these were not very successful.

30. See C. H. Waddington, *OR in World War 2: Operational Research against the U-Boat* (London, Paul Elek Scientific Books, 1973), especially Chapter 4.

31. The German experience with maritime aircraft forms an interesting corrective to the view that the British allocation of four-engined aircraft in 1943 was an unparalleled blunder. See, for example, Barnett, Chapter 15. Another way to

express this is that Dönitz would have loved to have had the problems about aircraft that the Admiralty had in 1943. See also Chapter 4 of this book.

32. Initial capitalisation of Reconnaissance, Closure and Attack means that the term is being used not generally but as defined in Chapter 5.

33. Hessler I, 57, 62 and 64.

34. The submarine losses figure would have been even worse for the Allies had there not been a late flurry in December when no less than 10 were lost. Barley and Waters, 1A, 253.

35. Hessler I, Diagram 14.

36. Some writers, such as Clay Blair, have said that SC stood for Slow Convoy but this does not appear in any of the documentation. Perhaps, like some other wartime designations it is remembered in an easy and popular, rather than accurate form, for example PLUTO.

37. As might be expected, there was an imbalance in favour of imports. Later in the war this was to result in the net export of stone ballast from the United Kingdom to the USA, to which at least one New York City road owes its origins – an on-site observation from Professor David Syrett.

38. It was nevertheless necessary to institute convoy systems in other parts of Africa and the Middle East from time to time. See Chapter 9.

39. It was also the case that the numbers deployed per operation were much higher.

40. Admittedly one quite large, the *Terje Viken* of 20 000 tons: Jürgen Rohwer, *Axis Submarine Successes*, 45.

41. Hessler I, 69–70 and Diagram 10.

42. Erroneously described in Hessler I, 76 and Diagram 11 as 'OS'?. This does not make sense for two reason; the OS series of convoys had not been instituted at this point and, in any case, it was far too far to the west for this designation to be feasible.

43. It might be thought reasonable that this failure to convert an aircraft sighting into submarine contact might be attributable to Ultra but it would seem more likely that this was attributable to the well-known coordination problems of German air forces and the navy – as had been seen earlier when Ultra was less advanced – and because no such claim has ever been entered for Ultra on this occasion.

44. Measuring strength of escort forces is relatively easy to do as data exists to permit a calculus of numbers and types. Measurement of competence is more difficult and, to some extent, subjective. The opinion of the enemy is, perhaps, as reliable a guide as any.

45. See p. 163.

46. See p. 161.

47. E. M. Forster; *Howards End* (London, Penguin Books, 1989), title page.

48. Paul M. Sutcliffe, 'Operational Research in the Battle of the Atlantic', in Stephen Howarth and Derek Law (eds), *The Battle of the Atlantic 1939–1945: the 50th Anniversary International Naval Conference* (London, Greenhill Books, 1994), 426.

49. The first of these is the main reason for the move attributed to Dönitz by Graham Rhys-Jones in his paper *The Riddle of the Convoys: Admiral Dönitz and the U-Boat Campaign of 1941* (Newport, Rhode Island, Naval War College, 1992 (unpublished).

50. It is not possible to be certain of the service speeds of all of the independents sunk in this period, but of those for which data is known, a significant proportion operated in this speed bracket. Data from E. C. Talbot-Booth, *Merchant Ships 1940* (London, Sampson-Low Marston, 1940).
51. Hinsley, *British Intelligence*, 2, 169.
52. Patrick Beesly, 'Special Intelligence and the Battle of the Atlantic: the British View' in Robert W. Love, Jr, *Changing Interpretations and New Sources in Naval History: Papers from the Third United States Naval Academy History Symposium* (New York, Garland Publishing, 1980), 416.
53. Patrick Beesly, *Very Special Intelligence: the Story of the Admiralty's Operational Intelligence Centre 1939–1945* (London, Hamish Hamilton, 1977), 262.
54. These range from the apparently Olympian claim of Clive Ponting, *Armageddon: the Second World War* (London, Sinclair Stevenson, 1995), 120, who attributes equal credit to radar, and Patrick Howarth, the biographer of the JIC's chairman, who claims this as Ultra's greatest-ever achievement. Patrick Howarth; *Intelligence Chief Extraordinary: the life of the Ninth Duke of Portland* (London, Bodley Head, 1986), 147.
55. Noel Annan, *Changing Enemies: the Defeat and Regeneration of Germany* (London, HarperCollins, 1995), 52.
56. Allan R. Millet and Williamson Murray (eds), *Military Effectiveness* (Boston, Allen and Unwin, 1988), Vol. III: *The Second World War*, 116–7. The data referred to is Roskill's tabular enumeration of monthly losses.
57. Specifically Christopher Andrew and David Dilks (eds), *The Missing Dimension; Governments and Intelligence Communities in the Twentieth Century* (Macmillan, London, 1984), 165; David A. Charters, Marc Milner and J. Brent Wilson (eds), *Military History and the Military Profession* (Westport, Connecticut, Greenwood Publishing Group, 1992), 83, and David Syrett, 'Communications Intelligence and the Battle of the Atlantic, 1943–1945', *Archives*, XXII (April 1995), 48. In none of these instances is the working revealed.
58. Harry Hinsley; 'The Enigma of Ultra' in *History Today*, September 1993, 19.
59. Hinsley, *British Intelligence*, 2, 169 for instance, makes the first point very cogently.
60. W. J. R. Gardner, 'The Battle of the Atlantic, 1941 – the First Turning Point' in Geoffrey Till, *Seapower: Theory and Practice* (Ilford, Essex, Frank Cass, 1994), 116.
61. Hinsley, *British Intelligence*, 2, 170.
62. This is obtained by considering the mean number of boat-days committed per operation per month against the number of operations, then considering the mean number and tons sunk per operation in which some sinkings were achieved.
63. For the general phenomenon of over-claiming, see Blair.
64. Karl Dönitz, *Memoirs: Ten Years and Twenty Days* (London, Greenhill Books, 1990), 157–163, Hessler I, 85, 88–92; BdU KTB, 1941.
65. There is an excellent unwritten thesis on what might flippantly be called 'The influence of the Eighth Army on the Battle of the Atlantic', if only as a partial corrective to the 'Mediterranean theatre as strategic waste' school of history.
66. The choice of the word 'coupling' is very deliberate and not intended for any salacious or sensational purpose. 'Triplings' were rare, unidimensional and poor in quality. Like the internal governance of the Third Reich,

✓   sequential bilateral meetings were much preferred to open and simultaneous communication among all concerned.

67. See Chapter 9, especially the commitment of submarines to operations in
the periods August–September 1943 and April–May 1943, when there is a
ratio of greater effort leading to lesser results.

9   Case-Study II – Mid-1942 to Mid-1943

1. For one critique of this, see Michael Gannon, *Operation Drumbeat: the
Dramatic True Story of Germany's First U-Boat Attacks along the American
Coast in World War II* (New York, Harper Perennial, 1991), although his
views are challenged by some, notably Robert W. Love, Jr, 'The US Navy
and Operation Roll of Drums, 1942', in Timothy J. Runyan and Jan M.
Copes (eds), *To Die Gallantly: the Battle of the Atlantic* (Boulder, Colorado,
Westview Press, 1994), 95–120.

✓ 2. Normally translated as 'happy time' and first used of the period following
the acquisition of the Biscay bases.

3. PRO ADM 234/67, The U-Boat war in the Atlantic (hereafter Hessler), II,
Section 258.

4. See Chapter 2 for a discussion of different ways of looking at time.

5. PRO ADM 186/802 The U-Boat war in the Atlantic (hereafter Hessler) I,
Section 154. The objection was twofold. Firstly, he was concerned that
various subsidiary deployments such as the Mediterranean and in the
Northern theatre after the attack on Russia were strategic distractions from
the main Atlantic task. However, Northern U-boats were potentially retriev-
able whereas the complex current system in the Strait of Gibraltar pre-
✓✓   cluded their return. No U-boat which successfully passed the Strait
eastbound ever returned. See Barley and Waters, Appendix 8. See also
Chapter 8, p. 150.

6. The full story of this convoy is told in David Syrett, 'The Sinking of HMS
FREDRAKE and the Battle for Convoy ON153', in *The American Neptune* 51,
Spring 1991, 105–11.

✓ 7. Seventy-nine per cent by number of ships.

8. It might be considered wrong to categorise the operation which involved
the two convoys HX229 and SC122, generating such large numbers of
engaged submarines and casualties as a single operation, but any detailed
study makes it clear that it is very difficult to disentangle the actions involving the convoys. See also Jürgen Rohwer, *The Critical Convoy Battles of March
1943: the Battle for HX229/SC122* (Shepperton, Surrey, Ian Allan, 1977).

9. Hessler II, Section 333. Quoting BdU KTB of 24 May 1943.

10. S. W. Roskill, *The War at Sea* (London, HMSO, 1954–61), 3 volumes in 4;
Donald Macintyre, *The Battle of the Atlantic* (London, Batsford, 1961); John
Costello and Terry Hughes, *The Battle of the Atlantic* (London, Book Club
Associates, 1977); W. J. R. Gardner, 'Prelude to Victory: the Battle of the
Atlantic 1942–1943', in *The Mariner's Mirror*, Vol. 79, No. 3 (August 1993),
305–17; David Syrett, 'The Battle for Convoy ONS-154, 26–31 December
1942', in *The Northern Mariner/Le marin du nord*, Vol. VII No. 2 (April 1997),
41–50 are a few examples.

11. See Chapter 3.

12. Jürgen Rohwer and W. A. B. Douglas, '"The Most Thankless Task" Revisited' in James Boutilier (ed.), *The RCN in Retrospect, 1910–1968* (Vancouver, Canada, University of British Columbia Press, 1982), 191.

13. See the classification of the phases of convoy attack in Chapter 5.

14. It has been pointed out by Arnold Hague that the proper distinction between ON and ONS did not exist until March 1943 when the ONS series started at 1 (to avoid confusion with faster ships run under ON numbers). Nevertheless there are many references in the literature to ONS numbers before this time and it is not intended to change these. Further, as there is no major analysis in this book which draws any significant distinction between slow and fast convoys, it is felt unnecessary to enforce the distinction.

15. It does not, of course, include any occasion on which non-pack attack occurred but as any chance sightings were rare, and the submarine was supposed to report in the first instance to allow the closure of others, this can safely be discounted as a significant cause of the loss of convoy shipping.

16. Hessler II, Diagrams 19 and 20. See also p. 182 for January.

17. Brian McCue, *U-Boats in the Bay of Biscay: an Essay in Operational Analysis* (Washington DC, National Defense University, 1990). In particular, see the diagram on page 10 which indicates some of relationships involved.

18. McCue does point out, however, that this facet appeared to receive more attention during the war, at least from Morse and Kimball, than it did subsequently and that Dönitz himself was well aware of the 'repair quagmire'. McCue 17, 100–107.

19. PRO ADM 234/579, Defeat of the Enemy Attack on Shipping (hereafter Barley and Waters), 1B, Plan 9.

20. J. D. Brown, 'The Battle of the Atlantic, 1941–1943: Peaks and Troughs' in Runyan and Copes, 152–3.

21. A rare exception is in McCue 133–44, results summarised in Table 21, 143.

22. Karl Dönitz, *Memoirs: 10 Years and 20 Days* (London, Greenhill Books, 1990), 252.

23. Again it is necessary to acknowledge David Syrett's work.

24. There were few limits as to how far afield German submarines actually went. See David Stevens, *U-Boat far from Home: the Epic Voyage of U 862 to Australia and New Zealand* (St Leonards, NSW, Australia; Allen & Unwin; 1997) for an account of a patrol to Australian and New Zealand waters, admittedly in 1944. Although an interesting and significant achievement in terms of endurance, little was done as tonnage warfare.

25. See Chapter 5 for a full description of these phases.

26. See, for example, the wealth of material in PRO ADM223/120, /170 and, for a later period, ADM223/8.

27. See Chapter 8.

28. The deficiencies of Ultra in tactical terms are adequately demonstrated by David Syrett in *The Defeat of the German U-Boats: the Battle of the Atlantic* (Columbia, South Carolina, University of South Carolina Press, 1994), 148–61.

29. Ralph Erskine, 'Ultra and Some US Navy Carrier Operations', *Cryptologia*, XIX, No. 1, (January 1995), 81–96.

30. McCue, 143. This is largely seen as a benefit of eliminating the increasingly time-absorbent returns to the Biscay bases.

31. PRO ADM 234/68, The U-Boat War in the Atlantic (referred to as Hessler), III, 32.

32. This was relatively exceptional and less pressing before May 1943. It was usually done as a method of extending the endurance and operational flexibility of submarines with weapons remaining but low on fuel, from submarines in the opposite condition, it being much easier to transfer fuel than torpedoes.

33. Hessler III, 32.

34. Ralph Erskine, 'Ultra and Some US Navy Carrier Operations'.

35. For a full account of the Bay battles, see Alfred Price, *Aircraft versus Submarine: the Evolution of the Antisubmarine Aircraft, 1912 to 1980* (London, Jane's Publishing, 1980), especially Chapter 8.

36. Price, Chapter 4 notes air activities in 1941; the first air-kill recorded there was in July 1942; PRO ADM 234/578, Defeat of the Enemy Attack on Shipping (hereafter Barley and Waters), 1A, 254, although the first kill there was credited to a British submarine as early as August 1940; Barley and Waters, 252.

37. This stands in distinction to the case of the refuelling rendezvous where its timeliness was often ensured by the Germans often broadcasting rendezvous days in advance of the event, thus obviating the normal deleterious effects of decoding delays. See NARA RG 457, SRH-008 (Bray edition), 100–1.

38. NARA RG 38 Tenth Fleet ASW Analysis and Statistics Section Box 49; Cominch 0556 1 June 1943.

10 Conclusion

1. W. J. R. Gardner, 'An Allied Perspective', in Stephen Howarth and Derek Law, *The Battle of the Atlantic 1939–1945: the Battle of the Atlantic 1939–1945* (London, Greenhill Books, 1994, 531.

2. F. W. Winterbotham, *The Ultra Secret* (London, Weidenfeld and Nicolson, 1974).

3. It might be argued that recording of live performances diminishes this point but, as any competent actor will be able to attest, playing to a camera – or even a microphone – and an audience are quite different things. Thus most films of live performances fail in one or both ways.

4. See Chapter 7.

5. Some more are suggested at pp. 213–14.

6. See Chapters 8 and 9.

7. A severe caution has to be entered here about the hierarchical nature of the levels of warfare. Although it would be natural to assume that 'strategic' is more important than 'operational', far less 'tactical' levels, the nation that believes that excellence at one level means that others can be neglected is liable to suffer in war.

8. See Chapter 8.

9. It is only fair to point out that the locus of many of the redeployments was such that a reversion to direct convoy support would have been relatively easy.

10. Harry Hinsley, 'The Enigma of Ultra', *History Today* (September 1993), 20.

References and Bibliography

Primary Sources

Public Record Office, United Kingdom

Admiralty

ADM 137/1392
ADM 186/802
ADM 199/575
ADM 199/576
ADM 199/580
ADM 199/1489
ADM 199/1491
ADM 219
ADM 223/7
ADM 223/8
ADM 223/120
ADM 223/170
ADM 223/172
ADM 223/261
ADM 223/358
ADM 234/67
ADM 234/68
ADM 234/322
ADM 234/560
ADM 234/578
ADM 234/579

Air Ministry

AIR 10/5555

Cabinet Office

CAB 86/1
CAB 86/2
CAB 86/3
CAB 86/4

National Archives and Records Administration, United States of America

RG 38 10th Fleet Box ASM-42
RG 38 10th Fleet ASW Analysis and Statistics Section Box 49
RG 242 PG 30280-30301/b T1022, 4063.

RG 457 SRH-008
RG 457 SRH-009
RG 457 SRH-024
RG 457 SRH-025
RG 457 SRH-277
RG 457 SRH-368
RG 457 SRM-054

Secondary Sources

Books

Abbazia, Patrick; *Mr Roosevelt's Navy: the Private War of the US Atlantic Fleet* (Annapolis, Maryland; Naval Institute Press, 1975)

Andrew, Christopher and Dilks, David (eds), *The Missing Dimension: Governments and Intelligence Communities in the Twentieth Century* (London, Macmillan, 1984)

Andrew, Christopher and Noakes, Jeremy (eds), *Intelligence and International Relations 1900–1945* (Exeter, Exeter University Publications, 1987)

Annan, Noel, *Changing Enemies: the Defeat and Regeneration of Germany* (London, HarperCollins, 1995)

Anon., *Fuehrer Conferences* (London, Greenhill Books, 1990)

Anon., *The U-Boat Commander's Handbook* (English translation; Gettysburg, Pennsylvania; Thomas Publications, 1989)

Bailey, Thomas A. and Ryan, Paul B., *Hitler vs. Roosevelt : the Undeclared Naval War* (New York, Free Press/Macmillan, 1979)

Baker, Richard, *The Terror of Tobermory: Vice-Admiral Sir Gilbert Stephenson, KBE, CBE, CMG* (London, W. H. Allen, 1972)

Barley, Freddie and Waters, David, *The Defeat of the Enemy Attack on Shipping: a Study of Policy and Operations* (London, Historical Section, Admiralty; 1957) 2 vols; also (London, Navy Records Society, 1998). See also PRO ADM 234/578 and /579.

Barnett, Corelli, *Engage the Enemy More Closely: the Royal Navy in the Second World War* (London, Hodder & Stoughton, 1991)

Baxter, James Phinney, *Scientists against Time* (Boston Massachusetts; Little, Brown, 1947)

Beesly, Patrick, *Very Special Admiral: the life of Admiral J. H. Godfrey, CB* (London, Hamish Hamilton, 1980)

Beesly, Patrick, *Very Special Intelligence: the Story of the Admiralty's Operational Intelligence Centre, 1939–1945* (London, Hamish Hamilton, 1977)

Behrens, C. B. A., *Merchant Shipping and the Demands of War* (London, HMSO, 1955)

Blair, Clay, *Hitler's U-Boat War: the Hunters* (New York, Random House, 1996)

Bonatz, Heinz, *Seekrieg im Äther: die Leistungen der Marine-Funkaufklärung 1939–1945* (Herford, Germany; Mittler, 1981)

Boutilier, James A (ed.), *The RCN in Retrospect, 1910–1968* (Vancouver, Canada; University of British Columbia Press, 1982)

Bruijn, Jaap R., *The Dutch Navy of the Seventeenth and Eighteenth Centuries;* (Columbia, South Carolina; University of South Carolina Press, 1993)

Bucheim, Lothar-Günther, *U-Boat* (London, Collins, 1974) (published in German as *Das Boot*)

Bullock, Alan, *Hitler and Stalin: Parallel Lives* (London, BCA, 1991)

Campbell, John, *Naval Weapons of World War Two* (London, Conway Maritime Press, 1985)

Chalmers, W. S., *Max Horton and the Western Approaches: a Biography of Admiral Sir Max Kennedy Horton, GCB, DSO* (London, Hodder and Stoughton, 1954)

Charters, David A., et al. (eds); *Military History and the Military Profession* (Westport, Praeger, 1992)

Corbett, Julian S, *Drake and the Tudor Navy: with a History of the Rise of England as a Maritime Power* (Aldershot, Hampshire, Temple Smith, Gower Publishing, 1988)

Costello, John and Hughes, Terry, *The Battle of the Atlantic* (London, Book Club Associates, 1977)

Creighton, Kenelm, Rear Admiral, *Convoy Commodore* (London, William Kimber, 1956)

Crowther, J. G. and Whiddington, R., *Science at War* (London, HMSO, 1947)

Deighton, Len, *Blitzkrieg: from the Rise of Hitler to the Fall of Dunkirk* (London, Pimlico, 1996)

Dimbleby, David and Reynolds, David, *An Ocean Apart: the Relationship between Britain and America in the Twentieth Century* (London, Hodder and Stoughton, 1988)

Dixon, Norman, *On the Psychology of Military Incompetence* (London, Jonathan Cape, 1976)

Döenitz, Karl, *Memoirs: Ten Years and Twenty Days* (London, Greenhill Books, 1990)

Doughty, Martin, *Merchant Shipping and War: a Study in Defence Planning* (London, Royal Historical Society, 1982)

Ellis, John, *Brute Force: Allied Strategy and Tactics in the Second World War* (London, André Deutsch, 1990)

Ellis, L. F. and Warhurst, A. E., *Victory in the West: the Defeat of Germany,* (London, HMSO, 1968)

Elton, G. R., *The Practice of History* (London, Harper Collins, 1987)

Farrago, Ladislas, *The Tenth Fleet* (New York, Ivan Obolensky, 1962)

Friedman, Norman, *Submarine Design and Development* (London, Conway Maritime Press, 1984)

Gannon, Michael, *Black May: the Epic story of the Allies' Defeat of the German U-Boats in May 1943* (New York, Harper Collins, 1998)

Gannon, Michael, *Operation Drumbeat: the Dramatic True Story of Germany's First U-Boat Attacks along the American Coast in World War II* (New York, Harper Perennial, 1991)

Gardner, W. J. R., *Anti-Submarine Warfare* (London, Brassey's, 1996)

Gordon, Andrew, *The Rules of the Game: Jutland and British Naval Command* (London, John Murray, 1996)

Gorshkov, S. G., *The Sea Power of the State* (Annapolis, Maryland; Naval Institute Press, 1979)

Gretton, Peter, *Crisis Convoy: the Story of HX231* (London, Peter Davies, 1974)

Gretton, Peter, *Convoy Escort Commander* (London, Cassell, 1964)

Gunther, John, *Inside Europe* (London, Hamish Hamilton, 1936)

Hackmann, Willem; *Seek and Strike: Sonar, Anti-Submarine Warfare and the Royal Navy 1914–1954* (London, HMSO, 1984)

Hague, Arnold, *Sloops 1926–1946*; (Kendal, World Ship Society, 1993)

Hague, Arnold, *The Towns: a History of the Fifty Destroyers Transferred from the United States to Great Britain in 1940*; (Kendal, World Ship Society, 1988)

Halpern, Paul, *A Naval History of World War I* (Annapolis, Maryland; Naval Institute Press, 1994)

Hancock, W. K. and Gowing, M. M., *British War Economy* (London, HMSO, 1949)

Harding, Richard, *Atlantic Seapower and Naval Warfare, 1650–1830* (London, University of London Press, 1999)

Hessler, Gunther, *The U-Boat War in the Atlantic* (London, HMSO, 1989) (see also PRO ADM 186/802, ADM 234/67 and /68.)

Hezlet, Arthur, *The Electron and Sea Power* (London, Peter Davies, 1975)

Hezlet, Arthur, *The Submarine and Sea Power* (London, Peter Davies, 1967)

Hinsley, F. H. and Stripp, Alan, *Codebreakers: the Inside story of Bletchley Park* (Oxford, Oxford University, 1993)

Hinsley, F. H., Thomas, E. E. et al., *British Intelligence in the Second World War: Its Influence on Strategy and Operations*, 3 vols in 4 (London, HMSO, 1984)

Hobbs, David, *Aircraft Carriers of the Royal and Commonwealth Navies: the Complete Illustrated Encyclopedia from World War I to the Present* (London, Greenhill Books, 1996)

Howard Bailey, Chris, *The Royal Naval Museum Book of the Battle of the Atlantic: the Corvettes and Their Crews: an Oral History* (Stroud, Alan Sutton, 1994)

Howarth, Patrick, *Intelligence Chief Extraordinary: the Life of the Ninth Duke of Portland* (London, Bodley Head, 1986)

Howarth, Stephen (ed.), *Men of War: Great Naval Leaders of World War II* (London, Weidenfeld and Nicolson, 1992)

Howarth, Stephen and Law, Derek, *The Battle of the Atlantic 1939–1945: the 50th Anniversary International Naval Conference* (London, Greenhill Books, 1994)

Howse, Derek (ed.), *Radar at Sea: the Royal Navy in World War 2* (London, Macmillan, 1993)

Jones, R. V., *Reflections on Intelligence* (London, William Heinemann, 1989)

Jones, R. V., *Most Secret War: British Scientific Intelligence 1939–1945* (London, Coronet, 1978)

Kahn, David, *Seizing the Enigma: the Race to Break the German U-Boat Codes 1939–1943* (London, Souvenir Press, 1991)

Kemp, Peter, *Decision at Sea: the Convoy Escorts* (New York, Elsevier-Dutton, 1978)

Kimball, Warren F., *Forged in War: Churchill, Roosevelt and the Second World War* (London, Harper Collins, 1997)

Kimball, Warren F., *Churchill and Roosevelt: the Complete Correspondence* (London, Collins, 1984), 3 vols

Kingsley, F. A. (ed.), *The Development of Radar Equipments for the Royal Navy, 1935–1945* (London, Macmillan, 1995)

Lane, Frederic C., *Ships for Victory: a History of Shipbuilding under the US Maritime Commission in World War II* (Baltimore, Maryland; Johns Hopkins University Press, 1951)

Law, Derek G., *The Royal Navy in World War Two: an Annotated Bibliography* (London, Greenhill Books, 1988)

Les Marines de Guerre du Dreadnought au Nucléaire (Chateâu de Vincennes, France; Service historique de la Marine, 1988)

Love, Robert William, Jr, *Changing Interpretations in Naval History: Papers from the Third United States Naval Academy History Symposium* (New York, Garland, 1980)

Macintyre, Donald, *The Battle of the Atlantic* (London, Batsford, 1961)

Mackesy, Kenneth, *Guderian: Panzer General* (London, Purnell Book Services, 1975)

Martiensen, Anthony, *Hitler and His Admirals* (London, Secker and Warburg, 1948)

McCue, Brian, *U-Boats in the Bay of Biscay: an Essay in Operations Analysis* (Washington, DC; National Defense University Press, 1990)

McLachlan, Donald, *Room 39: Naval Intelligence in Action 1939–1945* (London, Weidenfeld and Nicolson, 1968)

Meigs, Montgomery C., *Slide Rules and Submarines: American Scientists and Subsurface Warfare in World War II* (Washington, National Defense University Press, 1989)

Middlebrook, Martin, *Convoy: the Battle for Convoys SC122 and HX229* (London, Allen Lane 1976)

Millett, Allan R. and Murray, Williamson (eds), *Military Effectiveness: Vol. III – The Second World War* (Boston, Allen and Unwin, 1988)

Milner, Marc, *The U-Boat Hunters: the Royal Canadian Navy and the Offensive against Germany's Submarines* (Annapolis, Maryland; Naval Institute Press, 1994)

Milner, Marc, *North Atlantic Run: the Royal Canadian Navy and the Battle for the Convoys* (Toronto, University of Toronto Press, 1985)

Ministry of Defence, United Kingdom, *The Fundamentals of British Maritime Doctrine* (London HMSO, 1995)

Morison, S. E., *The History of United States Naval Operations in World War II, Volume X: the Atlantic Battle Won, May 1943–May 1945* (Boston, Massachusetts; Little, Brown, 1956)

Morison, S. E., *History of United States Naval Operations in World War II, Volume I: The Battle of the Atlantic, September 1939–May 1943* (Boston, Massachusetts, Little, Brown, 1947)

Neitzel, Sönke, *Der Einsatz der deutschen Luftwaffe über dem Atlantik und der Nordsee 1939–1945* (Bonn, Germany; Bernard & Graefe, 1995)

Overy, Richard, *Why the Allies Won* (London, Jonathan Cape, 1995)

Padfield, Peter, *War Beneath the Sea: Submarine Conflict 1939–1945* (London, Pimlico, 1997)

Padfield, Peter, *Dönitz, the Last Führer: Portrait of a Nazi War Leader* (London, Victor Gollancz, 1984)

Parrish, Thomas, *The Ultra Americans: the U.S. Role in Breaking the Nazi Codes* (New York, Stein and Day, 1986)

Pawle, Gerald, *The Secret War: 1939–1945* (London, George G. Harrap, 1956)

Payton Smith, D. J., *Oil* (London, HMSO, 1971)

Poland, E. N., *The Torpedomen: HMS Vernon's Story 1872–1986* (no place of publication or publisher given, 1993)

Ponting, Clive, *Armageddon: the Second World War* (London, Sinclair-Stevenson, 1995)

Poolman, Kenneth, *Allied Escort Carriers of World War Two in Action* (London, Blandford Press, 1988)

Postan, M. M., *British War Production* (London, HMSO, 1952)

Prados, John, *Combined Fleet Decoded: the Secret History of American Intelligence and the Japanese Navy in World War II* (New York, Random House, 1995)

Price, Alfred, *Aircraft versus Submarine: the Evolution of the Anti-Submarine Aircraft, 1912 to 1980* (London, Jane's Publishing, 1980)

Pugh, Philip, *The Cost of Seapower: the Influence of Money on Naval Affairs from 1815 to the Present* (London, Conway Maritime Press, 1986)

Rayner, D. A. (edited by Roskill, S. W.), *Escort: the Battle of the Atlantic* (London, William Kimber, 1955)

Rich, Norman, *Hitler's War Aims: the Establishment of the New Order* (New York, Norton, 1974)

Roberts, William R. and Sweetman, Jack, *New Interpretations in Naval History: Selected Papers from the Ninth Naval History Symposium, US Naval Academy 18–20 October 1989* (Annapolis, Maryland; Naval Institute Press, 1991)

Rohwer, Jürgen, *Axis Submarine Successes 1939–1945* (Cambridge, Patrick Stephens, 1983)

Rohwer, Jürgen, *The Critical Convoy Battles of March 1943: the Battle for HX229/SC122* (Shepperton, Ian Allan, 1977)

Rohwer, J. and Hummelchen, G., *Chronology of the War: the Naval History of World War Two* (London, Greenhill Books, 1992)

Roskill, S. W., *The War at Sea*; 3 vols in 4 (London, HMSO, 1954–61)

Roskill, S. W., *The Secret Capture* (London, Collins, 1959)

Roskill, S. W., *Churchill and the Admirals* (London, Collins, 1977)

Rössler, Eberhard, *The U-Boat: the Evolution and Technical History of German Submarines* (London, Arms and Armour, 1981)

Runyan, Timothy J. and Copes, Jan M., *To Die Gallantly: the Battle of the Atlantic* (Boulder, Colorado; Westview Press, 1994)

Rust, Eric C., *Naval Officers under Hitler: the Story of Crew 34* (New York, Praeger, 1991)

Savage, C. I., *Inland Transport* (London, HMSO, 1957)

Savas, Theodore P. (ed.), *Silent Hunters: German U-Boat Commanders of World II* (Campbell, California; Savas, 1997)

Scott, J. D. and Hughes, R., *The Administration of War Production* (London, HMSO, 1955)

Seth, Ronald, *The Fiercest Battle: the Story of North Atlantic Convoy ONS5, 22 April–7 May 1943* (London, Hutchinson, 1961)

Smith, Bradley F., *The Ultra-Magic Deals and the Most Secret Special Relationship, 1940–1946* (Novato, California; Presidio Press, 1993)

Smith, Kevin, *Conflict over Convoys: Anglo-American Logistics Diplomacy in the Second World War* (Cambridge, Cambridge University Press, 1996)

Snyder, Louis L., *Encyclopedia of the Third Reich* (London, Blandford, 1989)

Stefanick, Tom, *Strategic Antisubmarine Warfare and Naval Strategy* (Lexington, Massachusetts; Institute for Defense and Disarmament Studies/Lexington Books, 1987)

Stern, Robert C., *Type VII U-Boats* (London, Arms and Armour, 1991)

Stevens, David; *U-Boat Far from Home: the Epic Voyage of U-862 to Australia and New Zealand* (St Leonards, NSW, Australia; Allen and Unwin, 1997)

Syrett, David (ed.), *Signals Intelligence and the Battle of the Atlantic* (London, Navy Records Society, 1998)

Syrett, David, *The Defeat of the German U-Boats: the Battle of the Atlantic* (Columbia, South Carolina; University of South Carolina, 1994)

Talbot-Booth, E. C., *Merchant Ships 1940* (London, Sampson-Low Marston, 1940)

Tarrant, V. E., *The U-Boat Offensive 1914–1945* (London, Arms and Armour, 1989)

Terraine, John, *Business in Great Waters: the U-Boat Wars 1916–1945* (London, Leo Cooper, 1989)

Terrell, Edward, *Admiralty Brief: the Story of Inventions that Contributed to the Battle of the Atlantic* (London, George G. Harrap, 1958)

Tidman, Keith R., *The Operations Analysis Group: a History of Naval Operations Analysis* (Annapolis, Maryland; Naval Institute Press, 1984)

Till, Geoffrey (ed.), *Seapower: Theory and Practice* (Ilford, Frank Cass, 1994)

Vaeth, J. Gordon, *Blimps and U-Boats: US Navy Airships in the Battle of the Atlantic* (Annapolis, Naval Institute Press, 1992)

van der Vat, Dan, *The Atlantic Campaign: the Great Struggle at Sea 1939–1945*; (London, Hodder and Stoughton, 1988)

Vause, Jordan, *U-Boat Ace: the Story of Wolfgang Lüth* (Annapolis, Naval Institute Press, 1990)

Waddington, C. H., *OR in World War 2: Operational Research against the U-Boat* (London, Paul Elek (Scientific Books), 1973)

Werner, Herbert A., *Iron Coffins: a Personal Account of the German U-Boat Battles of World War II* (New York, Holt, Rinehart and Winston, 1969)

Whinney, Bob, *The U-Boat Peril: an Anti-Submarine Commander's War* (Poole, Blandford Press, 1986)

Williams, Kathleen Broome *Secret Weapon: U.S. High-Frequency Direction Finding in the Battle of the Atlantic* (Annapolis, Maryland; Naval Institute Press, 1996)

Williams, Mark, *Captain Gilbert Roberts R N and the Anti-U-Boat School* (London, Cassell, 1979)

Willmott, H. P., *Grave of a Dozen Schemes* (Annapolis, Naval Institute Press, 1996)

Wilson, Thomas, *Churchill and the Prof* (London, Cassell, 1995)

Wilt, Alan F., *War from the Top: German and British Military Decision Making during World War II* (London, I. B. Tauris, 1990)

Winterbotham, F. W., *The Ultra Secret* (London, Weidenfeld and Nicolson, 1974)

Y' Blood, William T., *Hunter-Killer: U.S. Escort Carriers in the Battle of the Atlantic* (Annapolis, Maryland; Naval Institute Press, 1983)

Zimmerman, David, *The Great Naval Battle of Ottawa* (Toronto, Canada; University of Toronto Press, 1989)

Articles

Erskine, Ralph, 'Kriegsmarine Signal Indicators', *Cryptologia* XX, No. 4 (October 1996), 330–40

Erskine, Ralph, 'Naval Enigma: an Astonishing Blunder', *Intelligence and National Security*, Vol. 3, No. 1 (July 1996), 468–73

Erskine, Ralph, 'Ultra and Some US Navy Carrier Operations', *Cryptologia* XIX, No. 1 (January 1995), 81–96

Erskine, Ralph, 'The German Naval Grid in World War II', *Cryptologia* (January 1992), 39–51

Erskine, Ralph, 'Naval Enigma: a Missing Link' *International Journal of Intelligence and Counterintelligence*, Vol. 3, No. 4 (Winter 1989), 493–508

Erskine, Ralph, 'Naval Enigma: the Breaking of Heimisch and Triton', *Intelligence and National Security*, Vol. 3, No. 1 (January 1988), 162–83

Erskine, Ralph, 'Naval Enigma: M4 and its Rotors', *Cryptologia*, No. 11 (October 1987), 235–44

Erskine, Ralph, 'U-Boats, Homing Signals and HFDF', *Intelligence and National Security*, No. 2 (April 1987), 324–30

Gardner, W. J. R., 'Prelude to Victory: the Battle of the Atlantic 1942–1943', *The Mariner's Mirror*, Vol. 79, No. 3 (August 1993), 305–17

Hinsley, Harry, 'The Enigma of Ultra', *History Today* (September 1993), 15–20

Milner, Marc, 'The Battle of the Atlantic', *The Journal of Strategic Studies* (March 1990), 45–66

Milner, Marc, 'The Dawn of Modern ASW: Allied Responses to the U-Boat, 1943–1945', *Journal of the RUSI*, Vol. 134, No. 1 (Spring 1989), 61–8

Syrett, David, 'The Battle for Convoy ONS-154, 26–31 December 1942', *The Northern Mariner/Le Marin du Nord* (April 1997), 41–50

Syrett, David, 'Prelude to Victory: the Battle for Convoy HX231, 4–7 April 1943', *Historical Research*, Vol. 70, No. 171 (February 1997), 99–109

Syrett, David, 'The Battle for Convoy UC-1, 23–27 February 1943', *The Northern Mariner/Le Marin du nord*, (January 1996), 21–27

Syrett, David, 'Communications Intelligence and the Battle of the Atlantic, 1943–1945', *Archives*, Vol. XXI (April 1995), 45–59

Syrett, David; 'The sinking of HMS Firedrake and the Battle for Convoy ON153', *The American Neptune*, No. 51, (Spring 1991), 105–11

Waters, D. W., 'The Mathematics of Convoy', *Navy International*, (May 1978), 25–26, 78

Index

Perception in late 1942 of Allied
dominance 194
Post-May 1943 strategies 204–7
pragmatism 202
Rationale for continuing operations
after May 1943 53
Tonnage warfare, knowledge and
objectives 46–8
'Tying down' doctrine of May 1943
63
U-boats to the Mediterranean
150, 175
Douglas, W. A. B. 185, 187

Economics 12, 24, Chapter 3, 157,
200, 217
Electrical 93, 97, 98, 133, 134
Electro-boat 95
Encryption 132
Endurance 94, 110–12
English Channel 158
Enigma 120, 133–8, 172, 217
Environment 79–80, 99, 160
Equipment
Sensors: *Fliege* 97; Metox 67, 97,
139; *Wanze* 97
Weapons: Ahead-thrown weapons
109; FAT (German torpedo)
48, 99; G7a (German torpedo)
98; G7e (German torpedo)
98; Hs293Glider bomb 208;
LUT (German torpedo) 48,
99; Mark 24 homing torpedo
(also mine or Fido) 109;
Mousetrap 109; Retro-bomb
108; Squid 109; T5 homing
torpedo, also Gnat 99, 113;
TMA(German mine) 100;
TMB(German mine) 100
Other: *Alberich* 100, 101; Aphrodite
101; *Bold* 101, 139, 186, 187;
Foxer 113; *Knickebein* 120;
Kurier 100, 102, 105; *Sonne*
100, 120; Squash 100, 102;
Starshell 102; Submarine
Bubble Target (SBT), *see also Bold*
101; Thetis 101
Erskine, Ralph 204, 207
Escort 70, 76–83, 88, 201

Escort aircraft carrier (CVE) 112,
139, 144, 203, 205
Escort Force Commander 27, 32, 76,
202
Escort group 76–8, 129, 162, 208
Exchange rate 42, 192, 197
Eye 96, 102, 105, 114
E-bar (type of German signal) 131

Flak 112, 207
Flanigan, Captain H. A. (Pat) USN
116, 118
Flares 102
Focke-Wulf 200 12, 15
Four-rotor (Enigma) 137, 140
Frames (Time analysis concept)
23–5
Frontboote 149, 150, 173, 189, 190,
197
Führer, see Hitler
Führerprinzip 57
F-211 (USN organisation) 136

German Naval High Command
(OKM) 175
Gibraltar 150, 157, 163–7, 175,
184
glückliche Zeit (Ger., fortunate time)
19, 20, 179
Godt, Rear Admiral Eberhardt
(German) 58, 60
Gordon, Andrew 31, 112
Gorshkov, S. G., Admiral of the Fleet
of the Soviet Union 53
Government Code and Cipher School
(GC&CS) 140, 141
Grand Alliance 7, 146
Grand strategy 26, 67, 185, 218
Great Circle 80
Greenland 74, 147, 165–6
Grid 136
Groundwave 123
Gulf of Mexico 20, 179

Halifax 79, 163
Harlinghausen, Oberstleutnant
(Luftwaffe) 159
Hessler, Fregattenkapitän 65–7, 155,
191